Three Guineas

Three Guineas

VIRGINIA WOOLF

Annotated and with an introduction
by Jane Marcus

Mark Hussey, General Editor

A Harvest Book • Harcourt, Inc.
Orlando Austin New York San Diego Toronto London

www.HarcourtBooks.com

Letters by Virginia Woolf reprinted with kind permission of the Society of Authors,
as the literary representative of the estate of Virginia Woolf.

Virginia Woolf's scrapbook pages reproduced courtesy of
the University of Sussex Library, England.

Library of Congress Cataloging-in-Publication Data
Woolf, Virginia, 1882–1941.
Three guineas/Virginia Woolf; annotated and with
an introduction by Jane Marcus; Mark Hussey, general editor.—Annotated ed., 1st ed.
p.   cm.— (A Harvest book)
Includes bibliographical references.
1. War—Prevention.   2. Women—England—Social conditions.
I. Marcus, Jane.   II. Hussey, Mark, 1956–   III. Title.
PR6045.O72T5   2006
823'.912—dc22   2006006360
ISBN-13: 978-0-15-603163-9   ISBN-10: 0-15-603163-9

Text set in Garamond MT
Designed by Cathy Riggs

Printed in the United States of America

First edition
C E G I K J H F D B

Contents

Three Guineas

VIRGINIA WOOLF

VIRGINIA WOOLF was born into what she once described as "a very communicative, literate, letter writing, visiting, articulate, late nineteenth century world." Her parents, Leslie and Julia Stephen, both previously widowed, began their marriage in 1878 with four young children: Laura (1870–1945), the daughter of Leslie Stephen and his first wife, Harriet Thackeray (1840–1875); and George (1868–1934), Gerald (1870–1937), and Stella Duckworth (1869–1897), the children of Julia Prinsep (1846–1895) and Herbert Duckworth (1833–1870). In the first five years of their marriage, the Stephens had four more children. Their third child, Virginia, was born in 1882, the year her father began work on the monumental *Dictionary of National Biography* that would earn him a knighthood in 1902. Virginia, her sister, Vanessa (1879–1961), and brothers, Thoby (1880–1906) and Adrian (1883–1948), all were born in the tall house at 22 Hyde Park Gate in London where the eight children lived with numerous servants, their eminent and irascible father, and their beautiful mother, who, in Woolf's words, was "in the very centre of that great Cathedral space that was childhood."

Woolf's parents knew many of the intellectual luminaries of the late Victorian era well, counting among their close friends novelists such as George Meredith, Thomas Hardy, and Henry James. Woolf's great-aunt Julia Margaret Cameron was a pioneering photographer who made portraits of the poets Alfred

Tennyson and Robert Browning, of the naturalist Charles Darwin, and of the philosopher and historian Thomas Carlyle, among many others. Beginning in the year Woolf was born, the entire Stephen family moved to Talland House in St. Ives, Cornwall, for the summer. There the younger children would spend their days playing cricket in the garden, frolicking on the beach, or taking walks along the coast, from where they could look out across the bay to the Godrevy lighthouse.

The early years of Woolf's life were marred by traumatic events. When she was thirteen, her mother, exhausted by a punishing schedule of charitable visits among the sick and poor, died from a bout of influenza. Woolf's half sister Stella took over the household responsibilities and bore the brunt of their self-pitying father's sorrow until she escaped into marriage in 1897 with Jack Hills, a young man who had been a favorite of Julia's. Within three months, Stella (who was pregnant) was dead, most likely from peritonitis. In this year, which she called "the first really *lived* year of my life," Woolf began a diary. Over the next twelve years, she would record in its pages her voracious reading, her impressions of people and places, feelings about her siblings, and events in the daily life of the large household.[1]

In addition to the premature deaths of her mother and half sister, there were other miseries in Woolf's childhood. In autobiographical writings and letters, Woolf referred to the sexual abuse she suffered at the hands of her two older half brothers, George and Gerald Duckworth. George, in one instance, explained his behavior to a family doctor as his effort to comfort his half sister for the fatal illness of their father. Sir Leslie died

---

[1] Woolf's early diary is published as *A Passionate Apprentice: The Early Journals, 1897–1909,* edited by Mitchell A. Leaska. A 1909 notebook discovered in 2002 has been published as *Carlyle's House and Other Sketches,* edited by David Bradshaw (London: Hesperus, 2003).

from cancer in 1904, and shortly thereafter the four Stephen children—Vanessa, Virginia, Thoby, and Adrian—moved together to the then-unfashionable London neighborhood of Bloomsbury. When Thoby Stephen began to bring his Cambridge University friends to the house on Thursday evenings, what would later become famous as the "Bloomsbury Group" began to form.

In an article marking the centenary of her father's birth, Woolf recalled his "allowing a girl of fifteen the free run of a large and quite unexpurgated library"—an unusual opportunity for a Victorian young woman, and evidence of the high regard Sir Leslie had for his daughter's intellectual talents. In her diary, she recorded the many different kinds of books her father recommended to her—biographies and memoirs, philosophy, history, and poetry. Although he believed that women should be "as well educated as men," Woolf's mother held that "to serve is the fulfilment of women's highest nature." The young Stephen children were first taught at home by their mother and father, with little success. Woolf herself received no formal education beyond some classes in Greek and Latin in the Ladies' Department of King's College in London, beginning in the fall of 1897. In 1899 she began lessons in Greek with Clara Pater, sister of the renowned Victorian critic Walter Pater, and in 1902 she was tutored in the classics by Janet Case (who also later involved her in work for women's suffrage). Such homeschooling was a source of some bitterness later in her life, as she recognized the advantages that derived from the expensive educations her brothers and half brothers received at private schools and university. Yet she also realized that her father's encouragement of her obviously keen intellect had given her an eclectic foundation. In the early years of Bloomsbury, she reveled in the opportunity to discuss ideas with her brother Thoby and his friends, among whom were Lytton Strachey, Clive Bell, and

E. M. Forster. From them, she heard, too, about an intense young man named Leonard Woolf, whom she had met briefly when visiting Thoby at Cambridge, and also in 1904 when he came to dinner at Gordon Square just before leaving for Ceylon (now called Sri Lanka), where he was to administer a far-flung outpost of the British Empire.

Virginia Woolf's first publications were unsigned reviews and essays in an Anglo-Catholic newspaper called the *Guardian*, beginning in December 1904. In the fall of 1906, she and Vanessa went with a family friend, Violet Dickinson, to meet their brothers in Greece. The trip was spoiled by Vanessa's falling ill, and when she returned to London, Virginia found both her brother Thoby—who had returned earlier—and her sister seriously ill. After a misdiagnosis by his doctors, Thoby died from typhoid fever on November 20, leaving Virginia to maintain a cheerful front while her sister and Violet Dickinson recovered from their own illnesses. Two days after Thoby's death, Vanessa agreed to marry his close friend Clive Bell.

While living in Bloomsbury, Woolf had begun to write a novel that would go through many drafts before it was published in 1915 as *The Voyage Out*. In these early years of independence, her social circle widened. She became close to the art critic Roger Fry, organizer of the First Post-Impressionist Exhibition in London in 1910, and also entered the orbit of the famed literary hostess Lady Ottoline Morrell (cruelly caricatured as Hermione Roddice in D. H. Lawrence's 1920 novel *Women in Love*). Her political consciousness also began to emerge. In 1910 she volunteered for the movement for women's suffrage. She also participated that February in a daring hoax that embarrassed the British Navy and led to questions being asked in the House of Commons: She and her brother Adrian, together with some other Cambridge friends, gained access to a secret warship by dressing up and posing as the Emperor of Abyssinia and his retinue. The "Dreadnought Hoax" was front-page news, complete with photographs of the phony Ethiopians with flowing robes, blackened faces, and false beards.

To the British establishment, one of the most embarrassing aspects of the Dreadnought affair was that a woman had taken part in the hoax. Vanessa Bell was concerned at what might have happened to her sister had she been discovered on the ship. She was also increasingly worried about Virginia's erratic health, and by the early summer 1910 had discussed with Dr. George Savage, one of the family's doctors, the debilitating headaches her sister suffered; Dr. Savage prescribed several weeks in a nursing home. Another element in Vanessa's concern was that Virginia was twenty-eight and still unmarried. Clive Bell and Virginia had, in fact, engaged in a hurtful flirtation soon after the birth of Vanessa's first child in 1908. Although she had been proposed to twice in 1909 and once in 1911, Virginia had not taken these offers very seriously.

Dropping by Vanessa's house on a July evening in 1911, Virginia met Leonard Woolf, recently back on leave from Ceylon. Soon after this, Leonard became a lodger at the house Virginia shared with Adrian, the economist John Maynard Keynes, and the painter Duncan Grant. Leonard decided to resign from the Colonial Service, hoping that Virginia would agree to marry him. After some considerable hesitation, she did, and they married in August 1912.

By the end of that year, Woolf was again suffering from the tremendous headaches that afflicted her throughout her life, and in 1913 she was again sent to a nursing home for what was then called a "rest cure." In September of that year, she took an overdose of a sleeping drug and was under care until the following spring. In early 1915 she suffered a severe breakdown and was ill throughout most of the year in which her first novel was published.

Despite this difficult beginning, Virginia and Leonard Woolf's marriage eventually settled into a pattern of immense productivity and mutual support. Leonard worked for a time for the Women's Cooperative Guild, and became increasingly involved with advising the Labour Party and writing on international politics, as well as editing several periodicals. Virginia began to establish herself as an important novelist and influential critic. In 1917 the Woolfs set up their own publishing house, the Hogarth Press, in their home in Richmond. Their first publication was *Two Stories*—Leonard's "Three Jews" and Virginia's experimental "The Mark on the Wall." They had decided to make their livings by writing, and in 1919, a few months before Woolf's second novel, *Night and Day,* was published, they bought a cottage in the village of Rodmell in Sussex. After moving back into London from Richmond in 1923, Woolf would spend summers at Monk's House, returning to the social whirl of the city in the fall.

"The Mark on the Wall" was one of a number of what Woolf called "sketches" that she began to write around the time she and Leonard bought their printing press. *Night and Day* was the last of her books to be published in England by another press. In 1919 Hogarth published her short story *Kew Gardens,* with two woodcuts by Vanessa Bell, and two years later came *Monday or Tuesday,* the only collection of her short fiction published in Woolf's lifetime. Her next novel was *Jacob's Room* (1922), a slim elegy to the generation of 1914, and to her beloved brother Thoby, whose life of great promise had also been cut short so suddenly. Woolf had written to her friend Margaret Llewelyn Davies in 1916 that the Great War, as it was then called, was a "preposterous masculine fiction" that made her "steadily more feminist," and in her fiction and nonfiction she began to articulate and illuminate the connections between the patriarchal status quo, the relatively subordinate position of women, and war making. Thinking about a novel she was calling "The Hours," Woolf wrote in her diary in 1923 that she wanted to criticize "the social system." Her inclusion in the novel of a shell-shocked war veteran named Septimus Warren Smith would confuse many of the early reviewers of her fourth novel, *Mrs. Dalloway* (1925), but others recognized that Woolf was breaking new ground in the way she rendered consciousness and her understanding of human subjectivity.

By the time she wrote *Mrs. Dalloway,* Woolf was also a sought-after essayist and reviewer who, like many of her celebrated contemporaries, was staking out her own particular piece of modernist territory. The Hogarth Press published radical young writers like Katherine Mansfield, T. S. Eliot, and Gertrude Stein. Approached by Harriet Shaw Weaver with part of the manuscript of James Joyce's *Ulysses* in 1918, the Woolfs turned it down. Their own small press could not cope with the long and complex manuscript, nor could Leonard Woolf find a commercial printer willing to risk prosecution for obscenity by producing it. In 1924 the Hogarth Press became the official English publisher of the works of Sigmund Freud, translated by Lytton Strachey's brother James. Woolf's own literary criticism was collected in a volume published in 1925, *The Common Reader*—a title signaling her distrust of academics and love of broad, eclectic reading.

The staggering range of Woolf's reading is reflected in the more than five hundred essays and reviews she published during her lifetime. Her critical writing is concerned not only with the canonical works of English literature from Chaucer to her contemporaries, but also ranges widely through lives of the obscure, memoirs, diaries, letters, and biographies. Models of the form, her essays comprise a body of work that has only recently begun to attract the kind of recognition her fiction has received.

In 1922 Woolf met "the lovely and gifted aristocrat" Vita Sackville-West, already a well-known poet and novelist. Their close friendship slowly turned into a love affair, glowing most intensely from about 1925 to 1928, before modulating into friendship once more in the 1930s. The period of their intimacy was extremely creative for both writers, Woolf publishing essays such as "Mr. Bennett and Mrs. Brown" and "Letter to a Young Poet," as well as three very different novels: *To the Lighthouse* (1927), which evoked her own childhood and had at its center the figure of a modernist woman artist, Lily Briscoe; *Orlando* (1928), a fantastic biography inspired by Vita's own remarkable family history; and *The Waves* (1931), a mystical and profoundly meditative work that pushed Woolf's concept of novel form to its limit. Woolf also published a second *Common Reader* in 1932, and the "biography" of *Flush,* Elizabeth Barrett Browning's dog (1933). She went with Sackville-West to Cambridge in the fall of 1928 to deliver the second of the two lectures on which her great feminist essay *A Room of One's Own* (1929) is based.

As the political situation in Europe in the 1930s moved inexorably to its crisis in 1939, Woolf began to collect newspaper clippings about the relations between the sexes in England, France, Germany, and Italy. The scrapbooks she made became the matrix from which developed the perspectives of her penultimate novel, *The Years* (1937), and the arguments of her pacifist-feminist polemic *Three Guineas* (1938). In 1937 Vanessa's eldest son, Julian Bell, was killed serving as an ambulance driver in the Spanish Civil War. Woolf later wrote to Vanessa that she had written *Three Guineas* partly as an argument with Julian. Her work on *The Years* was grindingly slow and difficult. Ironically, given Woolf's reputation as a highbrow, it became a bestseller in the United States, even being published in an Armed Services edition. While she labored over the novel in 1934, the news came of the death of Roger Fry, one of her oldest and closest friends and the former lover of her sister, Vanessa. Reluctantly, given her distaste for the conventions of biography, Woolf agreed to write his life, which was published in 1940.

In 1939, to relieve the strain of writing Fry's biography, Woolf began to write a memoir, "A Sketch of the Past," which remained unpublished until 1976, when the manuscripts were edited by Jeanne Schulkind for a collection of Woolf's autobiographical writings, *Moments of Being.* Withdrawing with Leonard to Monk's House in Sussex, where they could see the German airplanes flying low overhead on their way to bomb London, Woolf continued to write for peace and correspond with antiwar activists in Europe and the United States. She began to write her last novel, *Between the Acts,* in the spring of 1938, but by early 1941 was dissatisfied with it. Before completing her final revisions, Woolf ended her own life, walking into the River Ouse on the morning of March 28, 1941. To her sister, Vanessa, she wrote, "I can hardly think clearly any more. If I could I would tell you what you and the children have meant to me. I think you know." In her last note to Leonard, she told him he had given her "complete happiness," and asked him to destroy all her papers.

BY THE END of the twentieth century, Virginia Woolf had become an iconic figure, a touchstone for the feminism that revived in the 1960s as well as for the conservative backlash of the 1980s. Hailed by many as a radical writer of genius, she has also been dismissed as a narrowly focused snob. Her image adorns T-shirts, postcards, and even a beer advertisement, while phrases from her writings occur in all kinds of contexts, from peace-march slogans to highbrow book reviews. That Woolf is one of those figures upon whom the myriad competing narratives of twentieth- and twenty-first-century Western culture inscribe themselves is testified to by the enormous number of biographical works about her published in the decades since her nephew Quentin Bell broke the ground in 1972 with his two-volume biography of his aunt.

Argument continues about the work and life of Virginia Woolf: about her experience of incest, her madness, her class attitudes, her sexuality, the difficulty of her prose, her politics, her feminism, and her legacy. Perhaps, though, these words from her essay "How Should One Read a Book?" are our best guide: "The only advice, indeed, that one person can give another about reading is to take no advice, to follow your own instincts, to use your own reason, to come to your own conclusions."

—MARK HUSSEY, GENERAL EDITOR

CHRONOLOGY

Information is arranged in this order: 1. Virginia Woolf's family and her works; 2. Cultural and political events; 3. Significant publications and works of art.

1878   Marriage of Woolf's parents, Leslie Stephen (1832–1904) and Julia Prinsep Duckworth (née Jackson) (1846–1895). Leslie Stephen publishes *Samuel Johnson,* first volume in the English Men of Letters series.
England at war in Afghanistan.

1879   Vanessa Stephen (Bell) born (d. 1961). Edward Burne-Jones paints Julia Stephen as the Virgin Mary in "The Annunciation." Leslie Stephen, *Hours in a Library,* 3rd series.
Somerville and Lady Margaret Hall Colleges for women founded at Oxford University.
Anglo-Zulu war in South Africa.

1880   Thoby Stephen born (d. 1906).
William Gladstone becomes prime minister for second time. First Boer War begins (1880–81). Deaths of Gustave Flaubert (b. 1821) and George Eliot (b. 1819). Lytton Strachey born (d. 1932).
Fyodor Dostoyevsky, *The Brothers Karamazov.*

1881   Leslie Stephen buys lease of Talland House, St. Ives, Cornwall.

Cambridge University Tripos exams opened to women. Henrik Ibsen, *Ghosts;* Henry James, *The Portrait of a Lady, Washington Square;* Christina Rossetti, *A Pageant and Other Poems;* D. G. Rossetti, *Ballads and Sonnets;* Oscar Wilde, *Poems.*

1882   Adeline Virginia Stephen (Virginia Woolf) born January 25. Leslie Stephen begins work as editor of the *Dictionary of National Biography (DNB)*; publishes *The Science of Ethics.* The Stephen family spends its first summer at Talland House.

Married Women's Property Act enables women to buy, sell, and own property and keep their own earnings. Triple Alliance between Germany, Italy, and Austria. Phoenix Park murders of British officials in Dublin, Ireland. James Joyce born (d. 1941). Death of Charles Darwin (b. 1809).

1883   Adrian Leslie Stephen born (d. 1948). Julia Stephen's *Notes from Sick Rooms* published.

Olive Schreiner, *The Story of an African Farm;* Robert Louis Stevenson, *Treasure Island.*

1884   Leslie Stephen delivers the Clark Lectures at Cambridge University.

Third Reform Act extends the franchise in England. Friedrich Engels, *The Origin of the Family, Private Property and the State;* John Ruskin, *The Storm-Cloud of the Nineteenth Century;* Mark Twain, *The Adventures of Huckleberry Finn.*

1885   First volume of Leslie Stephen's *Dictionary of National Biography* published.

Redistribution Act further extends the franchise in England. Ezra Pound born (d. 1972); D. H. Lawrence born (d. 1930).

George Meredith, *Diana of the Crossways;* Émile Zola, *Germinal.*

1887   Queen Victoria's Golden Jubilee.

Arthur Conan Doyle, *A Study in Scarlet;* H. Rider Haggard, *She;* Thomas Hardy, *The Woodlanders.*

1891   Leslie Stephen gives up the *DNB* editorship. Laura Stephen (1870–1945) is placed in an asylum.

William Gladstone elected prime minister of England a fourth time.

Thomas Hardy, *Tess of the D'Urbervilles;* Oscar Wilde, *The Picture of Dorian Gray.*

1895   Death of Julia Stephen.

Armenian Massacres in Turkey. Discovery of X-rays by William Röntgen; Guglielmo Marconi discovers radio; invention of the cinematograph. Trials of Oscar Wilde.

Thomas Hardy, *Jude the Obscure;* H. G. Wells, *The Time Machine;* Oscar Wilde, *The Importance of Being Earnest.*

1896   Vanessa Stephen begins drawing classes three afternoons a week.

Death of William Morris (b. 1834); F. Scott Fitzgerald born (d. 1940).

Anton Chekhov, *The Seagull.*

1897   Woolf attends Greek and history classes at King's College, London, and begins to keep a regular diary. Vanessa, Virginia, and Thoby watch Queen Victoria's Diamond Jubilee procession. Stella Duckworth (b. 1869) marries Jack Hills in April, but dies in July. Gerald Duckworth (1870–1937) establishes a publishing house.
Paul Gauguin, *Where Do We Come From? What Are We? Where Are We Going?*; Bram Stoker, *Dracula.*

1898   Spanish-American War (1898–99). Marie Curie discovers radium. Death of Stéphane Mallarmé (b. 1842).
H. G. Wells, *The War of the Worlds;* Oscar Wilde, *The Ballad of Reading Gaol.*

1899   Woolf begins Latin and Greek lessons with Clara Pater. Thoby Stephen goes up to Trinity College, Cambridge University, entering with Lytton Strachey, Leonard Woolf (1880–1969), and Clive Bell (1881–1964).
The Second Boer War begins (1899–1902) in South Africa. Ernest Hemingway born (d. 1961).

1900   Woolf and Vanessa attend the Trinity College Ball at Cambridge University.
Deaths of Friedrich Nietzsche (b. 1844), John Ruskin (b. 1819), and Oscar Wilde (b. 1854).
Sigmund Freud, *The Interpretation of Dreams.*

1901   Vanessa enters Royal Academy Schools.
Queen Victoria dies January 22. Edward VII becomes king. Marconi sends messages by wireless telegraphy from Cornwall to Newfoundland.

1902   Woolf begins classics lessons with Janet Case. Adrian
        Stephen enters Trinity College, Cambridge University.
        Leslie Stephen is knighted.
        Joseph Conrad, *Heart of Darkness;* Henry James, *The
        Wings of the Dove;* William James, *The Varieties of Religious
        Experience.*

1903   The Wright Brothers fly a biplane 852 feet. Women's
        Social and Political Union founded in England by Em-
        meline Pankhurst.

1904   Sir Leslie Stephen dies. George Duckworth (1868–
        1934) marries Lady Margaret Herbert. The Stephen
        children—Vanessa, Virginia, Thoby, and Adrian—move
        to 46 Gordon Square, in the Bloomsbury district of
        London. Woolf contributes to F. W. Maitland's biogra-
        phy of her father. Leonard Woolf comes to dine before
        sailing for Ceylon. Woolf travels in Italy and France.
        Her first publication is an unsigned review in the
        Guardian, a church weekly.
        "Empire Day" inaugurated in London and in Britain's
        colonies.
        Anton Chekhov, *The Cherry Orchard;* Henry James, *The
        Golden Bowl.*

1905   Woolf begins teaching weekly adult education classes at
        Morley College. Thoby invites Cambridge friends to
        their home for "Thursday Evenings"—the beginnings
        of the Bloomsbury Group. Woolf travels with Adrian to
        Portugal and Spain. The Stephens visit Cornwall for the
        first time since their mother's death.
        Revolution in Russia.

Albert Einstein, *Special Theory of Relativity;* E. M. Forster, *Where Angels Fear to Tread;* Sigmund Freud, *Essays in the Theory of Sexuality;* Edith Wharton, *The House of Mirth;* Oscar Wilde, *De Profundis.*

1906 The Stephens travel to Greece. Vanessa and Thoby fall ill. Thoby dies November 20; on November 22, Vanessa agrees to marry Clive Bell.
Deaths of Paul Cézanne (b. 1839) and Henrik Ibsen (b. 1828). Samuel Beckett born (d. 1989).

1907 Woolf moves with her brother Adrian to Fitzroy Square. Vanessa marries Clive Bell.
First Cubist exhibition in Paris. W. H. Auden born (d. 1973).
Joseph Conrad, *The Secret Agent;* E. M. Forster, *The Longest Journey;* Edmund Gosse, *Father and Son;* Pablo Picasso, *Demoiselles d'Avignon.*

1908 Birth of Vanessa Bell's first child, Julian. Woolf travels to Italy with Vanessa and Clive Bell.
Herbert Asquith becomes prime minister.
E. M. Forster, *A Room with a View;* Gertrude Stein, *Three Lives.*

1909 Woolf receives a legacy of £2,500 on the death of her Quaker aunt, Caroline Emelia Stephen. Lytton Strachey proposes marriage to Woolf, but they both quickly realize this would be a mistake. Woolf meets Lady Ottoline Morrell for the first time. She travels to the Wagner festival in Bayreuth.
Chancellor of the Exchequer David Lloyd George (1863–1945) introduces a "People's Budget," taxing

wealth to pay for social reforms. A constitutional crisis ensues when the House of Lords rejects it. Death of George Meredith (b. 1828).

Filippo Marinetti, "The Founding and Manifesto of Futurism"; Henri Matisse, *Dance.*

1910   Woolf participates in the Dreadnought Hoax. She volunteers for the cause of women's suffrage. Birth of Vanessa Bell's second child, Quentin (d. 1996).

First Post-Impressionist Exhibition ("Manet and the Post-Impressionists") organized by Roger Fry (1866–1934) at the Grafton Galleries in London. Edward VII dies May 6. George V becomes king. Death of Leo Tolstoy (b. 1828).

E. M. Forster, *Howards End;* Igor Stravinsky, *The Firebird.*

1911   Woolf rents Little Talland House in Sussex. Leonard Woolf returns from Ceylon; in November, he, Adrian Stephen, John Maynard Keynes (1883–1946), Woolf, and Duncan Grant (1885–1978) share a house together at Brunswick Square in London.

Ernest Rutherford makes first model of atomic structure. Rupert Brooke, *Poems;* Joseph Conrad, *Under Western Eyes;* D. H. Lawrence, *The White Peacock;* Katherine Mansfield, *In a German Pension;* Ezra Pound, *Canzoni;* Edith Wharton, *Ethan Frome.*

1912   Woolf leases Asheham House in Sussex. Marries Leonard on August 10; they move to Clifford's Inn, London.

Captain Robert Scott's expedition reaches the South Pole, but he and his companions die on the return

journey. The *Titanic* sinks. Second Post-Impressionist Exhibition, for which Leonard Woolf serves as
secretary.

Marcel Duchamp, *Nude Descending a Staircase;* Wassily
Kandinsky, *Concerning the Spiritual in Art;* Thomas
Mann, *Death in Venice;* George Bernard Shaw, *Pygmalion.*

1913 *The Voyage Out* manuscript delivered to Gerald Duckworth. Woolf enters a nursing home in July; in September, she attempts suicide.

Roger Fry founds the Omega Workshops.

Sigmund Freud, *Totem and Taboo;* D. H. Lawrence, *Sons
and Lovers;* Marcel Proust, *Du côté de chez Swann;* Igor
Stravinsky, *Le Sacre du printemps.*

1914 Leonard Woolf, *The Wise Virgins;* he reviews Freud's
The Psychopathology of Everyday Life.

World War I ("The Great War") begins in August.
Home Rule Bill for Ireland passed.

Clive Bell, *Art;* James Joyce, *Dubliners;* Wyndham Lewis
et al., "Vorticist Manifesto" (in *Blast*); Gertrude Stein,
Tender Buttons.

1915 *The Voyage Out,* Woolf's first novel, published by Duck-
worth. In April the Woolfs move to Hogarth House in
Richmond. Woolf begins again to keep a regular diary.
First Zeppelin attack on London. Death of Rupert
Brooke (b. 1887).

Joseph Conrad, *Victory;* Ford Madox Ford, *The Good Soldier;* D. H. Lawrence, *The Rainbow;* Dorothy Richardson,
Pointed Roofs.

1916   Woolf discovers Charleston, where her sister, Vanessa
       (no longer living with her husband, Clive), moves in
       October with her sons, Julian and Quentin, and Dun-
       can Grant (with whom she is in love) and David Gar-
       nett (with whom Duncan is in love).
       Easter Rising in Dublin. Death of Henry James (b.
       1843).
       Albert Einstein, *General Theory of Relativity;* James Joyce,
       A Portrait of the Artist as a Young Man; Dorothy Richard-
       son, *Backwater.*

1917   The Hogarth Press established by Leonard and Virginia
       Woolf in Richmond. Their first publication is their
       own *Two Stories,* with woodcuts by Dora Carrington
       (1893–1932).
       Russian Bolshevik Revolution destroys the rule of the
       czar. The United States enters the European war.
       T. S. Eliot, *Prufrock and Other Observations;* Sigmund
       Freud, *Introduction to Psychoanalysis;* Carl Jung, *The Uncon-
       scious;* Dorothy Richardson, *Honeycomb;* W. B. Yeats, *The
       Wild Swans at Coole.*

1918   Woolf meets T. S. Eliot (1888–1965). Harriet Shaw
       Weaver comes to tea with the manuscript of James
       Joyce's *Ulysses.* Vanessa Bell and Duncan Grant's daugh-
       ter, Angelica Garnett, born; her paternity is kept secret
       from all but a very few intimates.
       Armistice signed November 11; Parliamentary Reform
       Act gives votes in Britain to women of thirty and older
       and to all men.
       G. M. Hopkins, *Poems;* James Joyce, *Exiles;* Katherine
       Mansfield, *Prelude* (Hogarth Press); Marcel Proust, *À*

l'ombre des jeunes filles en fleurs; Lytton Strachey, *Eminent Victorians;* Rebecca West, *The Return of the Soldier.*

1919 The Woolfs buy Monk's House in Sussex. Woolf's second novel, *Night and Day,* is published by Duckworth. Her essay "Modern Novels" (republished in 1925 as "Modern Fiction") appears in the *Times Literary Supplement; Kew Gardens* published by Hogarth Press.

Bauhaus founded by Walter Gropius in Weimar. Sex Disqualification (Removal) Act opens many professions and public offices to women. Election of first woman member of Parliament, Nancy Astor. Treaty of Versailles imposes harsh conditions on postwar Germany, opposed by John Maynard Keynes, who writes *The Economic Consequences of the Peace.* League of Nations created. T. S. Eliot, "Tradition and the Individual Talent," *Poems;* Dorothy Richardson, *The Tunnel, Interim;* Robert Wiene, *The Cabinet of Dr. Caligari* (film).

1920 The Memoir Club, comprising thirteen original members of the Bloomsbury Group, meets for the first time. *The Voyage Out* and *Night and Day* are published in the United States by George H. Doran.

Mohandas Gandhi initiates mass passive resistance against British rule in India.

T. S. Eliot, *The Sacred Wood;* Sigmund Freud, *Beyond the Pleasure Principle;* Roger Fry, *Vision and Design;* D. H. Lawrence, *Women in Love;* Katherine Mansfield, *Bliss and Other Stories;* Ezra Pound, *Hugh Selwyn Mauberley;* Marcel Proust, *Le Côté de Guermantes I;* Edith Wharton, *The Age of Innocence.*

1921 Woolf's short story collection *Monday or Tuesday* published by Hogarth Press, which will from this time publish all her books in England. The book is also published in the United States by Harcourt Brace, which from now on is her American publisher.

Aldous Huxley, *Crome Yellow;* Pablo Picasso, *Three Musicians;* Luigi Pirandello, *Six Characters in Search of an Author;* Marcel Proust, *Le Côté de Guermantes II, Sodome et Gomorrhe I;* Dorothy Richardson, *Deadlock;* Lytton Strachey, *Queen Victoria.*

1922   *Jacob's Room* published. Woolf meets Vita Sackville-West (1892–1962) for the first time.

Bonar Law elected prime minister. Mussolini comes to power in Italy. Irish Free State established. British Broadcasting Company (BBC) formed. Discovery of Tutankhamen's tomb in Egypt. Death of Marcel Proust (b. 1871).

T. S. Eliot, *The Waste Land;* James Joyce, *Ulysses;* Katherine Mansfield, *The Garden Party;* Marcel Proust, *Sodome et Gomorrhe II;* Ludwig Wittgenstein, *Tractatus Logico-Philosophicus.*

1923   The Woolfs travel to Spain, stopping in Paris on the way home. Hogarth Press publishes *The Waste Land.*

Stanley Baldwin succeeds Bonar Law as prime minister. Death of Katherine Mansfield (b. 1888).

Mina Loy, *Lunar Baedeker;* Marcel Proust, *La Prisonnière;* Dorothy Richardson, *Revolving Lights;* Rainer Maria Rilke, *Duino Elegies.*

1924   The Woolfs move to Tavistock Square. Woolf lectures on "Character in Fiction" to the Heretics Society at Cambridge University.

The Labour Party takes office for the first time under

the leadership of Ramsay MacDonald but is voted out within the year. Death of Joseph Conrad (b. 1857).

E. M. Forster, *A Passage to India;* Thomas Mann, *The Magic Mountain.*

1925   *Mrs. Dalloway* and *The Common Reader* published. Woolf stays with Vita Sackville-West at her house, Long Barn, for the first time.

Nancy Cunard, *Parallax;* F. Scott Fitzgerald, *The Great Gatsby;* Ernest Hemingway, *In Our Time;* Adolf Hitler, *Mein Kampf;* Franz Kafka, *The Trial;* Alain Locke, ed., *The New Negro;* Marcel Proust, *Albertine disparue;* Dorothy Richardson, *The Trap;* Gertrude Stein, *The Making of Americans.*

1926   Woolf lectures on "How Should One Read a Book?" at Hayes Court School. "Cinema" published in *Arts* (New York), "Impassioned Prose" in *Times Literary Supplement,* and "On Being Ill" in *New Criterion.* Meets Gertrude Stein (1874–1946).

The General Strike in support of mine workers in England lasts nearly two weeks.

Ernest Hemingway, *The Sun Also Rises;* Langston Hughes, *The Weary Blues;* Franz Kafka, *The Castle;* A. A. Milne, *Winnie-the-Pooh.*

1927   *To the Lighthouse,* "The Art of Fiction," "Poetry, Fiction and the Future," and "Street Haunting" published. The Woolfs travel with Vita Sackville-West and her husband, Harold Nicolson, to Yorkshire to see the total eclipse of the sun. They buy their first car.

Charles Lindbergh flies the Atlantic solo.

E. M. Forster, *Aspects of the Novel;* Ernest Hemingway, *Men without Women;* Franz Kafka, *Amerika;* Marcel

Proust, *Le Temps retrouvé;* Gertrude Stein, *Four Saints in Three Acts.*

1928 *Orlando, A Biography* published. In October, Woolf delivers two lectures at Cambridge on which she will base *A Room of One's Own.* Femina-Vie Heureuse prize awarded to *To the Lighthouse.*

The Equal Franchise Act gives the vote to all women over twenty-one. Sound films introduced. Death of Thomas Hardy (b. 1840).

Djuna Barnes, *Ladies Almanack;* Radclyffe Hall, *The Well of Loneliness;* D. H. Lawrence, *Lady Chatterley's Lover;* Evelyn Waugh, *Decline and Fall;* W. B. Yeats, *The Tower.*

1929 *A Room of One's Own* published. "Women and Fiction" in *The Forum* (New York).

Labour Party returned to power under Prime Minister MacDonald. Discovery of penicillin. Museum of Modern Art opens in New York. Wall Street crash.

William Faulkner, *The Sound and the Fury;* Ernest Hemingway, *A Farewell to Arms;* Nella Larsen, *Passing.*

1930 Woolf meets the pioneering composer, writer, and suffragette Ethel Smyth (1858–1944), with whom she forms a close friendship.

Death of D. H. Lawrence (b. 1885).

W. H. Auden, *Poems;* T. S. Eliot, *Ash Wednesday;* William Faulkner, *As I Lay Dying;* Sigmund Freud, *Civilisation and Its Discontents.*

1931 *The Waves* is published. First of six articles by Woolf about London published in *Good Housekeeping;* "Introductory Letter" to *Life As We Have Known It.* Lectures to London branch of National Society for Women's Service on "Professions for Women." Meets John Lehmann (1907–1987), who will become a partner in the Hogarth Press.

Growing financial crisis throughout Europe and beginning of the Great Depression.

1932 *The Common Reader, Second Series* and "Letter to a Young Poet" published. Woolf invited to give the 1933 Clark Lectures at Cambridge, which she declines.

Death of Lytton Strachey (b. 1880).

Aldous Huxley, *Brave New World*.

1933 *Flush, A Biography,* published. The Woolfs travel by car to Italy.

Adolf Hitler becomes chancellor of Germany, establishing the totalitarian dictatorship of his National Socialist (Nazi) Party.

T. S. Eliot, *The Use of Poetry and the Use of Criticism;* George Orwell, *Down and Out in Paris and London;* Gertrude Stein, *The Autobiography of Alice B. Toklas;* Nathanael West, *Miss Lonelyhearts;* W. B. Yeats, *The Collected Poems*.

1934 Woolf meets W. B. Yeats at Ottoline Morrell's house. Writes "Walter Sickert: A Conversation."

George Duckworth dies. Roger Fry dies.

Samuel Beckett, *More Pricks Than Kicks;* Nancy Cunard, ed., *Negro: An Anthology;* F. Scott Fitzgerald, *Tender Is the Night;* Wyndham Lewis, *Men Without Art;* Henry Miller, *Tropic of Cancer;* Ezra Pound, *ABC of Reading;* Evelyn Waugh, *A Handful of Dust*.

1935   The Woolfs travel to Germany, where they accidentally get caught up in a parade for Göring. They return to England via Italy and France.

1936   Woolf reads "Am I a Snob?" to the Memoir Club, and publishes "Why Art Today Follows Politics" in the *Daily Worker*.
Death of George V, who is succeeded by Edward VIII, who then abdicates to marry Wallis Simpson. George VI becomes king. Spanish Civil War (1936–38) begins when General Franco, assisted by Germany and Italy, attacks the Republican government. BBC television begins.
Djuna Barnes, *Nightwood;* Charlie Chaplin, *Modern Times* (film); Aldous Huxley, *Eyeless in Gaza;* J. M. Keynes, *The General Theory of Employment, Interest and Money;* Rose Macaulay, *Personal Pleasures;* Margaret Mitchell, *Gone with the Wind.*

1937   *The Years* published. Woolf's nephew Julian Bell killed in the Spanish Civil War.
Neville Chamberlain becomes prime minister.
Zora Neale Hurston, *Their Eyes Were Watching God;* David Jones, *In Parenthesis;* Pablo Picasso, *Guernica;* John Steinbeck, *Of Mice and Men;* J. R. R. Tolkien, *The Hobbit.*

1938   *Three Guineas* published.
Germany annexes Austria. Chamberlain negotiates the Munich Agreement ("Peace in our time"), ceding Czech territory to Hitler.
Samuel Beckett, *Murphy;* Elizabeth Bowen, *The Death of the Heart;* Jean-Paul Sartre, *La Nausée.*

1939   The Woolfs visit Sigmund Freud, living in exile in London having fled the Nazis. They move to Mecklenburgh Square.

Germany occupies Czechoslovakia; Italy occupies Albania; Russia makes a nonaggression pact with Germany. Germany invades Poland and war is declared by Britain and France on Germany, September 3. Deaths of W. B. Yeats (b. 1865), Sigmund Freud (b. 1856), and Ford Madox Ford (b. 1873).

James Joyce, *Finnegans Wake;* John Steinbeck, *The Grapes of Wrath;* Nathanael West, *The Day of the Locust.*

1940   *Roger Fry: A Biography* published. "Thoughts on Peace in an Air Raid" in the *New Republic.* Woolf lectures on "The Leaning Tower" to the Workers Educational Association in Brighton.

The Battle of Britain leads to German night bombings of English cities. The Woolfs' house at Mecklenburgh Square is severely damaged, as is their former house at Tavistock Square. Hogarth Press is moved out of London.

Ernest Hemingway, *For Whom the Bell Tolls;* Christina Stead, *The Man Who Loved Children.*

1941   Woolf drowns herself, March 28, in the River Ouse in Sussex. *Between the Acts* published in July.

Death of James Joyce (b. 1882).

Rebecca West, *Black Lamb and Grey Falcon.*

INTRODUCTION
BY JANE MARCUS

THREE GUINEAS is a very radical book. For those who think of Virginia Woolf only as a Modernist English novelist, it will be a revelation. She was also a major European thinker. Here we have Virginia Woolf's last words as a public intellectual, a late pronouncement in a series of works that define her as an important European theorist of feminism, pacifism, and socialism.[1] We know that she wanted the American reader to respond to her attack on fascism because she published *Three Guineas* in the United States in a version especially for American readers with many changes, deletions, and additions.[2] Also, in May and June 1938, she published a shortened version called "Women Must Weep — Or Unite Against War" in two issues of the highly respected and widely read "highbrow" American journal, the *Atlantic Monthly*. Doubtless she was capitalizing (I use the word advisedly) on the enormous popular success of her fictional version of the same themes and issues in *The Years* in the previous year (1937) when she appeared on the cover of *Time* magazine on April 12 in Man Ray's controversial photograph with dark red lipstick and a shingled haircut. Her image in the United States changed utterly. Mrs. Woolf was no longer the Victorian lady of Bloomsbury but a hard-hitting feminist who had a great deal to say about public issues. The *Atlantic Monthly*'s audience was huge and quite different from the literary audience for her novels. Skeptics may argue from her well-known anti-Americanism and remarks in her diaries and letters that she published so much of her last work (reviews and short stories) in the United States for the sake of the money, but it would be an irony at odds with the anticapitalist thrust of her book.

Although Brenda Silver and Anna Snaith, in studying the response to the book, have documented that many letters from American readers, especially women and working-class men, praised her work and many began corresponding with her, educated men, including men on the Left, as in Britain, remained in the dark.[3] American women were dealing with different patriarchal institutions, of course, but they experienced the same "tyrannies and servilities" (*Three Guineas* 168) as English women. Woolf's idea was that the gender issue was inseparable from the buildup to war and the power of fascism to rule the state. But the atmosphere in the United States was tense and uncertain as well as undecided on the issue of the rise of fascism in Europe, the Spanish Civil War (see the note to page 14), the Nazis, and Mussolini's Italy. Before publishing two large sections of *Three Guineas,* which was sparked by her horror at photographs of children killed by Franco's bombs in Spain, the editor of the *Atlantic Monthly* himself published an article congratulating Franco.[4]

While the work of Silver and Snaith gives us a good idea of what the response to *Three Guineas* was like at the time — essentially violently mixed in pros and cons — no one was lukewarm. That response is evident again today, during another militaristic moment in western history. We cannot know how many readers were converted to Woolf's ideals because of this book, but we may remember the importance it had in the foundational debates of Second Wave feminism in the United States, Britain, Europe, and abroad. The appearance of work by feminist literary critics, philosophers, historians, and political scientists in the late '70s established *A Room of One's Own* and *Three Guineas* as the "Bible" of a new feminist movement for social change that succeeded the struggle of Woolf's generation. The public debate was exciting, and women in the professions, Woolf's next generation of "educated women," were following her lead in arguing the issues of gender and identity, women and citizenship, patriotism and pacifism, motherhood and creativity, and using her books as instruction manuals. In the United States, the Vietnam War served as the impetus to debate woman's role, just as the rise of fascism determined the arguments of *Three Guineas.* Woolf's pamphlets were among the things the new feminist researchers carried to the libraries and professional meetings to invent new ways of thinking about gender. We read aloud from these texts at demonstrations and many still march against war under her banners.

The work of Tillie Olsen, Berenice Carroll, Blanche Wiesen Cook, Sandi Cooper, Amy Swerdlow, Naomi Black, and Brenda Silver brought Woolf's ideas into intellectual currency again. The Berkshire Women's History meeting echoed with Woolf's words, as did the Modern Language Association (MLA); the newly formed Virginia Woolf Society, inspired by J. J. Wilson's session at the 1970 MLA convention on "The Uses of Manuscripts in Virginia Woolf Studies," was as deeply influenced by Woolf's ideas as we were by her novels. Brenda Silver's pioneering work studying Woolf's notebooks and scrapbooks for *Three Guineas* gave us a model for the intellectual life of radical women. The newspaper clippings that Woolf collected throughout the 1930s, now online due to the work of Merry Pawlowski and Vara Neverow,[5] inspired us to stay politically engaged and activist despite our academic work as feminists. Keeping track of fascism and patriarchy in her own day, Virginia Woolf inspired us to do the same. It seemed that the fictional version of Woolf's ideas, her novel *The Years,* and the "factual" (or feminist counterfactual) effort of *Three Guineas* was repeated in Doris Lessing's later experiment *The Golden Notebook* (1962). Both political writers took that domestic staple of family life, the scrapbook, and used it for recording public events. For a brief time, I, too, kept a scrap-book of news clippings, Peace and Freedom pamphlets, and photographs of the police beating demonstrators during the Vietnam War. Woolf used her scrapbooks to produce a universal protest from that particular European fascism.

The 1970s debate over Sara Ruddick's ideas, eventually published in *Maternal Thinking,* and the question of whether women were less inclined than men to make war because they bore children, was a memorable part of the discussion. On the Left, Lillian Robinson debated class issues in the new feminist classics, and in England the women of the Greenham Common Peace Encampment carried *Three Guineas* under their arms and read aloud from it during their vigils at the U.S. Air Force base. Misreadings of the text were common, and some agreed with Vita Sackville-West that it was full of "misleading arguments" (Sackville-West 412). But it is clear that Woolf did not believe that nonviolence was innate in women. She had been thinking about this issue for decades. Her quotation from one of the Spanish Civil War pamphlets that inspired her book makes this clear: "If sanctioned the fighting instinct easily develops" (*Three Guineas* 210), she writes, and gives the following example:

> —Come nearer Amalia—orders the commandant. She pushes her horse towards us and salutes her chief with the sword.
> —Sergeant Amalia Bonilla—continues the chief of the squadron—how old are you?—Thirty-six.—Where were you born?—In Granada.—Why have you joined the army?—My two daughters were militiawomen. The younger has been killed in the Alto de Leon. I thought I had to supersede her and avenge her.—And how many enemies have you killed to avenge her?—You know it,

commandant, five. The sixth is not sure.—No, but you
have taken his horse. The amazon Amalia rides in fact a
magnificent dapple-grey horse.... (210)

Woolf is quoting from *The Martyrdom of Madrid: Inedited Witnesses*, published by the French reporter Louis Delaprée in
Madrid in 1937 (see Laurence, "Facts and Fugue"). His pamphlet includes many stories and details that his Paris newspaper
refused to print, including photographs of "dead children," a
phrase that, in the mourning mode of lamentation ("Women
must weep"), becomes the Dies Irae–like refrain of *Three Guineas*.

Since the heyday of these arguments, few have doubted
women's capacity for violence. But not all American feminists
adopted Virginia Woolf as their role model. The critics were
split on her significance, and the "lupines," as they were called
by Woolf's nephew and biographer, Quentin Bell, continued to
discuss her politics despite his disdain for his subject's feminism
and pacifism. But others feared that "the ultimate room of one's
own is the grave" (Showalter 297), based on their reading of
Bell's biography, which emphasized Woolf's illnesses, construct-
ing her as a madwoman and writing the life backward from the
suicide. How could such a woman be the role model for a new
feminism?

In Britain, critics in the circle of sociologist Michèle Barrett
debated the issue, disturbed more than Americans by class issues and the elitism attributed to Virginia Woolf and Bloomsbury by a smear campaign by the Cambridge University critic
F. R. Leavis and his wife, Queenie (Q. D. Leavis), who set Woolf
against D. H. Lawrence, the "true" working-class English writer.
Many university English departments and left-wing and socialist men had been educated on these lines by Leavis and his fol-
lowers, so it took a bit longer for British critics to embrace the
writer and to interpret her writing for themselves. Gillian Beer

was an early independent exception in Britain in terms of taking Woolf's intellect seriously.

This complicated history is a classic example of uneven developments. In *British Writers of the Thirties* (1988), Valentine Cunningham could still with impunity dismiss *Three Guineas* as "skittishly wayward," ranking it among the low points of the decade with Aldous Huxley's 1936 Peace Pledge Union pamphlet *What Are You Going to Do About It? The Case for Constructive Peace* (70). Woolf's nephew Julian Bell is sneeringly traced from the "Bloomsbury . . . pacifism" of his *We Did Not Fight* (1935) "then steadily backtracking, and finally dying in Spain driving a conscience-appeasing ambulance" (70). Leonard Woolf, despite his Labour Party activism, work for the League of Nations, and his many important political works in this decade, is merely mentioned as Virginia Woolf's "Jewish husband" (40).

Recently, the center of Woolf studies has shifted somewhat from the United States to Britain, producing, among other things, new Penguin editions of the novels and essays, edited by Julia Briggs with introductions by a new generation of Woolf scholars, and a new biography by Hermione Lee, based on three decades of critical, biographical, and textual work done by mostly American critics. Finally, the new biography by Julia Briggs (2005) treats Woolf as an already established canonical English novelist, ignoring the previous conflict and turmoil about the life and concentrating on the writer and her writing.

Feminist Politics

DESPITE HAVING licked a few envelopes in the cause of the Adult Suffrage League during the women's suffrage movement in 1910 (*Letters* 1: 421), Woolf was not an activist. Neither her health nor her temperament allowed her to experience the violent demonstrations of the radical decade of feminist revolt at the beginning of the twentieth century or the equally violent anti-fascist demonstrations of the 1930s. Thinking was her fighting, she said (*Diary* 5: 285), and "by writing, I am doing what is far more necessary than anything else" ("A Sketch" 73): *Three Guineas* is paramount in its verbally aggressive attacks on the enemies of peace and the origins of war in patriarchy. But, we must remember, publishing was her fighting as well, and we see clearly her commitment to feminism, socialism, pacifism, anti-imperialism, and antifascism (as well as experimental writing) in her publications at the Hogarth Press. Owning her own press gave Virginia Woolf the freedom to publish what she believed in and to say what she wanted in her own work. *Three Guineas* was published in a Hogarth series of feminist books, including important works by Willa Muir and Ray Strachey.[6]

Her allegiance to "Adult Suffrage," instead of to any of the more exclusively feminist organizations (like the Women's Social and Political Union of Emmeline and Christabel Pankhurst), to obtain votes for women should make clear her early commitment to the principle that working-class men were, like all women, victims of patriarchy, and she supported the socialist-feminist group that advocated that men, especially returning soldiers and sailors, be granted the right to vote despite the fact that they did not own property (Oldfield 16–18). The nature of Woolf's socialist feminism is often misunderstood. Her lifelong concern for working-class women may be seen in the "Introductory Letter" to Margaret Llewelyn Davies' *Life As We Have Known It* (1931).

Here she also uses the epistolary form instead of a preface; she uses it again in "Letter to a Young Poet" (1932). The persona of the letter writer is clearly female, because women have been allowed to practice this minor form of writing where truth has not been an issue, but in *Three Guineas* she (and the speaker is clearly female) seems to be created by the writers who have asked for money and readers of both sides of the correspondence. That means you and me. There is a valiant but (I think) failed attempt on the part of the writer to create a discursive community based on our interest in the causes of peace, women's education, and antifascism, perhaps using as the model for her "Society of Outsiders" the "we" created by the letter and its reply. One of the working titles for *Three Guineas* was "On Being Despised," but another was "Answers to Correspondents." We know that Woolf's genius as a letter writer was based in her imagining of the face on the other side of the page and that she took on various personalities in order to shape her reply to the reader she had created. One of the difficulties of reading this book is following the multiple voices of the speaker and assuming the multiple roles in which she casts us.

Money

A WELL-DEVELOPED class consciousness lies behind Woolf's assessment of the struggles of working-class women and the limitations placed on the help women of her own class might give to their sisters. Since she believed that women like herself were hindered in their wish to change policy and politics by a lack of formal education and access to the public institutions where power resides, her book, like her earlier feminist manifesto *A Room of One's Own*, focuses on money. The £500 a year she demands for the woman artist to live in freedom has, since that book was revived by American feminists in the 1970s, become an icon of our age. From the three guineas of the later work's title, with their origin in Britain's economic interest in the slave trade (both as a nation and as individual men), to the difference in funds possessed by women and men to the enormous amounts of money the British government was devoting to its war chest, she breaks all the rules about ladies not talking about money. In naming her book for the coins minted with the proceeds from African slavery, Woolf invests her text with outrage at the exploits of English imperialists and makes the connection between race, capitalism, and patriarchy (see the note on the book's title, page 223). Money and its origins are her subject.

In fact, she talks about little else in this book, packed as it is with references to pounds and shillings and pence, pointing a finger at women's poverty while the coffers of the church, the state, the military, the universities, and the men's colleges obscenely overflow. The finer points of the subject of women and money do not escape her. She points out that Sophia Jex-Blake's father would not allow her to accept wages for her work as a doctor because it would reflect badly on him (*Three Guineas* 79, 156). Women of her class must "work" only as volunteers, and there is a running joke about women organizing bazaars as fund-raisers. Vanessa Bell's jacket for the book, with its obsolete quill pen and checkbook in the same nursery pink and blue of her design for the jacket of *A Room of One's Own,* is a very mild cover for the modern clink of coins and the shuffling of paper that resound through the text.[7] In fact, one may say that the pound sign £ is the most important signifier in the book. Money, money, money. The pound sign appears so often in the text that the typesetters must have thought it was a new letter in the alphabet. (I count seventy-one instances of £ in the text and twenty-five in Woolf's notes. This does not include references to money in words.)

Woolf's Marxist economic analysis of women's oppression is very different from the writings of other feminists of the period in that the focus is on a struggle of the middle-class Englishwoman for emancipation from the economic dominance of her fathers and brothers. She believed firmly that leftists must organize in their own class before rushing off to organize the masses, and makes many hostile references in her writing of this political decade to what she considers to be the dishonest attempts of young men in the Left intelligentsia of Britain to avoid the responsibility of converting one's own class to principles of justice before going as missionaries to the working class. Woolf is following the dicta to write what she knows best, to organize in her own class, and to point out the dependence of capitalism on patriarchy. Women's forced allegiance to patriarchy was determined by their poverty. The basic argument is that women have supported patriarchy because they have been economically dependent on men. Because they did not participate in "production," their class position could not be calculated. Now that they have begun to enter the workforce, she shows women of her own class what their social and political responsibilities are. In part two, we are urged to embrace poverty, intellectual chastity, derision, and freedom from unreal loyalties as we enter the professions. It would be a daunting task to make the revolution she demands because she insists that on breaking any gender barrier we are ethically responsible for opening the doors to the other oppressed or excluded people who come after us.

The issues of gender, equality, identity, education, war, and peace that Woolf had been struggling with in all her writing are subject to a final burst of fury in *Three Guineas*. Here we have a devastating analysis of fascism at home and abroad. History may show England as the champion fighter against German and Italian fascism in World War II, but Woolf shows fascism at home in the English family. Politically, this is very much a thirties text, part of the discourse of a powerful debate among the European Left inspired by the dilemma of how to respond to the Spanish Civil War. To the harrowing question that tormented so many of her contemporaries—Was there ever a just war?—she answered no.

A Thirties Documentary

THREE GUINEAS was part of a major documentary project Virginia Woolf undertook in the 1930s but never completed. For a decade she kept news clippings on war, the rise of fascism, and the treatment of women in the labor force, education, and the church in a series of notebooks and scrapbooks (now in the University of Sussex Library), as if she were collecting pieces for a patchwork quilt. The notebooks are a source for *Three Guineas,* but they also inspired *The Years,* originally conceived as a series of fictional chapters to be interleaved with factual chapters from *Three Guineas* but then published separately as a novel when she feared the experiment would not work. The decision to cut "enormous chunks" of writing from *The Years* itself at the last minute, when it was already in galley proofs, indicates her disquiet about the mixed project that contained "enough powder to blow up St. Paul's" (*Diary* 4: 77). Another part of the project was a speech called "Professions for Women," drafts of which have been reprinted along with much of the deleted material from *The Years* in the posthumous *The Pargiters* (and see Woolf, "Speech"). Altogether, the novel and the pamphlet and the speech, along with the reading notebooks, the scrapbooks, and the discarded proofs of *The Years,* make a huge documentary that never quite came off. Ambitious readers may easily reconstruct the pieces.

An Interactive Text

WHILE *A Room of One's Own* has become a classic feminist text, *Three Guineas,* a much more formidable and savage denunciation of male privilege and its relation to private property and war, has had far fewer readers. It is difficult to read because the role of the reader in overhearing the narrator's responses is uncomfortable. We are eavesdroppers twisting our necks to hear what she says, and we are never sure we aren't being addressed as well, as part of the problem. Readers always want to be on the right side in a book's battles, but *Three Guineas* is a minefield and we are never sure of our footing in her literary no-man's-land. Even the practice of quotation of large passages of biographies and memoirs and newspapers and journals is so overdetermined that we question the practice itself, realizing that quoting is simply a way of producing authority. Woolf produces so much quotation to buttress her point that the exhausted reader cries "Enough!"—just what she was hoping we would do. She creates authority and then teaches the reader how to dismantle it.

The strictly rational reader is asked to flow with the text's digressive circling around the "mulberry tree" of private property (*Three Guineas* 72), in her figuring the compulsions of capitalism and patriarchy as a children's game. As always in Woolf's writing, the reference to the nursery rhyme has a purpose. If we are spellbound in a round dance around the mulberry bush, as she says we are, it will be a struggle to free ourselves from the witchcraft that keeps us loyal to an oppressive social structure. The song has several versions, including references to seventeenth-century silk workers, as the silkworms were fed on mulberries and many streets in London were named after the mulberry bush in the areas where they worked. One version is a compulsive repetition of work to be done on different days of the week: "Here we go round the mulberry bush" either "so early in the morning" or "on a cold and frosty morning." In another, with the refrain "Pop goes the weasel," the subject is the way the working class spends its money: "A penny for a spool of thread / A penny for a needle," or "Half a pound of twopenny rice and half a pound of treacle," a recipe for a worker's meal of rice and sugar syrup. There is a later reference to another nursery rhyme, "Sing a Song of Sixpence," in which the king is in his countinghouse counting out his money, a historical reference to Henry VIII, his beheading of his wives, and the dissolution of the monasteries that produced enormous wealth for the Crown.

The silkworms and other such creatures appear in the book as references to professional men so often that the critic Q. D. (Queenie) Leavis called her savage review of *Three Guineas* "Caterpillars of the Commonwealth, Unite!" The title includes a mocking reference to Woolf's attempt to write a *Communist Manifesto* for women, echoing the Left slogan, "Workers of the World, Unite," as well as a phrase from Shakespeare's *Richard II* referring to the courtiers Bushy, Bagot, and Green, the quintessential "insiders," sapping the state from within, as "caterpillars of the commonwealth" (act II, scene iii). The mulberry bushes and worms and caterpillars of *Three Guineas,* like the constant references to how much things cost, constitute a working-class linguistic subtext to the book's overt concern with the problems of "daughters of educated men." Queenie Leavis obviously did not miss the message and loudly announces her allegiance to the insiders. By talking so openly about money, Woolf attracts to her side (as fellow Outsiders) working-class men and women, many of whom wrote to her about their enjoyment of her pamphlet (see Snaith).

Much noisy page turning is required to read this book, as one moves from the page to Virginia Woolf's own notes, to this editor's notes, and then to the bookshelves or the Internet to chase an undocumented allusion or a puzzling phrase. Woolf's genius lies in her commitment to experimental writing: *Three Guineas* is an interactive text. Twenty-first-century readers, who use the Internet and other technological media, should be at home with this book in a way that earlier readers were not. Part of Woolf's advanced project in experimental writing was to involve the reader in both the reading and the "writing" of the script for her books. The first words of *A Room of One's Own* are "But, you may say . . . ," putting words into the mouth of the reader or listener and giving us permission to say "No" or to argue with her. She strips herself of authority and welcomes us into the text as fellow explorers of the questions she has been asked about the relation of women to fiction. Here, in *Three Guineas,* she asks us to join her in researching questions about the relation of women to "facts," and unsettles us by turning to sources in biography, autobiography, letters, and the daily newspaper, all notoriously excluded from the realms of academic, political, or historical factual reality. These unauthorized sources, we are being taught, are where we must search for the "truth" of women's experience.

It is here that *Three Guineas* had one of its most important effects on what is called Second Wave feminism from the 1970s on, by alerting women to untapped sources of their own history in "lost" letters and diaries. Her notes and the citations in the text are a model for feminist historians about where to look for women's history. Autobiography, memoir, biography, and literary texts make up the body of the references in the book. Such sources were considered unreliable in a serious historical or political work, so Woolf is making a conscious challenge to the patriarchal authority of "footnotes" and "texts" in foregrounding these so-called unreliable sources. Her other sources were the daily papers, notorious as well for their "unreliability." The fact that readers today are as distrustful of professional histories and their "facts" as she was in her day is in part due to the immense effect *Three Guineas* has had on the deflation of English cultural authority. In addition, Woolf and her Bloomsbury contemporaries were the first to see how personal is "the political" and how much truth occurs in fiction.

Her heavily allusive writing not only makes connections to the writing of the past but gives an example of how to keep women's history alive by citation and urges us to keep these sources in circulation. As a publisher at the Hogarth Press,

Woolf urged many women to write their autobiographies. For her, personal literature gave access to the "lives of the obscure" and offered a cultural antidote to the practice of history as a series of lives of great men. The names of women are repeated in this very repetitive text as a litany to lost lives and causes. *Three Guineas* has passed on this feminist political act. Its example has been followed by several decades of interest in the writing and reading of biography and memoir. It may be hard for readers today to see the relevance of this point given the current taste for the genre, but her contemporaries believed that memoirs were, like fiction, unreliable. Woolf, as we know, thought that fiction was always closer to "truth" than factual writing.[8]

Virginia Woolf's political commitment to undermining authority is enacted in the structure and voice of her writing. Her style and her politics are equally antiestablishment. If Woolf herself has opened the text up to share authority with the reader, then it follows that my role as editor or explainer of the text is antipathetic to her intentions and takes away from your responsibilities as readers. I want to make clear that this introduction and the annotations (as opposed to Virginia Woolf's own notes) have no authority unless you so invest them. If I have usurped your role as reader/fellow researcher that the text asks of you, then your role is to read me with suspicion and to go and look up the references yourself and write your own notes. Mine are here as my own response to the book.

What Kind of a Book Is It?

I GAVE UP correcting my students when they call *A Room of One's Own* a novel. While it is in fact a series of talks in essay form, it also charms us with its fictional characters and plot. *Three Guineas* is a manifesto, a polemic in the great age of polemics. It is peace propaganda written as Europe gears up for war, as Woolf's comrades in politics and intellectual debate who had been pacifists in the First World War called for artists to take arms in the struggle in Spain against Franco and fascism. The characters she brings into the text to witness the present struggles are feminist activists from earlier struggles—Mary Kingsley, the first Englishwoman to explore Africa; Sophia Jex-Blake, the first woman doctor allowed to practice; Anne Jemima Clough and the other pioneers of women's education; Emmeline Pankhurst; Millicent Fawcett and the other suffragists and suffragettes who fought for votes for women. The Harriet Martineaus, Josephine Butlers, Barbara Stephens, Barbara Bodichons, and other Victorian feminist reformers are like saints and martyrs marching through the footnotes, joined there by another cast of contemporary characters: Frau Pommer, who is going to be hanged by the Nazis, and Sergeant Amalia Bonilla, who has killed five men, and maybe a sixth, in revenge for the killing of her daughters in the Spanish Civil War. The activist woman reader is assured of being in that distinguished company if she will also bring the cause of women into the antiwar and antifascist struggles. If you do not know anything about the history of women in Britain, here is your reading list (as in *A Room of One's Own*). And here, also, in mind-numbing repetition, is the story of how little money they had to accomplish their tremendous goals in storming the medical schools, building the women's colleges, or venturing up the Niger.

A *Communist Manifesto* for Women

THE SPANISH Civil War produced an avalanche of artistic response, in painting and propaganda, powerful posters never surpassed in artistic power since the Russian Revolution, poetry, fiction, journalism, and even music like *The Songs of the Lincoln Brigade*. George Orwell's *Homage to Catalonia* (1938), which is one of the few works that survive the historical moment, is also a hybrid text, a diary, a war journal, and an anticommunist manifesto. I fear that Orwell's book survives not so much as war writing but because of its anticommunism. In the same way one might argue that *Three Guineas* did not survive because its pacifism could not be separated from its feminism and neither -ism could be separated from Woolf's own brand of communism, a view so often misread and reversed and called "elitism." She says, "Let us try to translate the kitchenmaid's cry into the language of educated people" (103). Woolf never assumed she could speak for workingwomen or workingmen.

The guineas of the title mark her class and the fact that she could, in those days when such privileges were rare, write a check on a bank. The Spanish Civil War was clearly her impetus to put her pieces of propaganda together literally as a book and intellectually as related causes. She donated some manuscript pages of *Three Guineas* (now in the Berg Collection of the New York Public Library) to be sold for the aid of refugees from the Spanish Civil War (see *Letters* 6: 314 and 319). The sight of a group of Basque refugee children moved her to tears (*Diary* 5: 97). Such great propaganda campaigns, in which artists donate their work to political causes, were begun in the West by the international groups supporting the Republicans in Spain. "Authors Take Sides on the Spanish Civil War," organized by Nancy Cunard and published in the *Left Review* in 1937, was the first of such letters, and they are still being used today. Leonard Woolf signed it in support of the Republicans, but Virginia Woolf did not. Such appeals are common now, along with letters to the editors of newspapers signed by intellectuals to protest war and atrocity. But they were a new and exciting combination of the verbal and the visual in the late 1930s.

Like others on the Left, Woolf chose carefully among ways
to speak out from specific positions; she wrote as a member of
her class, as a woman, and as an artist. While others spoke as
party members or as members of their religions or as national
citizens, she was rigorously correct about identifying herself in
an ethically impeccable way. She thought very seriously about
the role of the artist in politics, explaining later to Ben Nicolson:

> What puzzles me is that people who had infinitely
> greater gifts than any of us had—I mean Keats, Shelley,
> Wordsworth, Coleridge and so on—were unable to influ-
> ence society. They didn't have anything like the influence
> they should have had upon 19th century politics. And so
> we drifted into imperialism and all the other horrors that
> led to 1914. Would they have had more influence if they
> had taken an active part in politics? Or would they only
> have written worse poetry? (*Letters* 6: 421)

Thirties' forms of protest literature are clearly at work in
Woolf's pamphlet, and it may be studied as well in the context
of other antiwar protests. What is interesting for us as readers
is to see how she begins to break down the barriers between the
private letter and this new form of writing, the public letter.
When we say that *Three Guineas* consists of three private letters
in response to three public letters, it is clear that both "threes"
are general, not specific, and include the speakers' receipt of and
response to hundreds of such appeals from intellectuals and
artists on the Left.

In fact, it is not too much to say that in *Three Guineas,* Virginia Woolf invents herself as the female Marx and writes the
Communist Manifesto for women. A major element in Karl Marx's
internationalism was his argument that workers had no countries, that their nationality was determined by the needs of cap-

italism for workforces. One of the most quoted passages of
Three Guineas is: "As a woman, I have no country. As a woman
I want no country. As a woman my country is the whole world"
(129). Women took the nationality of their spouses, and she de-
fines the statelessness that Marx attributed to the working class
as the condition of women. But Woolf was suspicious of all
nationalisms and maintained the internationalism of her men-
tors Jane Ellen Harrison and Margaret Llewelyn Davies. Workers do have their place in *Three Guineas,* though they are not as
prominent as the figure of the working-class woman who is
washing the dishes during Woolf's lectures in *A Room of One's
Own,* whose descendant is destined to become the future Judith
Shakespeare. Here, workers are the allies of women in a future
egalitarian society and fellow members of her Society of Outsiders. When Woolf substitutes women for workers in Marx's for-
mulation, though a careful reading suggests that she was actually
adding women to workers, not replacing them, her idealism was
stretched to the limit, a limit not acknowledged by many readers. While her attacks on middle-class professional men were
right on target, her hopes for an alliance of all the alienated
workers and disaffected women of all classes were not fulfilled.
One could argue that she was following yet another of Marx's
formulations, this time the dictum that one should organize in
one's own class. This explains the point that Lillian Robinson
makes in "Who's Afraid of *A Room of One's Own?*" about the
problems one has with the limitation of Woolf's rigorous Marxist analysis to the plight of herself and her own class, "daughters
of educated men." Her passionate adherence to this principle is
expressed in what may be seen as yet another spin-off from the
enormous *Three Guineas/The Years/The Pargiters/*"Professions for
Women" thirties documentary project that occupied Woolf during the whole decade. The essay "The Leaning Tower" chastises
Auden and Spender and the poets of the '30s for their adulation

of working-class men while neglecting to convert their own fathers to the cause of socialism. They are her counterparts as educated men themselves or the sons of educated men, and she is deeply scornful of their pro-proletarian spectacles.

The Opposition

DOSES OF antifascism were to be taken straight, not clouded by the other issues Woolf argues are central to its power. This accounts for the rage expressed by her nephew and biographer Quentin Bell at her insisting on the intimate relations between patriarchy and war, capitalism and fascism. E. M. Forster perhaps expressed the prevalent male point of view on Woolf's feminism in his memorial Rede Lecture given on her death in 1941, comparing it to a disease that breaks out in spots all over her work (195). Critics and historians since then have been as wary of *Three Guineas* and its ideas as if it, too, were carrying a contagious disease. Forster may have had in mind syphilis, or perhaps he was thinking of measles. Today we could not help but think of AIDS. Whatever the spots were, they have frightened off many readers besides Forster. It is shocking to note that such indiscriminate male tirades against Woolf's political philosophy and her book were fired off again by Nigel Nicolson in his edition of Woolf's letters (see especially volume three).

Such animus expressed so recently must encourage us to take this work seriously. The beginnings of fascist ideology are described by Woolf in graphic imagery of poisonous worms and evil eggs, caterpillars, and insects "on a leaf, but in the heart of England" (65). We may want to compare her figures of speech with E. M. Forster's. How was it possible for two members of the Bloomsbury Group to hold such antipathetic views? It was a very narrow liberalism that considered feminism and anti-imperialism to be a plague. But then again, it was a very wide feminism that could embrace Marxist economic views in a pitched battle against the plague of fascism. *Three Guineas* begs women to enter the professions without being "contaminated" by patriarchal institutions. Narrow feminists, only concerned with women's rights and not the larger political issues, are exhorted to "help all properly qualified people, of whatever sex, class or colour, to enter your profession" (96). Woolf's three-pronged philosophy had few partisans who shared all aspects of her vision. Certainly her brother-in-law, Clive Bell, whose more direct peace pamphlet was called "Warmongers," was not a feminist. The anger in Woolf's book is specifically directed at her male contemporaries like H. G. Wells who fault women for not financing the revolution. She makes him look foolish by suggesting that he thinks women have a "stocking full of guineas" hidden under their bed (52). The image is a telling one. Of course it would have to be an opaque black stocking, suitable for the stingy spinsters of Wells's imagination.

As I write in 2005, the English *Times Literary Supplement* has published a laudatory review of a book attacking *Three Guineas* as one of the major causes of the collapse of English values. The reviewer of *Our Culture: What's Left of It: The Mandarins and the Masses* (Chicago: Ivan R. Dee, 2005) praises Theodore Dalrymple's "angry, funny chapter [that] gives a devastating reading of Virginia Woolf's *Three Guineas,* which he thinks would be better titled *How to Be Privileged and Yet Feel Extremely Aggrieved.*" "Can it really be right," the reviewer asks, "to attribute the sordidness of contemporary Britain to the fact that, as he claims, Virginia Woolf's cast of mind in *Three Guineas*—'shallow, dishonest, resentful, envious, snobbish, self-absorbed, trivial, philistine, and ultimately brutal'—has triumphed among Western cultural elites?" (Davenport-Hines).

KEEP OUT! THE IDEAS IN THIS DOCUMENT ARE DANGEROUS. Are you wearing gloves? This pamphlet could make you into a feminist. It surely will make you into a pacifist and an antifascist. But the pamphlet takes a very strange form. It imagines a middle-class woman, the daughter of an educated man, writing replies to letters. We see her at her writing table, when suddenly she is transformed into what her friend Gerald Brenan once called "a Lapland Witch." Ink is spilled. The lady shouts and curses, laughs hysterically, weeps and wheedles and cajoles the poor recipient of her letters, summoned forth from space to be lectured and scolded, begged and then dismissed. So much for the polite reply. This drama takes place in three long, breathless outbursts. It is followed by three sections of "Notes and References," in the form of further digressions, stories, lectures, and other disquisitions. Did you ever get a letter with footnotes? How would you feel if you got one? Is there some kind of deliberate alienation of the reader going on here? While a parody of scholarly footnoting is indeed at work here, an alternative historical practice of citing the uncited is also introduced. Once these alternative sources have been dignified by citation in these footnotes, they become acceptable sources.

Letters from the Home Front

THE FORM of this book, a set of answers to correspondents, bolstered by a set of awesome footnotes, is distinctly odd, original, and provoking—for it brings Virginia Woolf's writerly talents to a readerly form, the letter. In this case there are three letters in question, though some enthusiastic critics have claimed that there are as many as fourteen. Now regarded as one of the most important letter writers of the twentieth century, Woolf spins and tortures the form of the semiprivate letter in *Three*

Guineas to show how difficult it is for a woman citizen in England in 1936 and 1937 to reply to requests for money for good causes. Her replies (our text) also follow the private letter into the public domain. The relative values of the peace movement, the Republican struggle in the Spanish Civil War, and support of the poor women's colleges that desperately need help are weighed and measured, twisted and turned inside out. Their arguments are left in shreds, their logic exploded. The civility of the private letter is lost in the new thirties political discourse of the public letter.

The letter, as it is written in *Three Guineas,* or, to be exact, the reply, is transformed from the light, airy, and witty entertainment composed to charm her friends and family, for which she is now justly famous, to a ferocious political pamphlet. Imagine responding like Woolf to the begging requests we get today from the same peace movement, the fast-disappearing women's colleges, or the groups trying to stop AIDS in Africa or the war in Iraq. Could one say, as she does, that important as these issues are, we cannot fully support them because we ourselves are not fully free? Would one say further that these groups and institutions are compromised by their relations with patriarchy, capitalism, and empire?

In *Three Guineas,* the letter of reply becomes a long disquisition, a collective self-justification, on the moral duty of those excluded from the system, whom she calls the Society of Outsiders, to challenge the deeper sources of their oppression. It was a difficult stand to take in 1938 and it is a difficult position to justify now. The book alienated many of her friends and it drew the praise of the brave minority who shared her values. Woolf's strategy for enlisting her reader's support is to build up the authority of her replies with a massive set of footnotes, reshaping the privacy of the personal letter as both a loud public letter and a dramatic scholarly essay with voices on stage and off and ourselves called in every so often to play the parts the narrator chooses for us. She worried about this new clamor in politics and demonstrations in the 1930s, debating the influence of the loudspeaker on the human voice. It is a very complicated strategy and it is not clear that it fully succeeds.

One thing is very clear: Virginia Woolf wants to trump all the societies that ask for her support with her own society, the Society of Outsiders, a group that seems to have begun with her earlier vision of a women's group comparable to the Cambridge Apostles in "A Society"; readers are meant to rush to line up to join this new antisociety, searching their hearts to shed what she calls "unreal loyalties" (96), those loyalties that have traditionally held society together. Are we pure enough? we ask ourselves uneasily. Could we act like Antigone and defy the state and its wars? But Phyllis Lassner reminds us that the issue was more complicated than that, that "Woolf's was not a lone voice but one of many in a vital feminist debate on war and fascism in the thirties" (29). Arguing that there was more than one kind of courage in these anguished debates, Lassner asks us to consider the convictions of Rose Macaulay and Naomi Mitchison in relation to Woolf's stance on war and fascism and also to consider the real events of World War II when it did explode.[9]

The "educated man's daughter," as the narrator calls herself, like Virginia Woolf herself, had no formal education. She was by our standards splendidly self-educated in history, letters, and languages, but she resented not being allowed to go to school and university. It may seem to some readers ironic that a woman so privileged should claim the status of a victim, but there is no doubt that, like other autodidacts, she was insecure and resentful. In *A Room of One's Own,* woman is always cast as a daughter, a victim of patriarchal power, and the tropes of slavery are used to rouse pity and anger at the plight of women "locked up, beaten and flung about the room." The "educated man's daughter" has come a long way from "slavery," but is oppressed mentally, not physically (though Woolf cites many women who, like Antigone, have died for their beliefs). The ring of those olden golden guineas ritually invoked by the title reminds us again and again that this civilization is based on slavery, that the English empire and its present democracy derived much of its capital power from the buying and selling of slaves and the use of their labor. We are meant to connect this fact to the patriarchal use of the unpaid labor of women.

The Notes

THE ERUDITE set of notes and references bolstering the authority of *Three Guineas* as a political pamphlet comes, like some intricate and complicated, finely worked needlepoint pillows, from a list of books that a woman of her class would read. They are almost all the diaries and letters and memoirs of women. By some outrageous rhetorical trick, Woolf inscribes these formerly insubstantial autobiographies and "lives of the obscure" with authority by padding the arguments in the book with quotes from them. When the woman in question appears by name and by number in a note, we are reminded how trivial the educated man's daughter's interests were supposed to be, as well as what a strikingly unacknowledged source of social documentation these memoirs have been for scholarly historians. Woolf recognizes that historians have simultaneously derided the letters and memoirs of ladies while mining them for their best lines. Like the ellipses or three dots in *A Room of One's Own,* signifying women's absence from history, that send the curious reader to the library to look up her allusions, Woolf's notes in *Three Guineas* provide a reading list for an alternative history that includes the domestic with the national and international. And they create a role for certain readers as explorers in the lost texts and worlds of women of the past. (First assignment: Read the memoirs of those society hostesses who have influenced politics: the Duchess of Devonshire, Lady Palmerston, Lady Melbourne, Madame de Lieven, Lady Holland, Lady Ashburton [17]. One assumes you have already read the redoubtable Mary Kingsley, mentioned earlier, and that you will become an expert on all the women mentioned in the book.) Other readers are annoyed at the relentless logic of the game she plays, and they are beginning to itch.

On the Photographs in *Three Guineas*

THE IDEA of a war for peace disturbed Woolf viscerally, and much of the anguish and bitterness of the book reflects her struggle over revisions of pacifist principle, over what the poet Auden wrote (and later recanted) in his poem "Spain," "the conscious acceptance of guilt in the necessary murder." Fiction fails her as she faces the facts in *Three Guineas.*

But Woolf develops a new "weapon in the struggle" in the great age of documentary. All that she has learned from film, photography, newsreels, and propaganda photographs in newspapers and pamphlets she uses here in visualizing her opposition to war and fascism. Both the text and the notes burst with brilliant passages of descriptive writing as in the scene of professional men marching in their "sartorial splendours" (25), the chilling scene of the burning of the word "feminism" (121), because its aims have supposedly been achieved (conjuring up images of Nazi book burning and attacks on universities in Germany), and the description of "a crudely coloured photograph" of the "bridge which connects the private house with the world of public life" (22–23, and see Froula in the suggested readings).

Vivid as these scenes are, Woolf seems to be testing the limits of writing the visual against the actual pictures of "our fathers and brothers" (23).

The Spanish photographs of mutilated "dead children" and of "ruined houses" are ruthlessly referred to over and over again in the book. They are like a red flag or (perhaps) a Republican banner running through her agonizing argument that you can't stop force with force. She notes disapprovingly that the Madrid bombing photographs incite one to anger. She will not print them, lest they incite more volunteers to go off to war. But what are we to do with these bewigged and bemedaled men we see in the photographs in the book before us?

It is our hope in this edition to bring readers of European history and politics as well as lovers of literature to the pleasures of this very timely text for the twenty-first century. The debates Woolf raises about war and fascism, capitalism and patriarchy, are debates we need to hear again today. This is the first American edition of *Three Guineas* for many decades to include the photographs that were an essential part of the text. (Recent Oxford and Penguin paperbacks in England have restored the photographs.) It is unclear why the photographs were dropped, and there is no evidence to suggest foul play. But one may say with impunity that if you have read *Three Guineas* without the photographs, you have not read the book Virginia Woolf wrote. The photographs of English professional men in their garb of power, as mentioned above, are there to alert us to the origins of war and fascism. The five photographs are worth thousands of words, and clearly indicate the spending of thousands of guineas on finery and processions. The judge, the military man covered with medals, the procession of academics, the heralds blowing their trumpets, and the archbishop are not identified by name, though readers at the time may well have recognized them. They stand symbolically for the English patriarchy as Woolf envisioned it, propped up by pomp and circumstance, wigs and robes and ribbons and medals, music and public processions, marches and parades. What is the difference between these patriotic performances and those of Hitler and Mussolini? the pictures ask.

Woolf was a master of propaganda of the eye. She had already established her talent for visual discourse in the staged photographs (with personal connotations) in *Orlando* and *Flush*. The four men pictured in *Three Guineas* have been identified by Alice Staveley as representative patriarchs and individuals known to most readers at the time. The tiny little general covered with medals is Lord Baden-Powell, the military hero of Mafeking in the Boer War and the founder of the Boy Scouts; the picture calls up the controversy over the militarism of the scouts and the early training of marching and parading. The academic procession is led by former prime minister Stanley Baldwin, who was the chancellor of Cambridge University; a popular Conservative figure and patriotic speechmaker, he is used by Woolf often in the text regarding women in the professions in a mock battle between his opinions and Whitaker's *Almanack* (see the note to page 56). The judge was the sitting lord chancellor, Lord Hewart, and the priest was the archbishop of Canterbury, Cosmo Gordon Lang. It is clear that the generic captions hide another of Woolf's feminist subversions of the text, as she does in her notes. Students have found the proximity of the horses' rear ends to the state trumpeters of the Household Cavalry a Woolfian joke, but it is clear that the reader is meant to track down these much-decorated men to read what they wrote on the subjects of this book.

Leonard Woolf also used the visual to make his points in *Quack! Quack!* (1935), his antifascist argument that civilization was dying and savagery was taking over the world. Unlike his wife's rational document, Leonard Woolf's writings on war stress the emotional. He places photographs of Hitler and Mussolini next to images of primitive gods (see Duffy and Davis; Laurence, "A Writing Couple"), but the strategy is less effective than Virginia Woolf's because that is so obviously what propaganda does. As I argued in "Liberty, Sorority, Misogyny," it is the absence of such photographs in the text that makes *Three Guineas* a work of art. Woolf keeps the reader's experience of the atrocities of the deaths of women and children in the Spanish Civil War purely verbal. Atrocity photographs would incite us to fight and she refuses to show them.

The Pictures That Are Not There

THE SUBVERSIVE role played by the photographs cannot be exaggerated. Photographs, she writes in the beginning of the essay, are about facts—"they are simply statements of fact addressed to the eye" (14). She describes the photographs of dead bodies and ruined houses in Spain. It is 1936–37 and the Spanish government sends them twice a week. Republican Spain (1936–39) was under attack by right-wing military groups under General Franco, aided in arms and supplies by the Germans and Italians, who also sent their planes on bombing missions against civilians and cities in the first such massive attacks in modern warfare, presaging what was to happen in World War II. The fascist bombing of women and children was horrifying at the time, though it has become common practice. England and the Allies, including France and the United States, stood by and let the events unfold under a nonintervention pact, and they also blockaded the harbors so food and supplies could not get to the Republican fighters. Idealist leftists supported Spain, along with anarchists and communists. The Spanish Civil War inspired a huge mass of support from the Left in many countries who formed international brigades.[10] The literary response to the war was amazing, in poetry, journalism, and fiction, and "this revolutionary bomb of a book," as it was called in *Time and Tide* (June 4, 1938, 788–90), must certainly be counted in that literature. Artists were particularly upset at Franco's role in the murder of Federico García Lorca in 1936, and everyone, including the pacifist Virginia Woolf, watched with interest as women were mobilized to fight and the small and fiery figure of La Passionara urged them on.

Woolf wrote to her nephew Julian Bell, who had gone as an ambulance driver to Spain along with many radicals from around the world in international brigades, and who was killed in 1937: "This morning I got a packet of photographs from Spain all of dead children, killed by bombs" (November 14, 1936, *Letters* 6: 85). The bodies are "so mutilated" that they might be pigs, says a shocked Virginia Woolf. Pacifists of either sex, she says, respond with the same horror and disgust to these barbarities. The pictures invite a "violent" response, and this is one of the issues she works on in the text, as it repeats the refrain "dead children" and "ruined houses" (14). "Photographs are not . . . arguments" (13–14); they are addressed to the eye and are not rational, she muses. But she does not reproduce in her book pictures of the dangling birdcages in bombed buildings or the dead children of Madrid. Why not? The pictures described in words in the text are visually very present to us as we read. She never lets us forget that they are the occasion of her outburst. Are some things permissible only in words and not in pictures? Does she want to spare her readers the gruesome occasion of her writing? Does she have a secret desire to show us that verbal descriptions can also incite us to violence? "I strike the eye," she once wrote proudly, "and elderly gentlemen in particular get annoyed" (*Diary* 2: 29). There are two kinds of blows to batter the reader in *Three Guineas,* the pictures themselves and the pictures of pictures verbally rendered, black and white on black and white in words that call up horrific visions of the bombing of women and children and civilian houses. By leaving out the photographs of atrocities, she gives words the edge over pictures in carrying the weight of shock and awe. Governments regularly censor what the public may see in wartime. A perfect example is the ban on photos of soldiers' coffins in the U.S. media during the war in Iraq.

Many critics have traced the origins of *Three Guineas* through Woolf's diaries and letters, first as a feminist sequel to *A Room of One's Own* and then as a pacifist pamphlet and an antifascist position paper. To me, while the writing of the present text began with her bathtub revelation of 1931,[11] it is part of a series beginning with "A Society" (often called a short story but actually an early polemical piece), *A Room of One's Own,* the speech "Professions for Women," the introduction to Margaret Llewelyn Davies' *Life As We Have Known It,* and *The Years.* In all cases she asserted, "Women Must Weep." From the tears of the little girl who is elected president of the women's "Society" of the future in her early piece ("A Society" 136) to the character from Charles Kingsley's poem invoked in the *Atlantic Monthly* to the imagined complaints of the assembled characters of *Three Guineas,* the weeping female chorus asserts women's right to work.

Yes, we may say, Virginia Woolf wept. She wept at the sight of the refugees from Bilbao. There were many more to come when Franco defeated Barcelona. "A bitter cold wind. Thought of the refugees from Barcelona walking 40 miles, one with a baby in a parcel" (*Diary* 5: 203). She complained in letters about signing manifestos and going to meetings of "idiotic societies" (*Letters* 6: 46). But she also worked. She worked for peace and justice. She advocated a much more difficult position than war—fighting fascism at home in the patriarchal family, not in war, certainly not even in the Spanish Civil War, which all her friends agreed was a righteous war, not even in the war we call World War II, with its horrendous persecution of the Jews. She was willing to die with Leonard if the Germans invaded, but she was not willing to fight. She didn't fill in the forms in the questionnaires and pamphlets that arrived daily, to say "What I Believe," believing she had finally said all she believed in *Three Guineas*.

NOTES

[1]The revival of critical interest in Woolf's politics and feminism, it is commonly assumed, dates to the publication in 1976 of Jane Marcus's "'No More Horses': Virginia Woolf on Art and Propaganda," presented at the MLA convention in 1974, published in the Woolf issue of *Women's Studies* in 1976, and reprinted in *Art & Anger: Reading Like a Woman* (Columbus: Ohio State University Press, 1988). Political scientist Berenice Carroll's influential essay "'To Crush Him in Our Own Country': The Political Thought of Virginia Woolf" came out in *Feminist Studies* in 1978. Brenda Silver's pioneering work "*Three Guineas* Before and After: Further Answers to Correspondents," appeared in *Virginia Woolf: A Feminist Slant* (1983), edited by Jane Marcus, a volume that also included Canadian political scientist Naomi Black's "Virginia Woolf and the Women's Movement." Important to the interpretations of *Three Guineas* was Sara Ruddick's *Maternal Thinking* and Blanche Wiesen Cook's "'Women Alone Stir My Imagination.'" These essays initiated debate in the North American and British feminist movements (also in French, German, and Australian feminist circles and others) in the 1970s. The foundational work on the manuscript materials of *Three Guineas* was Brenda Silver's *Virginia Woolf's Reading Notebooks* (Princeton: Princeton University Press, 1983). See "Suggestions for Further Reading: *Three Guineas*" for details of these and other works.

[2]See the edition edited by Naomi Black for the Shakespeare Head Press (2001) for details on the differences between the English and American editions. Further work remains to be done on the manuscripts.

[3]Morton Dauwen Zabel, writing in the *Nation,* provides a classic example of American self-congratulation: "In the pioneer society of the United States, the feminist reformer never labored under the disabilities of her English sisterhood. Here, where the matriarchal ideal was strong from the first, women passed on a tradition of culture, taste and moral leadership. They had their

colleges, seminaries, property, household keys and citizenship" (October 8, 1938, 356). Quoted by Brenda Silver in "*Three Guineas* Before and After."

[4]Ellery Sedgwick. "On Franco's Side in Spain." *The New York Times,* February 13, 1938, and February 15, 1938.

[5]www.csub.edu/woolf_center/. Some examples are included in this edition in the appendix (249).

[6]Willa Muir's *Women: An Inquiry* was first published by the Hogarth Press in 1925. In its concern for studying gender differences, it was a powerful influence on both *A Room of One's Own* and *Three Guineas,* especially on Woolf's ideas about the psychology of the sexes. Muir was a professional psychologist who worked on "an analysis of the problems raised by sex in education." As an early feminist theorist, Muir anticipated many of the concerns of contemporary feminism. She was founder of the Women Students Suffrage Society at St. Andrews University and continued to work on feminist issues, especially regarding Scotland, throughout her life. Her work is collected in *Willa Muir: Imagined Selves,* edited by Kirsty Allen (Edinburgh: Canongate, 1996). Ray Strachey's *The Cause: A Short History of the Women's Movement in Great Britain* was published in 1928.

[7]An image of the cover can be seen at http://library.vicu.utoronto.ca/exhibitions/bloomsbury/covers/vbell/guineas.htm.

[8]For example, in "How Should One Read a Book?" she wrote: "Facts are a very inferior form of fiction. Thus the desire grows upon us to have done with half-statements and approximations; to cease from searching out the minute shades of human character, to enjoy the greater abstractness, the purer truth of fiction" (264).

[9]In addition to *British Women Writers of World War II,* see also Lassner's "'The Milk of Our Mother's Kindness Has Ceased to Flow': Virginia Woolf, Stevie Smith and the Representation of the Jew," in *Between "Race" and Culture: Representations of "the Jew" in English and American Literature,* edited by Bryan Cheyette, 129–44 (Stanford, CA: Stanford University Press, 1996).

[10]See Cunningham on the '30s, and the *Penguin Book of Spanish Civil War Verse* (Harmondsworth: Penguin, 1980). In *The Spanish Front: Writers on the Civil War* (New York: Oxford University Press, 2005), Cunningham reprints a section of *Three Guineas* that he titles "The Educated Man's Sister." He includes both sides: T. S. Eliot and other prominent English writers, for example, as well as pieces by Sylvia Townsend Warner and Valentine Ackland, Ethel Mannin,

Simone Weil, John Cornford, Julian Bell, George Orwell, Stephen Spender, and Louis MacNeice. A list of Spanish Civil War pamphlets in English, French, German, and Spanish appears in Hugh Thomas's *The Spanish Civil War* (New York: Modern Library, 2001), including Charlotte Haldane's *Truth Will Out*. Ernest Hemingway's *For Whom the Bell Tolls* is one of the most famous fictions of this war, and his journalism has been reprinted. There are many memoirs by American volunteers from the Lincoln Brigade, and Cary Nelson has written extensively about them, their letters, and their posters. On the posters, see *The Palette and the Flame: Posters of the Spanish Civil War,* edited by John Tisa (New York: International Publishers, 1979). For a more recent account of the war, see Paul Preston's *The Spanish Civil War: An Illustrated Chronicle 1936–39* (New York: Grove Press, 1986), and his subsequent books. Because Franco stayed in power so long, most of this story was told by English historians. Paul Preston has written the most interesting new accounts, and now that the Soviet archives have been opened, new versions of that history have begun to appear.

[11]"I have this moment, while having my bath, conceived an entire new book—a sequel to Room of Ones Own—about the sexual life of women: to be called Professions for Women perhaps—Lord how exciting!" (*Diary* 4: 6).

A NOTE ON THE COVER

"Nose-Diving on the City," 1939. Oil on plywood (detail).

Tullio Crali (1910–2000) was an Italian Futurist painter, part of that group who loved airplanes and war in the spirit of Filippo Marinetti's 1909 "Futurist Manifesto." They were known for their depictions of high-speed machines and their support of Mussolini and Italian fascism. The German and Italian bombing of Spain, photographs of which inspired *Three Guineas,* was the first modern bombing attack on cities and civilians. (Franz Borkenau's 1937 eyewitness account of the Spanish Civil War is called *The Spanish Cockpit.*)

Crali's brilliant painting is so abstract that the city being bombed could be Madrid or any other modern metropolis. What makes it so powerful is that we are placed behind the pilot's head, which is off-center and framed by the metal bars of the cockpit, as we sweep down on the city below, seeing as he sees in a dizzying and deadly dive at the target. Crali places the viewer in the position of the bomber. We, too, kill what we see. This uncanny view from above, with the advent of aerial photography in the Spanish Civil War, was a new and exciting tactic in the art and propaganda of the period. The photograph from above in

a poster of a child killed by a bomb is one of the key tropes in *Three Guineas.*
Woolf refuses to show such pictures, arguing that they incite to revenge. But
one may also consider here the problem of visual pleasure given by the "master of the universe" posture of seeing the dead from above, just as the child's
killers have seen her. It could well be argued that this is not only a Futurist and
Vorticist point of view, but also a Fascist point of view.

———————

I am grateful to those scholars who began the revival of interest in *Three
Guineas* in the 1970s by taking Woolf's politics seriously. Among them are
Brenda Silver, Sara Ruddick, Berenice Carroll, Michèle Barrett, Susan Squier,
Naomi Black, Blanche Wiesen Cook, Sybil Oldfield, and Peggy Comstock.
Thanks to Woolf scholars Mark Hussey, Julia Briggs, Merry Pawlowski, Vara
Neverow, Anna Snaith, Morag Shiach, Patricia Laurence; University of Sussex librarian Bet Inglis; the staff at the Berg Collection of the New York Public Library; and all who have contributed to our knowledge of *Three Guineas,*
its genesis, meanings, and political relevance in its time and in our time, both,
alas, "wartimes." I am indebted to the work and example of my colleagues,
feminist and pacifist activists and historians of feminist and peace movements, Blanche Wiesen Cook and Sandi Cooper, whose monumental volumes in the Garland Library of War and Peace should be consulted by readers
who wish to place Woolf's essay in the context of the history of intellectuals
who wrote and worked for peace. *Three Guineas* is a major text in modern
peace politics and should be read with Gandhi and Simone Weil. While Cook
and Cooper include several volumes of writing by Leonard Woolf, who was
not, in fact, a pacifist, on international government and the League of Nations, *Three Guineas* is missing from this important historical effort. I would
like to think of the present edition as a contribution to filling the gap where
Virginia Woolf belongs in the Garland Library so that *Three Guineas* may find
the place it deserves in the history of feminist peace polemics. Its title and its
rhetorical twists and turns, as well as its unpopular ideological positions, may
have obscured its importance to historians and political scientists, but it remains a brilliant piece of propaganda.

Also essential for my work has been the work and friendship of Angela
Ingram, Margaret Higonnet, and Phyllis Lassner. Many students have con-
tributed to my thinking about *Three Guineas,* including—at the University of
Texas—Mary Mathis, Marie-Luise Gattens, and Margot Backus, and—at
CUNY—June Dunn, Julia Duffy, Gay Wachman, Robin Hackett, and Lisa
Williams. Lillian Robinson's groundbreaking *Sex, Class, and Culture* is always

for me an essential text, despite and because of its analysis of the inadequacies of *Three Guineas* as a guide for contemporary feminist and pacifist action while pointing out the Marxist nature of Woolf's materialist analysis. Robinson's classic "Who's Afraid of *A Room of One's Own*?" remains a relevant question, especially in regard to *Three Guineas*. I am also indebted to my students in our *Three Guineas* seminars, Virginia Woolf as a Public Intellectual and A Virginia Woolf for the 21st Century at CUNY and CCNY, for their arguments and insights, to Jean Mills and Rebecca Wisor more recently for their work, and to Cori Gabbard for her help with this edition. To Michael Marcus I am grateful for technical, political, physical, and emotional support, as always.

WORKS CITED

Bell, Quentin. *Virginia Woolf: A Biography.* 2 vols. New York: Harcourt Brace Jovanovich, 1972.

Black, Naomi. "Virginia Woolf and the Women's Movement." In *Virginia Woolf: A Feminist Slant.* Edited by Jane Marcus, 180–97. Lincoln: University of Nebraska Press, 1983.

Cunningham, Valentine. *British Writers of the Thirties.* Oxford: Oxford University Press, 1988.

Davenport-Hines, Richard. "Britain's Lost Virtue." Review of Theodore Dalrymple, *Our Culture: What's Left of It: The Mandarins and the Masses. Times Literary Supplement* (October 26, 2005).

Duffy, Julia, and Lloyd Davis. "Demythologizing Facts and Photographs in *Three Guineas.*" In *Photo-Textualities: Reading Photographs and Literature.* Edited by Marsha Bryant, 128–40. Newark, NJ: University of Delaware Press, 1996.

Forster, E. M. "Virginia Woolf." In *Recollections of Virginia Woolf by Her Contemporaries.* Edited by Joan Russell Noble, 185–98. New York: William Morrow, 1972.

Lassner, Phyllis. *British Women Writers of World War II: Battlegrounds of Their Own.* New York: St. Martin's, 1998.

Laurence, Patricia. "The Facts and Fugue of War: From *Three Guineas* to *Between the Acts.*" In *Virginia Woolf and War: Fiction, Reality, and Myth.* Edited by Mark Hussey, 225–46. Syracuse, NY: Syracuse University Press, 1991.

———. "A Writing Couple: Shared Ideology in Virginia Woolf's *Three Guineas* and Leonard Woolf's *Quack, Quack!*" In *Women in the Milieu of Leonard and Virginia Woolf: Peace, Politics, and Education.* Edited by Wayne K. Chapman and Janet M. Manson, 125–43. New York: Pace University Press, 1998.

Leavis, Q. D. "Caterpillars of the Commonwealth, Unite!" *Scrutiny* (September 1938): 203–14.

Marcus, Jane. "Liberty, Sorority, Misogyny." In *Virginia Woolf and the Languages of Patriarchy*, 75–95. Bloomington: Indiana University Press, 1987.

Oldfield, Sybil. "Margaret Llewelyn Davies and Leonard Woolf." In *Women in the Milieu of Leonard and Virginia Woolf: Peace, Politics, and Education*. Edited by Wayne K. Chapman and Janet M. Manson, 3–32. New York: Pace University Press, 1998.

Robinson, Lillian S. "Who's Afraid of *A Room of One's Own?*" In *Sex, Class, and Culture*, 97–149. Bloomington: Indiana University Press, 1978.

Ruddick, Sara. *Maternal Thinking: Toward a Politics of Peace*. New York: Ballantine, 1989.

Sackville-West, Vita. *The Letters of Vita Sackville-West to Virginia Woolf*. Edited by Louise DeSalvo and Mitchell Leaska. New York: William R. Morrow, 1985.

Showalter, Elaine. "Virginia Woolf and the Flight into Androgyny." In *A Literature of Their Own*, 263–97. Princeton, NJ: Princeton University Press, 1977.

Silver, Brenda. "*Three Guineas* Before and After: Further Answers to Correspondents." In *Virginia Woolf: A Feminist Slant*. Edited by Jane Marcus, 254–76. Lincoln: University of Nebraska Press, 1983.

Snaith, Anna. "Wide Circles: The *Three Guineas* Letters." *Woolf Studies Annual* 6 (2000): 1–10, 11–168.

Staveley, Alice. "Name That Face." *Virginia Woolf Miscellany* 51 (Spring 1998): 4–5.

Woolf, Virginia. "How Should One Read a Book?" In *The Second Common Reader*. Edited and introduced by Andrew McNeillie, 258–70. San Diego: Harcourt, 1986.

———. "Introductory Letter to Margaret Llewelyn Davies." In *Life As We Have Known It, By Co-Operative Working Women*. Edited by Margaret Llewelyn Davies, xv–xxxix. New York: Norton, 1975. Originally published in 1931.

———. "The Leaning Tower." In *The Moment and Other Essays*, 128–54. New York: Harcourt Brace Jovanovich, 1974. Originally published in 1942.

———. "Letter to a Young Poet." In *The Death of the Moth and Other Essays*, 208–26. New York: Harcourt Brace Jovanovich, 1970. Originally published in 1942.

———. *The Pargiters by Virginia Woolf: The Novel-Essay Portion of* The Years. Edited and with an introduction by Mitchell A. Leaska. San Diego: Harcourt Brace Jovanovich, 1978.

————. "Professions for Women." In *The Death of the Moth and Other Essays,* 235–42. New York: Harcourt Brace Jovanovich, 1970. Originally published in 1942.

————. "A Sketch of the Past." In *Moments of Being.* Edited by Jeanne Schulkind. 2nd Edition. San Diego: Harcourt, 1985.

————. "A Society." In *The Complete Shorter Fiction of Virginia Woolf.* Edited by Susan Dick, 124–36. 2nd Edition. San Diego: Harcourt Brace & Company, 1989.

————. "Speech Before the London/National Society for Women's Service, January 21, 1931." In *The Pargiters by Virginia Woolf: The Novel-Essay Portion of* The Years. Edited and with an introduction by Mitchell A. Leaska, xxvii–xliv. San Diego: Harcourt Brace Jovanovich, 1978.

————. "Women Must Weep—Or Unite Against War." *Atlantic Monthly* 161.5 (May 1938): 585–94; and 161.6 (June 1938): 750–59.

Three Guineas

ILLUSTRATIONS

One

THREE YEARS is a long time to leave a letter unanswered, and your letter has been lying without an answer even longer than that. I had hoped that it would answer itself, or that other people would answer it for me. But there it is with its question—How in your opinion are we to prevent war?—still unanswered.

It is true that many answers have suggested themselves, but none that would not need explanation, and explanations take time. In this case, too, there are reasons why it is particularly difficult to avoid misunderstanding. A whole page could be filled with excuses and apologies; declarations of unfitness, incompetence, lack of knowledge, and experience: and they would be true. But even when they were said there would still remain some difficulties so fundamental that it may well prove impossible for you to understand or for us to explain. But one does not like to leave so remarkable a letter as yours—a letter perhaps unique in the history of human correspondence, since when before has an educated man asked a woman how in her opinion war can be prevented?—unanswered. Therefore let us make the attempt; even if it is doomed to failure.

In the first place let us draw what all letter-writers instinctively draw, a sketch of the person to whom the letter is addressed. Without someone warm and breathing on the other side of the page, letters are worthless. You, then, who ask the question, are a little grey on the temples; the hair is no longer thick on the top of your head. You have reached the middle years of life not without effort, at the Bar; but on the whole your journey has been prosperous. There is nothing parched, mean or dissatisfied in your expression. And without wishing to flatter you, your prosperity—wife, children, house—has been deserved. You have never sunk into the contented apathy of middle life, for, as your letter from an office in the heart of London shows, instead of turning on your pillow and prodding your pigs, pruning your pear trees—you have a few acres in Norfolk—you are writing letters, attending meetings, presiding over this and that, asking questions, with the sound of the guns in your ears. For the rest, you began your education at one of the great public schools and finished it at the university.

It is now that the first difficulty of communication between us appears. Let us rapidly indicate the reason. We both come of what, in this hybrid age when, though birth is mixed, classes still remain fixed, it is convenient to call the educated class. When we meet in the flesh we speak with the same accent; use knives and forks in the same way; expect maids to cook dinner and wash up after dinner; and can talk during dinner without much difficulty about politics and people; war and peace; barbarism and civilization—all the questions indeed suggested by your letter. Moreover, we both earn our livings. But . . . those three dots mark a precipice, a gulf so deeply cut between us that for three years and more I have been sitting on my side of it wondering whether it is any use to try to speak across it. Let us then ask someone else—it is Mary Kingsley—to speak for us. "I don't know if I ever revealed to you the fact that being allowed to learn German was *all* the paid-for education I ever had. Two thousand pounds was spent on my brother's, I still hope not in vain."[1] Mary Kingsley is not speaking for herself alone; she is speaking, still, for many of the daughters of educated men. And she is not merely speaking for them; she is also pointing to a very important fact about them, a fact that must profoundly influence all that follows: the fact of Arthur's Education Fund. You, who have read *Pendennis,* will remember how the mysterious letters A.E.F. figured in the household ledgers. Ever since the thirteenth century English families have been paying money into that account. From the Pastons to the Pendennises, all educated families from the thirteenth century to the present moment have paid money into that account. It is a voracious receptacle. Where there were many sons to educate it required a great effort on the part of the family to keep it full. For your education was not merely in book-learning; games educated your body; friends taught you more than books or games. Talk with them broadened your outlook and enriched your mind. In the holidays you travelled; acquired a taste for art; a knowledge of foreign politics; and then, before you could earn your own living, your father made you an allowance upon which it was possible for you to live while you learnt the profession which now entitles you to add the letters K.C. to your name. All this came out of Arthur's Education Fund. And to this your sisters, as Mary Kingsley indicates, made their contribution. Not only did their own education, save for such small sums as paid the German teacher, go into it; but many of those luxuries and trimmings which are, after all, an essential part of education — travel, society, solitude, a lodging apart from the family house — they were paid into it too. It was a voracious receptacle, a solid fact — Arthur's Education Fund — a fact so solid indeed that it cast a shadow over the entire landscape. And the result is that though we look at the same things, we see them differently. What is that congregation of buildings there, with a semi-monastic look, with chapels and halls and green playing-fields? To you it is your old school; Eton or Harrow; your old university, Oxford or Cambridge; the source of memories and of traditions innumerable.

But to us, who see it through the shadow of Arthur's Education Fund, it is a schoolroom table; an omnibus going to a class; a little woman with a red nose who is not well educated herself but has an invalid mother to support; an allowance of £50 a year with which to buy clothes, give presents and take journeys on coming to maturity. Such is the effect that Arthur's Education Fund has had upon us. So magically does it change the landscape that the noble courts and quadrangles of Oxford and Cambridge often appear to educated men's daughters[2] like petticoats with holes in them, cold legs of mutton, and the boat train starting for abroad while the guard slams the door in their faces.

The fact that Arthur's Education Fund changes the land-scape—the halls, the playing grounds, the sacred edifices—is an important one; but that aspect must be left for future discussion. Here we are only concerned with the obvious fact, when it comes to considering this important question—how we are to help you prevent war—that education makes a difference. Some knowledge of politics, of international relations, of economics, is obviously necessary in order to understand the causes which lead to war. Philosophy, theology even, might come in usefully. Now you the uneducated, you with an untrained mind, could not possibly deal with such questions satisfactorily. War, as the result of impersonal forces, is you will agree beyond the grasp of the untrained mind. But war as the result of human nature is another thing. Had you not believed that human nature, the reasons, the emotions of the ordinary man and woman, lead to war, you would not have written asking for our help. You must have argued, men and women, here and now, are able to exert their wills; they are not pawns and puppets dancing on a string held by invisible hands. They can act, and think for themselves. Perhaps even they can influence other people's thoughts and actions. Some such reasoning must have led you to apply to us; and with justification. For happily there is one branch of education which comes under the heading "unpaid-for education"—that understanding of human beings and their motives which, if the word is rid of its scientific associations, might be called psychology. Marriage, the one great profession open to our class since the dawn of time until the year 1919; marriage, the art of choosing the human being with whom to live life successfully, should have taught us some skill in that. But here again another difficulty confronts us. For though many instincts are held more or less in common by both sexes, to fight has always been the man's habit, not the woman's. Law and practice have developed that difference, whether innate or accidental. Scarcely a human being in the course of history has fallen to a woman's rifle; the vast majority of birds and beasts have been killed by you, not by us; and it is difficult to judge what we do not share.[3]

How then are we to understand your problem, and if we cannot, how can we answer your question, how to prevent war? The answer based upon our experience and our psychology— Why fight?—is not an answer of any value. Obviously there is for you some glory, some necessity, some satisfaction in fighting which we have never felt or enjoyed. Complete understanding could only be achieved by blood transfusion and memory transfusion—a miracle still beyond the reach of science. But we who live now have a substitute for blood transfusion and memory transfusion which must serve at a pinch. There is that marvellous, perpetually renewed, and as yet largely untapped aid to the understanding of human motives which is provided in our age by biography and autobiography. Also there is the daily paper, history in the raw. There is thus no longer any reason to be confined to the minute span of actual experience which is still, for us, so narrow, so circumscribed. We can supplement it by looking at the picture of the lives of others. It is of course only a picture at present, but as such it must serve. It is to biography then that we will turn first, quickly and briefly, in order to attempt to understand what war means to you. Let us extract a few sentences from a biography.

First, this from a soldier's life:

> I have had the happiest possible life, and have always been working for war, and have now got into the biggest in the prime of life for a soldier. . . . Thank God, we are off in an hour. Such a magnificent regiment! Such men, such horses! Within ten days I hope Francis and I will be riding side by side straight at the Germans.[4]

To which the biographer adds:

> From the first hour he had been supremely happy, for he had found his true calling.

To that let us add this from an airman's life:

> We talked of the League of Nations and the prospects of peace and disarmament. On this subject he was not so much militarist as martial. The difficulty to which he could find no answer was that if permanent peace were ever achieved, and armies and navies ceased to exist, there would be no outlet for the manly qualities which fighting developed, and that human physique and human character would deteriorate.[5]

Here, immediately, are three reasons which lead your sex to fight; war is a profession; a source of happiness and excitement; and it is also an outlet for manly qualities, without which men would deteriorate. But that these feelings and opinions are by no means universally held by your sex is proved by the following extract from another biography, the life of a poet who was killed in the European war: Wilfred Owen.

> Already I have comprehended a light which never will filter into the dogma of any national church: namely, that one of Christ's essential commands was: Passivity at any price! Suffer dishonour and disgrace, but never resort to arms. Be bullied, be outraged, be killed; but do not kill. . . . Thus you see how pure Christianity will not fit in with pure patriotism.

And among some notes for poems that he did not live to write are these:

> The unnaturalness of weapons. . . . Inhumanity of war. . . . The insupportability of war. . . . Horrible beastliness of war. . . . Foolishness of war.[6]

From these quotations it is obvious that the same sex holds very different opinions about the same thing. But also it is obvious, from today's newspaper, that however many dissentients there are, the great majority of your sex are today in favour of war. The Scarborough Conference of educated men, the Bournemouth Conference of working men are both agreed that to spend £300,000,000 annually upon arms is a necessity. They are of opinion that Wilfred Owen was wrong; that it is better to kill than to be killed. Yet since biography shows that differences of opinion are many, it is plain that there must be some one reason which prevails in order to bring about this overpowering unanimity. Shall we call it, for the sake of brevity, "patriotism"? What then, we must ask next, is this "patriotism" which leads you to go to war? Let the Lord Chief Justice of England interpret it for us:

Englishmen are proud of England. For those who have been trained in English schools and universities, and who have done the work of their lives in England, there are few loves stronger than the love we have for our country. When we consider other nations, when we judge the merits of the policy of this country or of that, it is the standard of our own country that we apply. . . . Liberty has made her abode in England. England is the home of democratic institutions. . . . It is true that in our midst there are many enemies of liberty—some of them, perhaps, in rather unexpected quarters. But we are standing firm. It has been said that an Englishman's Home is his Castle. The home of Liberty is in England. And it is a castle indeed—a castle that will be defended to the last. . . . Yes, we are greatly blessed, we Englishmen.[7]

That is a fair general statement of what patriotism means to an educated man and what duties it imposes upon him. But the educated man's sister—what does "patriotism" mean to her? Has she the same reasons for being proud of England, for loving England, for defending England? Has she been "greatly blessed" in England? History and biography when questioned would seem to show that her position in the home of freedom has been different from her brother's; and psychology would seem to hint that history is not without its effect upon mind and body. Therefore her interpretation of the word "patriotism" may well differ from his. And that difference may make it extremely difficult for her to understand his definition of patriotism and the duties it imposes. If then our answer to your question, "How in your opinion are we to prevent war?" depends upon understanding the reasons, the emotions, the loyalties which lead men to go to war, this letter had better be torn across and thrown into the waste-paper basket. For it seems plain that we cannot understand each other because of these differences. It seems plain that we think differently according as we are born differently; there is a Grenfell point of view; a Knebworth point of view; a Wilfred Owen point of view; a Lord Chief Justice's point of view and the point of view of an educated man's daughter. All differ. But is there no absolute point of view? Can we not find somewhere written up in letters of fire or gold, "This is right. This wrong"?—a moral judgment which we must all, whatever our differences, accept? Let us then refer the question of the rightness or wrongness of war to those who make morality their profession—the clergy. Surely if we ask the clergy the simple question: "Is war right or is war wrong?" they will give us a plain answer which we cannot deny. But no—the Church of England, which might be supposed able to abstract the question from its worldly confusions, is of two minds also. The bishops themselves are at loggerheads. The Bishop of London maintained that "the real danger to the peace of the world today were the pacifists. Bad as war was dishonour was far worse."[8] On the other hand, the Bishop of Birmingham[9] described himself as an "extreme pacifist. . . . I cannot see myself that war can be regarded as consonant with the spirit of Christ." So the Church itself gives us divided counsel—in some circumstances it is right to fight; in no circumstances is it right to fight. It is distressing, baffling, confusing, but the fact must be faced; there is no certainty in heaven above or on earth below. Indeed the more lives we read, the more speeches we listen to, the more opinions we consult, the greater the confusion becomes and the less possible it seems, since we cannot understand the impulses, the motives, or the morality which lead you to go to war, to make any suggestion that will help you to prevent war.

But besides these pictures of other people's lives and minds—these biographies and histories—there are also other pictures—pictures of actual facts; photographs. Photographs, of course, are not arguments addressed to the reason; they are simply statements of fact addressed to the eye. But in that very simplicity there may be some help. Let us see then whether when we look at the same photographs we feel the same things. Here then on the table before us are photographs. The Spanish Government sends them with patient pertinacity about twice a week.* They are not pleasant photographs to look upon. They are photographs of dead bodies for the most part. This morning's collection contains the photograph of what might be a man's body, or a woman's; it is so mutilated that it might, on the other hand, be the body of a pig. But those certainly are dead children, and that undoubtedly is the section of a house. A bomb has torn open the side; there is still a birdcage hanging in what was presumably the sitting-room, but the rest of the house looks like nothing so much as a bunch of spilikins suspended in mid-air.

Those photographs are not an argument; they are simply a crude statement of fact addressed to the eye. But the eye is connected with the brain; the brain with the nervous system. That system sends its messages in a flash through every past memory and present feeling. When we look at those photographs some fusion takes place within us; however different the education, the traditions behind us, our sensations are the same; and they are violent. You, Sir, call them "horror and disgust." We also call them horror and disgust. And the same words rise to our lips. War, you say, is an abomination; a barbarity; war must be stopped at whatever cost. And we echo your words. War is an abomination; a barbarity; war must be stopped. For now at last we are looking at the same picture; we are seeing with you the same dead bodies, the same ruined houses.

*Written in the winter of 1936–7.

Let us then give up, for the moment, the effort to answer your question, how we can help you to prevent war, by discussing the political, the patriotic or the psychological reasons which lead you to go to war. The emotion is too positive to suffer patient analysis. Let us concentrate upon the practical suggestions which you bring forward for our consideration. There are three of them. The first is to sign a letter to the newspapers; the second is to join a certain society; the third is to subscribe to its funds. Nothing on the face of it could sound simpler. To scribble a name on a sheet of paper is easy; to attend a meeting where pacific opinions are more or less rhetorically reiterated to people who already believe in them is also easy; and to write a cheque in support of those vaguely acceptable opinions, though not so easy, is a cheap way of quieting what may conveniently be called one's conscience. Yet there are reasons which make us hesitate; reasons into which we must enter, less superficially, later on. Here it is enough to say that though the three measures you suggest seem plausible, yet it also seems that, if we did what you ask, the emotion caused by the photographs would still remain unappeased. That emotion, that very positive emotion, demands something more positive than a name written on a sheet of paper; an hour spent listening to speeches; a cheque written for whatever sum we can afford—say one guinea. Some more energetic, some more active method of expressing our belief that war is barbarous, that war is inhuman, that war, as Wilfred Owen put it, is insupportable, horrible and beastly seems to be required. But, rhetoric apart, what active method is open to us? Let us consider and compare. You, of course, could once more take up arms—in Spain, as before in France—in defence of peace. But that presumably is a method that having tried you have rejected. At any rate that method is not open to us; both the Army and the Navy are closed to our sex. We are not allowed to fight. Nor again are we allowed to be members of the Stock Exchange. Thus we can use neither the pressure of force nor the pressure of money. The less direct but still effective weapons which our brothers, as educated men, possess in the diplomatic service, in the Church, are also denied to us. We cannot preach sermons or negotiate treaties. Then again although it is true that we can write articles or send letters to the Press, the control of the Press—the decision what to print, what not to print—is entirely in the hands of your sex. It is true that for the past twenty years we have been admitted to the Civil Service and to the Bar; but our position there is still very precarious and our authority of the slightest. Thus all the weapons with which an educated man can enforce his opinions are either beyond our grasp or so nearly beyond it that even if we used them we could scarcely inflict one scratch. If the men in your profession were to unite in any demand and were to say: "If it is not granted we will stop work," the laws of England would cease to be administered. If the women in your profession said the same thing it would make no difference to the laws of England whatever. Not only are we incomparably weaker than the men of our own class; we are weaker than the women of the working class. If the working women of the country were to say: "If you go to war, we will refuse to make munitions or to help in the production of goods," the difficulty of war-making would be seriously increased. But if all the daughters of educated men were to down tools tomorrow, nothing essential either to the life or to the war-making of the community would be embarrassed. Our class is the weakest of all the classes in the state. We have no weapon with which to enforce our will.[10]

The answer to that is so familiar that we can easily anticipate it. The daughters of educated men have no direct influence, it is true; but they possess the greatest power of all; that is, the influence that they can exert upon educated men. If this is true, if, that is, influence is still the strongest of our weapons and the only one that can be effective in helping you to prevent war, let us, before we sign your manifesto or join your society, consider what that influence amounts to. Clearly it is of such immense importance that it deserves profound and prolonged scrutiny. Ours cannot be profound; nor can it be prolonged; it must be rapid and imperfect—still, let us attempt it.

What influence then have we had in the past upon the profession that is most closely connected with war—upon politics? There again are the innumerable, the invaluable biographies, but it would puzzle an alchemist to extract from the massed lives of politicians that particular strain which is the influence upon them of women. Our analysis can only be slight and superficial; still if we narrow our enquiry to manageable limits, and run over the memoirs of a century and a half we can hardly deny that there have been women who have influenced politics. The famous Duchess of Devonshire, Lady Palmerston, Lady Melbourne, Madame de Lieven, Lady Holland, Lady Ashburton—to skip from one famous name to another—were all undoubtedly possessed of great political influence. Their famous houses and the parties that met in them play so large a part in the political memoirs of the time that we can hardly deny that English politics, even perhaps English wars, would have been different had those houses and those parties never existed. But there is one characteristic that all those memoirs possess in common; the names of the great political leaders—Pitt, Fox, Burke, Sheridan, Peel, Canning, Palmerston, Disraeli, Gladstone—are sprinkled on every page; but you will not find either at the head of the stairs receiving the guests, or in the more private apartments of the house, any daughter of an educated man. It may be that they were deficient in charm, in wit, in rank, or in clothing. Whatever the reason, you may turn page after page, volume after volume, and though you will find their brothers and husbands—Sheridan at Devonshire House, Macaulay at Holland House, Matthew Arnold at Lansdowne House, Carlyle even at Bath House, the names of Jane Austen, Charlotte Brontë, and George Eliot do not occur; and though Mrs. Carlyle went, Mrs. Carlyle seems on her own showing to have found herself ill at ease.

But, as you will point out, the daughters of educated men may have possessed another kind of influence—one that was independent of wealth and rank, of wine, food, dress and all the other amenities that make the great houses of the great ladies so seductive. Here indeed we are on firmer ground, for there was of course one political cause which the daughters of educated men had much at heart during the past 150 years: the franchise. But when we consider how long it took them to win that cause, and what labour, we can only conclude that influence has to be combined with wealth in order to be effective as a political weapon, and that influence of the kind that can be exerted by the daughters of educated men is very low in power, very slow in action, and very painful in use.[11] Certainly the one great political achievement of the educated man's daughter cost her over a century of the most exhausting and menial labour; kept her trudging in processions, working in offices, speaking at street corners; finally, because she used force, sent her to prison, and would very likely still keep her there, had it not been, paradoxically enough, that the help she gave her brothers when they used force at last gave her the right to call herself, if not a full daughter, still a stepdaughter of England.[12]

Influence then when put to the test would seem to be only fully effective when combined with rank, wealth and great houses. The influential are the daughters of noblemen, not the daughters of educated men. And that influence is of the kind described by a distinguished member of your own profession, the late Sir Ernest Wild.

He claimed that the great influence which women exerted over men always had been, and always ought to be, an indirect influence. Man liked to think he was doing his job himself when, in fact, he was doing just what the woman wanted, but the wise woman always let him think he was running the show when he was not. Any woman who chose to take an interest in politics had an immensely greater power without the vote than with it, because she could influence many voters. His feeling was that it was not right to bring women down to the level of men. He looked up to women, and wanted to continue to do so. He desired that the age of chivalry should not pass, because every man who had a woman to care about him liked to shine in her eyes.[13]

And so on.

If such is the real nature of our influence, and we all recognize the description and have noted the effects, it is either beyond our reach, for many of us are plain, poor and old; or beneath our contempt, for many of us would prefer to call ourselves prostitutes simply and to take our stand openly under the lamps of Piccadilly Circus rather than use it. If such is the real nature, the indirect nature, of this celebrated weapon, we must do without it; add our pigmy impetus to your more substantial forces, and have recourse, as you suggest, to letter signing, society joining and the drawing of an occasional exiguous cheque. Such would seem to be the inevitable, though depressing, conclusion of our enquiry into the nature of influence, were it not that for some reason, never satisfactorily explained, the right to vote, in itself by no means negligible,[14] was mysteriously connected with another right of such immense value to the daughters of educated men that almost every word in the dictionary has been changed by it, including the word "influence." You will not think these words exaggerated if we explain that they refer to the right to earn one's living.

That, Sir, was the right that was conferred upon us less than twenty years ago, in the year 1919, by an Act which unbarred the professions. The door of the private house was thrown open. In every purse there was, or might be, one bright new sixpence in whose light every thought, every sight, every action looked different. Twenty years is not, as time goes, a long time; nor is a sixpenny bit a very important coin; nor can we yet draw upon biography to supply us with a picture of the lives and minds of the new-sixpenny owners. But in imagination perhaps we can see the educated man's daughter, as she issues from the shadow of the private house, and stands on the bridge which lies between the old world and the new, and asks, as she twirls the sacred coin in her hand, "What shall I do with it? What do I see with it?" Through that light everything she saw looked different—men and women, cars and churches. The moon even, scarred as it is in fact with forgotten craters, seemed to her a white sixpence, a chaste sixpence, an altar upon which she vowed never to side with the servile, the signers-on, since it was hers to do what she liked with—the sacred sixpence that she had earned with her own hands herself. And if, checking imagination with prosaic good sense, you object that to depend upon a profession is only another form of slavery, you will admit from your own experience that to depend upon a profession is a less odious form of slavery than to depend upon a father. Recall the joy with which you received your first guinea for your first brief, and the deep breath of freedom that you drew when you realized that your days of dependence upon Arthur's Education Fund were over. From that guinea, as from one of the magic pellets to which children set fire and a tree rises, all that you most value—wife, children, home—and above all that influence which now enables you to influence other men, have sprung. What would that influence be if you were still drawing £40 a year from the family purse, and for any addition to that income were dependent even upon the most benevolent of fathers? But it is needless to expatiate. Whatever the reason, whether pride, or love of freedom, or hatred of hypocrisy, you will understand the excitement with which in 1919 your sisters began to earn not a guinea but a sixpenny bit, and will not scorn that pride, or deny that it was justly based, since it meant that they need no longer use the influence described by Sir Ernest Wild.

The word "influence" then has changed. The educated man's daughter has now at her disposal an influence which is different from any influence that she has possessed before. It is not the influence which the great lady, the Siren, possesses; nor is it the influence which the educated man's daughter possessed when she had no vote; nor is it the influence which she possessed when she had a vote but was debarred from the right to earn her living. It differs, because it is an influence from which the charm element has been removed; it is an influence from which the money element has been removed. She need no longer use her charm to procure money from her father or brother. Since it is beyond the power of her family to punish her financially she can express her own opinions. In place of the admirations and antipathies which were often unconsciously dictated by the need of money she can declare her genuine likes and dislikes. In short, she need not acquiesce; she can criticize. At last she is in possession of an influence that is disinterested.

Such in rough and rapid outlines is the nature of our new weapon, the influence which the educated man's daughter can exert now that she is able to earn her own living. The question that has next to be discussed, therefore, is how can she use this new weapon to help you to prevent war? And it is immediately plain that if there is no difference between men who earn their livings in the professions and women who earn their livings, then this letter can end; for if our point of view is the same as yours then we must add our sixpence to your guinea; follow your methods and repeat your words. But, whether fortunately or unfortunately, that is not true. The two classes still differ enormously. And to prove this, we need not have recourse to the dangerous and uncertain theories of psychologists and biologists; we can appeal to facts. Take the fact of education. Your class has been educated at public schools and universities for five or six hundred years, ours for sixty. Take the fact of property.[15] Your class possesses in its own right and not through marriage practically all the capital, all the land, all the valuables, and all the patronage in England. Our class possesses in its own right and not through marriage practically none of the capital, none of the land, none of the valuables, and none of the patronage in England. That such differences make for very considerable differences in mind and body, no psychologist or biologist would deny. It would seem to follow then as an indisputable fact that "we"—meaning by "we" a whole made up of body, brain and spirit, influenced by memory and tradition—must still differ in some essential respects from "you," whose body, brain and spirit have been so differently trained and are so differently influenced by memory and tradition. Though we see the same world, we see it through different eyes. Any help we can give you must be different from that you can give yourselves, and perhaps the value of that help may lie in the fact of that difference. Therefore before we agree to sign your manifesto or join your society, it might be well to discover where the difference lies, because then we may discover where the help lies also. Let us then by way of a very elementary beginning lay before you a photograph—a crudely coloured photograph—of your world as it appears to us who see it from the threshold of the private house; through the shadow of the veil that St. Paul still lays upon our eyes; from the bridge which connects the private house with the world of public life.

Your world, then, the world of professional, of public life, seen from this angle undoubtedly looks queer. At first sight it is enormously impressive. Within quite a small space are crowded together St. Paul's, the Bank of England, the Mansion House, the massive if funereal battlements of the Law Courts; and on the other side, Westminster Abbey and the Houses of Parliament. There, we say to ourselves, pausing, in this moment of transition on the bridge, our fathers and brothers have spent their lives. All these hundreds of years they have been mounting those steps, passing in and out of those doors, ascending those pulpits, preaching, money-making, administering justice. It is from this world that the private house (somewhere, roughly speaking, in the West End) has derived its creeds, its laws, its clothes and carpets, its beef and mutton. And then, as is now permissible, cautiously pushing aside the swing doors of one of these temples, we enter on tiptoe and survey the scene in greater detail. The first sensation of colossal size, of majestic masonry is broken up into a myriad points of amazement mixed with interrogation. Your clothes in the first place make us gape with astonishment.[16] How many, how splendid, how extremely ornate they are — the clothes worn by the educated man in his public capacity! Now you dress in violet; a jewelled crucifix swings on your breast; now your shoulders are covered with lace; now furred with ermine; now slung with many linked chains set with precious stones. Now you wear wigs on your heads; rows of graduated curls descend to your necks. Now your hats are boat-shaped, or cocked; now they mount in cones of black fur; now they are made of brass and scuttle-shaped; now plumes of red, now of blue hair surmount them. Sometimes gowns cover your legs; sometimes gaiters. Tabards embroidered with lions and unicorns swing from your shoulders; metal objects cut in star shapes or in circles glitter and twinkle upon your breasts. Ribbons of all colours—blue, purple, crimson—cross from shoulder to shoulder. After the comparative simplicity of your dress at home, the splendour of your public attire is dazzling.

But far stranger are two other facts that gradually reveal themselves when our eyes have recovered from their first amazement. Not only are whole bodies of men dressed alike summer and winter—a strange characteristic to a sex which changes its clothes according to the season, and for reasons of private taste and comfort—but every button, rosette and stripe seems to have some symbolical meaning. Some have the right to wear plain buttons only; others rosettes; some may wear a single stripe; others three, four or five. And each curl or stripe is sewn on at precisely the right distance apart—it may be one inch for one man, one inch and a quarter for another. Rules again regulate the gold wire on the shoulders, the braid on the trousers, the cockades on the hats—but no single pair of eyes can observe all these distinctions, let alone account for them accurately.

Even stranger, however, than the symbolic splendour of your clothes are the ceremonies that take place when you wear them. Here you kneel; there you bow; here you advance in procession behind a man carrying a silver poker; here you mount a carved chair; here you appear to do homage to a piece of painted wood; here you abase yourselves before tables covered with richly worked tapestry. And whatever these ceremonies may mean you perform them always together, always in step, always in the uniform proper to the man and the occasion.

Apart from the ceremonies, such decorative apparel appears to us at first sight strange in the extreme. For dress, as we use it, is comparatively simple. Besides the prime function of covering the body, it has two other offices—that it creates beauty for the eye, and that it attracts the admiration of your sex. Since marriage until the year 1919—less than twenty years ago—was

the only profession open to us, the enormous importance of dress to a woman can hardly be exaggerated. It was to her what clients are to you—dress was her chief, perhaps her only, method of becoming Lord Chancellor. But your dress in its immense elaboration has obviously another function. It not only covers nakedness, gratifies vanity, and creates pleasure for the eye, but it serves to advertise the social, professional, or intellectual standing of the wearer. If you will excuse the humble illustration, your dress fulfils the same function as the tickets in a grocer's shop. But, here, instead of saying, "This is margarine; this pure butter; this is the finest butter in the market," it says, "This man is a clever man—he is Master of Arts; this man is a very clever man—he is Doctor of Letters; this man is a most clever man—he is a Member of the Order of Merit." It is this function—the advertisement function—of your dress that seems to us most singular. In the opinion of St. Paul, such advertisement, at any rate for our sex, was unbecoming and immodest; until a very few years ago we were denied the use of it. And still the tradition, or belief, lingers among us that to express worth of any kind, whether intellectual or moral, by wearing pieces of metal, or ribbon, coloured hoods or gowns, is a barbarity which deserves the ridicule which we bestow upon the rites of savages. A woman who advertised her motherhood by a tuft of horsehair on the left shoulder would scarcely, you will agree, be a venerable object.

But what light does our difference here throw upon the problem before us? What connection is there between the sartorial splendours of the educated man and the photograph of ruined houses and dead bodies? Obviously the connection between dress and war is not far to seek; your finest clothes are those that you wear as soldiers. Since the red and the gold, the brass and the feathers are discarded upon active service, it is plain that their expensive and not, one might suppose, hygienic splendour is invented partly in order to impress the beholder with the majesty of the military office, partly in order through their vanity to induce young men to become soldiers. Here, then, our influence and our difference might have some effect; we, who are forbidden to wear such clothes ourselves, can express the opinion that the wearer is not to us a pleasing or an impressive spectacle. He is on the contrary a ridiculous, a barbarous, a displeasing spectacle. But as the daughters of educated men we can use our influence more effectively in another direction, upon our own class—the class of educated men. For there, in courts and universities, we find the same love of dress. There, too, are velvet and silk, fur and ermine. We can say that for educated men to emphasize their superiority over other people, either in birth or intellect, by dressing differently, or by adding titles before, or letters after their names are acts that rouse competition and jealousy—emotions which, as we need scarcely draw upon biography to prove, nor ask psychology to show, have their share in encouraging a disposition towards war. If then we express the opinion that such distinctions make those who possess them ridiculous and learning contemptible, we should do something, indirectly, to discourage the feelings that lead to war. Happily we can now do more than express an opinion; we can refuse all such distinctions and all such uniforms for ourselves. This would be a slight but definite contribution to the problem before us—how to prevent war; and one that a different training and a different tradition puts more easily within our reach than within yours.[17]

But our bird's-eye view of the outside of things is not altogether encouraging. The coloured photograph that we have been looking at presents some remarkable features, it is true; but it serves to remind us that there are many inner and secret chambers that we cannot enter. What real influence can we bring to bear upon law or business, religion or politics—we to whom many doors are still locked, or at best ajar, we who have neither capital nor force behind us? It seems as if our influence must stop short at the surface. When we have expressed an opinion upon the surface we have done all that we can do. It is true that the surface may have some connection with the depths, but if we are to help you to prevent war we must try to penetrate deeper beneath the skin. Let us then look in another direction—in a direction natural to educated men's daughters, in the direction of education itself.

Here, fortunately, the year, the sacred year 1919, comes to our help. Since that year put it into the power of educated men's daughters to earn their livings they have at last some real influence upon education. They have money. They have money to subscribe to causes. Honorary treasurers invoke their help. To prove it, here, opportunely, cheek by jowl with your letter, is a letter from one such treasurer asking for money with which to rebuild a women's college. And when honorary treasurers invoke help, it stands to reason that they can be bargained with. We have the right to say to her, "You shall only have our guinea with which to help you to rebuild your college if you will help this gentleman whose letter also lies before us to prevent war." We can say to her, "You must educate the young to hate war. You must teach them to feel the inhumanity, the beastliness, the insupportability of war." But what kind of education shall we bargain for? What sort of education will teach the young to hate war?

That is a question that is difficult enough in itself; and may well seem unanswerable by those who are of Mary Kingsley's persuasion—those who have had no direct experience of university education themselves. Yet the part that education plays in human life is so important, and the part that it might play in answering your question is so considerable that to shirk any

attempt to see how we can influence the young through education against war would be craven. Let us therefore turn from
our station on the bridge across the Thames to another bridge
over another river, this time in one of the great universities; for
both have rivers, and both have bridges, for us to stand upon.
Once more, how strange it looks, this world of domes and
spires, of lecture rooms and laboratories, from our vantage
point! How different it looks to us from what it must look to
you! To those who behold it from Mary Kingsley's angle—
"being allowed to learn German was *all* the paid education I
ever had"—it may well appear a world so remote, so formidable, so intricate in its ceremonies and traditions that any criticism or comment may well seem futile. Here, too, we marvel
at the brilliance of your clothes; here, too, we watch maces erect
themselves and processions form, and note with eyes too dazzled
to record the differences, let alone to explain them, the subtle
distinctions of hats and hoods, of purples and crimsons, of velvet and cloth, of cap and gown. It is a solemn spectacle. The
words of Arthur's song in *Pendennis* rise to our lips:

> Although I enter not,
> Yet round about the spot
>   Sometimes I hover,
> And at the sacred gate,
> With longing eyes I wait,
>   Expectant . . .

and again,

> I will not enter there,
> To sully your pure prayer
>   With thoughts unruly.

> But suffer me to pace
> Round the forbidden place,
>   Lingering a minute,
> Like outcast spirits, who wait
> And see through Heaven's gate
>   Angels within it.

But, since both you, Sir, and the honorary treasurer of the college rebuilding fund are waiting for answers to your letters we must cease to hang over old bridges humming old songs; we must attempt to deal with the question of education, however imperfectly.

What, then, is this "university education" of which Mary Kingsley's sisterhood have heard so much and to which they have contributed so painfully? What is this mysterious process that takes about three years to accomplish, costs a round sum in hard cash, and turns the crude and raw human being into the finished product—an educated man or woman? There can be no doubt in the first place of its supreme value. The witness of biography—that witness which anyone who can read English can consult on the shelves of any public library—is unanimous upon this point; the value of education is among the greatest of all human values. Biography proves this in two ways. First, there is the fact that the great majority of the men who have ruled England for the past 500 years, who are now ruling England in Parliament and the Civil Service, have received a university education. Second, there is the fact which is even more impressive if you consider what toil, what privation it implies—and of this, too, there is ample proof in biography—the fact of the immense sum of money that has been spent upon education in the past 500 years. The income of Oxford University is £435,656 (1933–4), the income of Cambridge University is £212,000 (1930). In

addition to the university income each college has its own separate income, which, judging only from the gifts and bequests announced from time to time in the newspapers, must in some
cases be of fabulous proportions.[18] If we add further the incomes enjoyed by the great public schools—Eton, Harrow,
Winchester, Rugby, to name the largest only—so huge a sum of
money is reached that there can be no doubt of the enormous
value that human beings place upon education. And the study of
biography—the lives of the poor, of the obscure, of the uneducated—proves that they will make any effort, any sacrifice to
procure an education at one of the great universities.[19]

But perhaps the greatest testimony to the value of education with which biography provides us is the fact that the sisters
of educated men not only made the sacrifices of comfort and
pleasure, which were needed in order to educate their brothers,
but actually desired to be educated themselves. When we consider the ruling of the Church on this subject, a ruling which we
learn from biography was in force only a few years ago—". . . I
was told that desire for learning in women was against the will
of God, . . ."[20]—we must allow that their desire must have been
strong. And if we reflect that all the professions for which a university education fitted her brothers were closed to her, her belief in the value of education must appear still stronger, since
she must have believed in education for itself. And if we reflect
further that the one profession that was open to her—marriage—was held to need no education, and indeed was of such
a nature that education unfitted women to practise it, then it
would have been no surprise to find that she had renounced
any wish or attempt to be educated herself, but had contented
herself with providing education for her brothers—the vast
majority of women, the nameless, the poor, by cutting down
household expenses; the minute minority, the titled, the rich, by
founding or endowing colleges for men. This indeed they did.

But so innate in human nature is the desire for education that you will find, if you consult biography, that the same desire, in spite of all the impediments that tradition, poverty and ridicule could put in its way, existed too among women. To prove this let us examine one life only—the life of Mary Astell.[21] Little is known about her, but enough to show that almost 250 years ago this obstinate and perhaps irreligious desire was alive in her; she actually proposed to found a college for women. What is almost as remarkable, the Princess Anne was ready to give her £10,000— a very considerable sum then, and, indeed, now, for any woman to have at her disposal—towards the expenses. And then— then we meet with a fact which is of extreme interest, both historically and psychologically: the Church intervened. Bishop Burnet was of opinion that to educate the sisters of educated men would be to encourage the wrong branch, that is to say, the Roman Catholic branch, of the Christian faith. The money went elsewhere; the college was never founded.

But these facts, as facts so often do, prove double-faced; for though they establish the value of education, they also prove that education is by no means a positive value; it is not good in all circumstances, and good for all people; it is only good for some people and for some purposes. It is good if it produces a belief in the Church of England; bad if it produces a belief in the Church of Rome; it is good for one sex and for some professions, but bad for another sex and for another profession.

Such at least would seem to be the answer of biography— the oracle is not dumb, but it is dubious. As, however, it is of great importance that we should use our influence through education to affect the young against war we must not be baffled by the evasions of biography or seduced by its charm. We must try to see what kind of education an educated man's sister receives at present, in order that we may do our utmost to use our influence in the universities where it properly belongs, and where it will have most chance of penetrating beneath the skin. Now happily we need no longer depend upon biography, which inevitably, since it is concerned with the private life, bristles with innumerable conflicts of private opinion. We have now to help us that record of the public life which is history. Even outsiders can consult the annals of those public bodies which record not the day-to-day opinions of private people, but use a larger accent and convey through the mouths of Parliaments and Senates the considered opinions of bodies of educated men.

History at once informs us that there are now, and have been since about 1870, colleges for the sisters of educated men both at Oxford and at Cambridge. But history also informs us of facts of such a nature about those colleges that all attempt to influence the young against war through the education they receive there must be abandoned. In face of them it is mere waste of time and breath to talk of "influencing the young"; useless to lay down terms, before allowing the honorary treasurer to have her guinea; better to take the first train to London than to haunt the sacred gates. But, you will interpose, what are these facts? these historical but deplorable facts? Therefore let us place them before you, warning you that they are taken only from such records as are available to an outsider and from the annals of the university which is not your own—Cambridge. Your judgment, therefore, will be undistorted by loyalty to old ties, or gratitude for benefits received, but it will be impartial and disinterested.

To begin then where we left off: Queen Anne died and Bishop Burnet died and Mary Astell died; but the desire to found a college for her own sex did not die. Indeed, it became stronger and stronger. By the middle of the nineteenth century it became so strong that a house was taken at Cambridge to lodge the students. It was not a nice house; it was a house without a garden in the middle of a noisy street. Then a second house was taken, a better house this time, though it is true that the water rushed through the dining-room in stormy weather and there was no playground. But that house was not sufficient; the desire for education was so urgent that more rooms were needed, a garden to walk in, a playground to play in. Therefore another house was needed. Now history tells us that in order to build this house, money was needed. You will not question that fact but you may well question the next—that the money was borrowed. It will seem to you more probable that the money was given. The other colleges, you will say, were rich; all derived their incomes indirectly, some directly, from their sisters. There is Gray's *Ode* to prove it. And you will quote the song with which he hails the benefactors: the Countess of Pembroke who founded Pembroke; the Countess of Clare who founded Clare; Margaret of Anjou who founded Queens'; the Countess of Richmond and Derby who founded St. John's and Christ's.

> What is grandeur, what is power?
> Heavier toil, superior pain.
> What the bright reward we gain?
> The grateful memory of the good.
> Sweet is the breath of vernal shower,
> The bee's collected treasures sweet,
> Sweet music's melting fall, but sweeter yet
> The still small voice of gratitude.[22]

Here, you will say in sober prose, was an opportunity to repay the debt. For what sum was needed? A beggarly £10,000—the very sum that the bishop intercepted about two centuries previously. That £10,000 surely was disgorged by the Church that had swallowed it? But churches do not easily disgorge what they have swallowed. Then the colleges, you will say, which had benefited, they must have given it gladly in memory of their noble benefactresses? What could £10,000 mean to St. John's, or

Clare, or Christ's? And the land belonged to St. John's. But the land, history says, was leased; and the £10,000 was not given; it was collected laboriously from private purses. Among them one lady must be for ever remembered because she gave £1,000; and Anon. must receive whatever thanks Anon. will consent to receive, because she gave sums ranging from £20 to £100. And another lady was able, owing to a legacy from her mother, to give her services as mistress without salary. And the students themselves subscribed—so far as students can—by making beds and washing dishes, by forgoing amenities and living on simple fare. Ten thousand pounds is not at all a beggarly sum when it has to be collected from the purses of the poor, from the bodies of the young. It takes time, energy, brains, to collect it; sacrifice to give it. Of course, several educated men were very kind; they lectured to their sisters; others were not so kind; they refused to lecture to their sisters. Some educated men were very kind and encouraged their sisters; others were not so kind, they discouraged their sisters.[23] Nevertheless, by hook or by crook, the day came at last, history tells us, when somebody passed an examination. And then the mistresses, principals or whatever they called themselves—for the title that should be worn by a woman who will not take a salary must be a matter of doubt—asked the Chancellors and the Masters about whose titles there need be no doubt, at any rate upon that score, whether the girls who had passed examinations might advertise the fact as those gentlemen themselves did by putting letters after their names. This was advisable, because, as the present Master of Trinity, Sir J. J. Thomson, O.M., F.R.S., after poking a little justifiable fun at the "pardonable vanity" of those who put letters after their names, informs us, "the general public who have not taken a degree themselves attach much more importance to B.A. after a person's name than those who have. Head mistresses of schools therefore prefer a belettered staff, so that students of Newnham and Girton, since they could not put B.A. after their names, were at a disadvantage in obtaining appointments." And in Heaven's name, we may both ask, what conceivable reason could there be for preventing them from putting the letters B.A. after their names if it helped them to obtain appointments? To that question history supplies no answer; we must look for it in psychology, in biography; but history supplies us with the fact. "The proposal, however," the Master of Trinity continues—the proposal, that is, that those who had passed examinations might call themselves B.A.—"met with the most determined opposition. . . . On the day of the voting there was a great influx of non-residents and the proposal was thrown out by the crushing majority of 1707 to 661. I believe the number of voters has never been equalled. . . . The behaviour of some of the undergraduates after the poll was declared in the Senate House was exceptionally deplorable and disgraceful. A large band of them left the Senate House, proceeded to Newnham and damaged the bronze gates which had been put up as a memorial to Miss Clough, the first Principal."[24]

Is that not enough? Need we collect more facts from history and biography to prove our statement that all attempt to influence the young against war through the education they receive at the universities must be abandoned? For do they not prove that education, the finest education in the world, does not teach people to hate force, but to use it? Do they not prove that education, far from teaching the educated generosity and magnanimity, makes them on the contrary so anxious to keep their possessions, that "grandeur and power" of which the poet speaks, in their own hands, that they will use not force but much subtler methods than force when they are asked to share them? And are not force and possessiveness very closely connected with war? Of what use then is a university education in influencing people to prevent war? But history goes on of course;

year succeeds to year. The years change things; slightly but imperceptibly they change them. And history tells us that at last, after spending time and strength whose value is immeasurable in repeatedly soliciting the authorities with the humility expected of our sex and proper to suppliants the right to impress head mistresses by putting the letters B.A. after the name was granted. But that right, history tells us, was only a titular right. At Cambridge, in the year 1937, the women's colleges—you will scarcely believe it, Sir, but once more it is the voice of fact that is speaking, not of fiction—the women's colleges are not allowed to be members of the university;[25] and the number of educated men's daughters who are allowed to receive a university education is still strictly limited; though both sexes contribute to the university funds.[26] As for poverty, *The Times* newspaper supplies us with figures; any ironmonger will provide us with a foot-rule; if we measure the money available for scholarships at the men's colleges with the money available for their sisters at the women's colleges, we shall save ourselves the trouble of adding up; and come to the conclusion that the colleges for the sisters of educated men are, compared with their brothers' colleges, unbelievably and shamefully poor.[27]

Proof of that last fact comes pat to hand in the honorary treasurer's letter, asking for money with which to rebuild her college. She has been asking for some time; she is still asking, it seems. But there is nothing, after what has been said above, that need puzzle us, either in the fact that she is poor, or in the fact that her college needs rebuilding. What is puzzling, and has become still more puzzling, in view of the facts given above, is this: What answer ought we to make her when she asks us to help her to rebuild her college? History, biography, and the daily paper between them make it difficult either to answer her letter or to dictate terms. For between them they have raised many questions. In the first place, what reason is there to think that a university education makes the educated against war? Again, if we help an educated man's daughter to go to Cambridge are we not forcing her to think not about education but about war?— not how she can learn, but how she can fight in order that she may win the same advantages as her brothers? Further, since the daughters of educated men are not members of Cambridge University they have no say in that education, therefore how can they alter that education, even if we ask them to? And then, of course, other questions arise—questions of a practical nature, which will easily be understood by a busy man, an honorary treasurer, like yourself, Sir. You will be the first to agree that to ask people who are so largely occupied in raising funds with which to rebuild a college to consider the nature of education and what effect it can have upon war is to heap another straw upon an already overburdened back. From an outsider, more-over, who has no right to speak, such a request may well de-serve, and perhaps receive, a reply too forcible to be quoted. But we have sworn that we will do all we can to help you to prevent war by using our influence—our earned money influence. And education is the obvious way. Since she is poor, since she is ask-ing for money, and since the giver of money is entitled to dic-tate terms, let us risk it and draft a letter to her, laying down the terms upon which she shall have our money to help to rebuild her college. Here, then, is an attempt:

"Your letter, Madam, has been waiting some time without an answer. But certain doubts and questions have arisen. May we put them to you, ignorantly as an outsider must, but frankly as an outsider should when asked to contribute money? You say, then, that you are asking for £100,000 with which to rebuild your college. But how can you be so foolish? Or are you so se-cluded among the nightingales and the willows, or so busy with profound questions of caps and gowns, and which is to walk first into the Provost's drawing-room—the Master's pug or the

Mistress's pom—that you have no time to read the daily papers? Or are you so harassed with the problem of drawing £100,000 gracefully from an indifferent public that you can only think of appeals and committees, bazaars and ices, strawberries and cream?

"Let us then inform you: we are spending three hundred millions annually upon the army and navy; for, according to a letter that lies cheek by jowl with your own, there is grave danger of war. How then can you seriously ask us to provide you with money with which to rebuild your college? If you reply that the college was built on the cheap, and that the college needs rebuilding, that may be true. But when you go on to say that the public is generous, and that the public is still capable of providing large sums for rebuilding colleges, let us draw your attention to a significant passage in the Master of Trinity's memoirs. It is this: 'Fortunately, however, soon after the beginning of this century the University began to receive a succession of very handsome bequests and donations, and these, aided by a liberal grant from the Government, have put the finances of the University in such a good position that it has been quite unnecessary to ask for any increase in the contribution from the Colleges. The income of the University from all sources has increased from about £60,000 in 1900 to £212,000 in 1930. It is not a very wild hypothesis to suppose that this has been to a large extent due to the important and very interesting discoveries which have been made in the University, and Cambridge may be quoted as an example of the practical results which come from Research for its own sake.'

"Consider only that last sentence. '. . . Cambridge may be quoted as an example of the practical results which come from Research for its own sake.' What has your college done to stimulate great manufacturers to endow it? Have you taken a leading part in the invention of the implements of war? How far have your students succeeded in business as capitalists? How then can you expect 'very handsome bequests and donations' to come your way? Again, are you a member of Cambridge University? You are not. How then can you fairly ask for any say in their distribution? You cannot. Therefore, Madam, it is plain that you must stand at the door, cap in hand, giving parties, spending your strength and your time in soliciting subscriptions. That is plain. But it is also plain that outsiders who find you thus occupied must ask themselves, when they receive a request for a contribution towards rebuilding your college, Shall I send it or shan't I? If I send it, what shall I ask them to do with it? Shall I ask them to rebuild the college on the old lines? Or shall I ask them to rebuild it, but differently? Or shall I ask them to buy rags and petrol and Bryant & May's matches and burn the college to the ground?

"These are the questions, Madam, that have kept your letter so long unanswered. They are questions of great difficulty and perhaps they are useless questions. But can we leave them unasked in view of this gentleman's questions? He is asking how we can help him to prevent war. He is asking us how we can help him to defend liberty; to defend culture. Also consider these photographs: they are pictures of dead bodies and ruined houses. Surely in view of these questions and pictures you must consider very carefully before you begin to rebuild your college what is the aim of education, what kind of society, what kind of human being it should seek to produce. At any rate I will only send you a guinea with which to rebuild your college if you can satisfy me that you will use it to produce the kind of society, the kind of people that will help to prevent war.

"Let us then discuss as quickly as we can the sort of education that is needed. Now since history and biography—the only evidence available to an outsider—seem to prove that the old education of the old colleges breeds neither a particular respect for liberty nor a particular hatred of war it is clear that you must rebuild your college differently. It is young and poor; let it therefore take advantage of those qualities and be founded on poverty and youth. Obviously, then, it must be an experimental college, an adventurous college. Let it be built on lines of its own. It must be built not of carved stone and stained glass, but of some cheap, easily combustible material which does not hoard dust and perpetrate traditions. Do not have chapels.[28] Do not have museums and libraries with chained books and first editions under glass cases. Let the pictures and the books be new and always changing. Let it be decorated afresh by each generation with their own hands cheaply. The work of the living is cheap; often they will give it for the sake of being allowed to do it. Next, what should be taught in the new college, the poor college? Not the arts of dominating other people; not the arts of ruling, of killing, of acquiring land and capital. They require too many overhead expenses; salaries and uniforms and ceremonies. The poor college must teach only the arts that can be taught cheaply and practised by poor people; such as medicine, mathematics, music, painting and literature. It should teach the arts of human intercourse; the art of understanding other people's lives and minds, and the little arts of talk, of dress, of cookery that are allied with them. The aim of the new college, the cheap college, should be not to segregate and specialize, but to combine. It should explore the ways in which mind and body can be made to co-operate; discover what new combinations make good wholes in human life. The teachers should be drawn from the good livers as well as from the good thinkers. There should be no difficulty in attracting them. For there would be none of the barriers of wealth and ceremony, of advertisement and competition which now make the old and rich universities such uneasy dwelling-places—cities of strife, cities where this is locked up and that is chained down; where nobody can walk freely or talk freely for fear of transgressing some chalk mark, of displeasing some dignitary. But if the college were poor it would have nothing to offer; competition would be abolished. Life would be open and easy. People who love learning for itself would gladly come there. Musicians, painters, writers, would teach there, because they would learn. What could be of greater help to a writer than to discuss the art of writing with people who were thinking not of examinations or degrees or of what honour or profit they could make literature give them but of the art itself?

"And so with the other arts and artists. They would come to the poor college and practise their arts there because it would be a place where society was free; not parcelled out into the miserable distinctions of rich and poor, of clever and stupid; but where all the different degrees and kinds of mind, body and soul merit co-operated. Let us then found this new college; this poor college; in which learning is sought for itself; where advertisement is abolished; and there are no degrees; and lectures are not given, and sermons are not preached, and the old poisoned vanities and parades which breed competition and jealousy . . ."

The letter broke off there. It was not from lack of things to say; the peroration indeed was only just beginning. It was because the face on the other side of the page — the face that a letter-writer always sees — appeared to be fixed with a certain melancholy, upon a passage in the book from which quotation has already been made. "Head mistresses of schools therefore prefer a belettered staff, so that students of Newnham and Girton, since they could not put B.A. after their name, were at a disadvantage in obtaining appointments." The honorary treasurer of the Rebuilding Fund had her eyes fixed on that. "What is the use of thinking how a college can be different," she seemed to say, "when it must be a place where students are taught to obtain appointments?" "Dream your dreams," she seemed to add, turning, rather wearily, to the table which she was arranging for some festival, "fire off your rhetoric, but we have to face realities."

That then was the "reality" on which her eyes were fixed; students must be taught to earn their livings. And since that reality meant that she must rebuild her college on the same lines as the others, it followed that the college for the daughters of educated men must also make Research produce practical results which will induce bequests and donations from rich men; it must encourage competition; it must accept degrees and coloured hoods; it must accumulate great wealth; it must exclude other people from a share of its wealth; and, therefore, in 500 years or so, that college, too, must ask the same question that you, Sir, are asking now: "How in your opinion are we to prevent war?"

An undesirable result that seemed; why then subscribe a guinea to procure it? That question at any rate was answered. No guinea of earned money should go to rebuilding the college on the old plan; just as certainly none could be spent upon building a college upon a new plan; therefore the guinea should be earmarked "Rags. Petrol. Matches." And this note should be attached to it. "Take this guinea and with it burn the college to the ground. Set fire to the old hypocrisies. Let the light of the burning building scare the nightingales and incarnadine the willows. And let the daughters of educated men dance round the fire and heap armful upon armful of dead leaves upon the flames. And let their mothers lean from the upper windows and cry, 'Let it blaze! Let it blaze! For we have done with this "education"!'"

That passage, Sir, is not empty rhetoric, for it is based upon the respectable opinion of the late head master of Eton, the present Dean of Durham.[29] Nevertheless, there is something hollow about it, as is shown by a moment's conflict with fact. We have said that the only influence which the daughters of educated men can at present exert against war is the disinterested influence that they possess through earning their livings. If there were no means of training them to earn their livings, there would be an end of that influence. They could not obtain appointments. If they could not obtain appointments they would again be dependent upon their fathers and brothers; and if they were again dependent upon their fathers and brothers they would again be consciously and unconsciously in favour of war. History would seem to put that beyond doubt. Therefore we must send a guinea to the honorary treasurer of the college rebuilding fund, and let her do what she can with it. It is useless as things are to attach conditions as to the way in which that guinea is to be spent.

Such then is the rather lame and depressing answer to our question whether we can ask the authorities of the colleges for the daughters of educated men to use their influence through education to prevent war. It appears that we can ask them to do nothing; they must follow the old road to the old end; our own influence as outsiders can only be of the most indirect sort. If we are asked to teach, we can examine very carefully into the aim of such teaching, and refuse to teach any art or science that encourages war. Further, we can pour mild scorn upon chapels, upon degrees, and upon the value of examinations. We can intimate that a prize poem can still have merit in spite of the fact that it has won a prize; and maintain that a book may still be worth reading in spite of the fact that its author took a first class with honours in the English tripos. If we are asked to lecture we can refuse to bolster up the vain and vicious system of lecturing by refusing to lecture.[30] And, of course, if we are offered honours and degrees for ourselves we can refuse them—how, indeed, in view of the facts, could we possibly do otherwise? But there is no blinking the fact that in the present state of things the most effective way in which we can help you through education to prevent war is to subscribe as generously as possible to the colleges for the daughters of educated men. For, to repeat, if those daughters are not going to be educated they are not going to earn their livings; if they are not going to earn their livings, they are going once more to be restricted to the education of the private house; and if they are going to be restricted to the education of the private house they are going, once more, to exert all their influence both consciously and unconsciously in favour of war. Of that there can be little doubt. Should you doubt it, should you ask proof, let us once more consult biography. Its testimony upon this point is so conclusive, but so voluminous, that we must try to condense many volumes into one story. Here, then, is the narrative of the life of an educated man's daughter who was dependent upon father and brother in the private house of the nineteenth century.

The day was hot, but she could not go out. "How many a long dull summer's day have I passed immured indoors because there was no room for me in the family carriage and no lady's maid who had time to walk out with me." The sun set; and out she went at last, dressed as well as could be managed upon an allowance of from £40 to £100 a year.[31] But "to any sort of entertainment she must be accompanied by father or mother or by some married woman." Whom did she meet at those entertainments thus dressed, thus accompanied? Educated men—"cabinet ministers, ambassadors, famous soldiers and the like, all splendidly dressed, wearing decorations." What did they talk about? Whatever refreshed the minds of busy men who wanted to forget their own work—"the gossip of the dancing world" did very well. The days passed. Saturday came. On Saturday "M.P.s and other busy men had leisure to enjoy society"; they came to tea and they came to dinner. Next day was Sunday. On Sundays "the great majority of us went as a matter of course to morning church." The seasons changed. It was summer. In the summer they entertained visitors, "mostly relatives" in the country. Now it was winter. In the winter "they studied history and literature and music, and tried to draw and paint. If they did not produce anything remarkable they learnt much in the process." And so with some visiting the sick and teaching the poor, the years passed. And what was the great end and aim of these years, of that education? Marriage, of course. "... it was not a question of *whether* we should marry, but simply of *whom* we should marry," says one of them. It was with a view to marriage that her mind was taught. It was with a view to marriage that she tinkled on the piano, but was not allowed to join an orchestra; sketched innocent domestic scenes, but was not allowed to study from the nude; read this book, but was not allowed to read that, charmed, and talked. It was with a view to marriage that her body was educated; a maid was provided for her; that the streets were shut to her; that the fields were shut to her; that solitude was denied her—all this was enforced upon her in order that she might preserve her body intact for her husband. In short, the thought of marriage influenced what she said, what she thought, what she did. How could it be otherwise? Marriage was the only profession open to her.[32]

The sight is so curious for what it shows of the educated man as well as of his daughter that it is tempting to linger. The influence of the pheasant upon love alone deserves a chapter to itself.[33] But we are not asking now the interesting question, what was the effect of that education upon the race? We are asking why did such an education make the person so educated consciously and unconsciously in favour of war? Because consciously, it is obvious, she was forced to use whatever influence she possessed to bolster up the system which provided her with maids; with carriages; with fine clothes; with fine parties—it was by these means that she achieved marriage. Consciously she must use whatever charm or beauty she possessed to flatter and cajole the busy men, the soldiers, the lawyers, the ambassadors, the cabinet ministers who wanted recreation after their day's work. Consciously she must accept their views, and fall in with their decrees because it was only so that she could wheedle them into giving her the means to marry or marriage itself.[34] In short, all her conscious effort must be in favour of what Lady Lovelace called "our splendid Empire" . . . "the price of which," she added, "is mainly paid by women." And who can doubt her, or that the price was heavy?

But her unconscious influence was even more strongly perhaps in favour of war. How else can we explain that amazing outburst in August 1914, when the daughters of educated men who had been educated thus rushed into hospitals, some still attended by their maids, drove lorries, worked in fields and munition factories, and used all their immense stores of charm, of sympathy, to persuade young men that to fight was heroic, and that the wounded in battle deserved all her care and all her praise? The reason lies in that same education. So profound was her unconscious loathing for the education of the private house with its cruelty, its poverty, its hypocrisy, its immorality, its inanity that she would undertake any task however menial, exercise any fascination however fatal that enabled her to escape. Thus consciously she desired "our splendid Empire"; unconsciously she desired our splendid war.

So, Sir, if you want us to help you to prevent war the conclusion seems to be inevitable; we must help to rebuild the college which, imperfect as it may be, is the only alternative to the education of the private house. We must hope that in time that education may be altered. That guinea must be given before we give you the guinea that you ask for your own society. But it is contributing to the same cause — the prevention of war. Guineas are rare; guineas are valuable, but let us send one without any condition attached to the honorary treasurer of the building fund, because by so doing we are making a positive contribution to the prevention of war.

Two

Now that we have given one guinea towards rebuilding a college we must consider whether there is not more that we can do to help you to prevent war. And it is at once obvious, if what we have said about influence is true, that we must turn to the professions, because if we could persuade those who can earn their livings, and thus actually hold in their hands this new weapon, our only weapon, the weapon of independent opinion based upon independent income, to use that weapon against war, we should do more to help you than by appealing to those who must teach the young to earn their livings; or by lingering, however long, round the forbidden places and sacred gates of the universities where they are thus taught. This, therefore, is a more important question than the other.

Let us then lay your letter asking for help to prevent war, before the independent, the mature, those who are earning their livings in the professions. There is no need of rhetoric; hardly, one would suppose, of argument. "Here is a man," one has only to say, "whom we all have reason to respect; he tells us that war is possible; perhaps probable; he asks us, who can earn our livings, to help him in any way we can to prevent war." That surely will be enough without pointing to the photographs that are all this time piling up on the table—photographs of more dead bodies, of more ruined houses, to call forth an answer, and an answer that will give you, Sir, the very help that you require. But ... it seems that there is some hesitation, some doubt—not certainly that war is horrible, that war is beastly, that war is insupportable and that war is inhuman, as Wilfred Owen said, or that we wish to do all we can to help you to prevent war. Nevertheless, doubts and hesitations there are; and the way to understand them is to place before you another letter, a letter as genuine as your own, a letter that happens to lie beside it on the table.[1]

It is a letter from another honorary treasurer, and it is again asking for money. "Will you," she writes, "send a subscription to" [a society to help the daughters of educated men to obtain employment in the professions] "in order to help us to earn our livings? Failing money," she goes on, "any gift will be acceptable—books, fruit or cast-off clothing that can be sold in a bazaar." Now that letter has so much bearing upon the doubts and hesitations referred to above, and upon the help we can give you, that it seems impossible either to send her a guinea or to send you a guinea until we have considered the questions which it raises.

The first question is obviously, Why is she asking for money? Why is she so poor, this representative of professional women, that she must beg for cast-off clothing for a bazaar? That is the first point to clear up, because if she is as poor as this letter indicates, then the weapon of independent opinion upon which we have been counting to help you to prevent war is not, to put it mildly, a very powerful weapon. On the other hand, poverty has its advantages; for if she is as poor as she pretends to be, then we can bargain with her, as we bargained with her sister at Cambridge, and exercise the right of potential givers to impose terms. Let us then question her about her financial position and certain other facts before we give her a guinea, or lay down the terms upon which she is to have it. Here is the draft of such a letter:

"Accept a thousand apologies, Madam, for keeping you waiting so long for an answer to your letter. The fact is, certain questions have arisen, to which we must ask you to reply before we send you a subscription. In the first place you are asking for money—money with which to pay your rent. But how can it be, how can it possibly be, my dear Madam, that you are so terribly poor? The professions have been open to the daughters of educated men for almost 20 years. Therefore, how can it be, that you, whom we take to be their representative, are standing, like your sister at Cambridge, hat in hand, pleading for money, or failing money, for fruit, books, or cast-off clothing to sell at a bazaar? How can it be, we repeat? Surely there must be some very grave defect, of common humanity, of common justice, or of common sense. Or can it simply be that you are pulling a long face and telling a tall story like the beggar at the street corner who has a stocking full of guineas safely hoarded under her bed at home? In any case, this perpetual asking for money and pleading of poverty is laying you open to very grave rebukes, not only from indolent outsiders who dislike thinking about practical affairs almost as much as they dislike signing cheques, but from educated men. You are drawing upon yourselves the censure and contempt of men of established reputation as philosophers and novelists—of men like Mr. Joad and Mr. Wells. Not only do they deny your poverty, but they accuse you of apathy and indifference. Let me draw your attention to the charges that they bring against you. Listen, in the first place, to what Mr. C. E. M. Joad has to say of you. He says: 'I doubt whether at any time during the last fifty years young women have been more politically apathetic, more socially indifferent than at the present time.' That is how he begins. And he goes on to say, very rightly, that it is not his business to tell you what you ought to do; but he adds, very kindly, that he will give you an example of what you might do. You might imitate your sisters in America.

You might found 'a society for the advertisement of peace.' He gives an example. This society explained, 'I know not with what truth, that the number of pounds spent by the world on armaments in the current year was exactly equal to the number of minutes (or was it seconds?) which had elapsed since the death of Christ, who taught that war is unchristian. . . .' Now why should not you, too, follow their example and create such a society in England? It would need money, of course; but—and this is the point that I wish particularly to emphasize—there can be no doubt that you have the money. Mr. Joad provides the proof. 'Before the war money poured into the coffers of the W.S.P.U. in order that women might win the vote which, it was hoped, would enable them to make war a thing of the past. The vote is won,' Mr. Joad continues, 'but war is very far from being a thing of the past.' That I can corroborate myself—witness this letter from a gentleman asking for help to prevent war, and there are certain photographs of dead bodies and ruined houses—but let Mr. Joad continue. 'Is it unreasonable,' he goes on, 'to ask that contemporary women should be prepared to give as much energy and money, to suffer as much obloquy and insult in the cause of peace, as their mothers gave and suffered in the cause of equality?' And again, I cannot help but echo, is it unreasonable to ask women to go on, from generation to generation, suffering obloquy and insult first from their brothers and then for their brothers? Is it not both perfectly reasonable and on the whole for their physical, moral and spiritual welfare? But let us not interrupt Mr. Joad. 'If it is, then the sooner they give up the pretence of playing with public affairs and return to private life the better. If they cannot make a job of the House of Commons, let them at least make something of their own houses. If they cannot learn to save men from the destruction which incurable male mischievousness bids fair to bring upon them, let women at least learn to feed them, before they destroy themselves.'2 Let us not pause to ask how even with a vote they can cure what Mr. Joad himself admits to be incurable, for the point is how, in the face of that statement, you have the effrontery to ask me for a guinea towards your rent? According to Mr. Joad you are not only extremely rich; you are also extremely idle; and so given over to the eating of peanuts and ice cream that you have not learnt to cook him a dinner before he destroys himself, let alone how to prevent that fatal act. But more serious charges are to follow. Your lethargy is such that you will not fight even to protect the freedom which your mothers won for you. That charge is made against you by the most famous of living English novelists—Mr. H. G. Wells. Mr. H. G. Wells says, 'There has been no perceptible woman's movement to resist the practical obliteration of their freedom by Fascists or Nazis.'3 Rich, idle, greedy and lethargic as you are, how have you the effrontery to ask me to subscribe to a society which helps the daughters of educated men to make their livings in the professions? For as these gentlemen prove in spite of the vote and the wealth which that vote must have brought with it, you have not ended war; in spite of the vote and the power which that vote must have brought with it, you have not resisted the practical obliteration of your freedom by Fascists or Nazis. What other conclusion then can one come to but that the whole of what was called 'the woman's movement' has proved itself a failure; and the guinea which I am sending you herewith is to be devoted not to paying your rent but to burning your building. And when that is burnt, retire once more to the kitchen, Madam, and learn, if you can, to cook the dinner which you may not share. . . ."4

There, Sir, the letter stopped; for on the face at the other side of the letter—the face that a letter-writer always sees—was an expression, of boredom was it, or was it of fatigue? The honorary treasurer's glance seemed to rest upon a little scrap of paper upon which were written two dull little facts which, since they have some bearing upon the question we are discussing, how the daughters of educated men who are earning their livings in the professions can help you to prevent war, may be copied here. The first fact was that the income of the W.S.P.U. upon which Mr. Joad has based his estimate of their wealth was (in the year 1912 at the height of their activity) £42,000.[5] The second fact was that: "To earn £250 a year is quite an achievement even for a highly qualified woman with years of experience."[6] The date of that statement is 1934.

Both facts are interesting; and since both have a direct bearing upon the question before us, let us examine them. To take the first fact first—that is interesting because it shows that one of the greatest political changes of our times was accomplished upon the incredibly minute income of £42,000 a year. "Incredibly minute" is, of course, a comparative term; it is incredibly minute, that is to say, compared with the income which the Conservative party, or the Liberal party—the parties to which the educated woman's brother belonged—had at their disposal for their political causes. It is considerably less than the income which the Labour party—the party to which the working woman's brother belongs—has at their disposal.[7] It is incredibly minute compared with the sums that a society like the Society for the Abolition of Slavery for example had at its disposal for the abolition of that slavery. It is incredibly minute compared with the sums which the educated man spends annually, not upon political causes, but upon sports and pleasure. But our amazement, whether at the poverty of educated men's daughters or at their economy, is a decidedly unpleasant emotion in this case, for it forces us to suspect that the honorary treasurer is telling the sober truth; she is poor; and it forces us to ask once more how, if £42,000 was all that the daughters of educated men could collect after many years of indefatigable labour for their own cause, they can help you to win yours? How much peace will £42,000 a year buy at the present moment when we are spending £300,000,000 annually upon arms?

But the second fact is the more startling and the more depressing of the two — the fact that now, almost 20 years, that is, after they have been admitted to the money-making professions "to earn £250 a year is quite an achievement even for a highly qualified woman with years of experience." Indeed, that fact, if it is a fact, is so startling and has so much bearing upon the question before us that we must pause for a moment to examine it. It is so important that it must be examined, moreover, by the white light of facts, not by the coloured light of biography. Let us have recourse then to some impersonal and impartial authority who has no more axe to grind or dinner to cook than Cleopatra's needle — Whitaker's Almanack, for example.

Whitaker, needless to say, is not only one of the most dispassionate of authors, but one of the most methodical. There, in his Almanack he has collected all the facts about all, or almost all, of the professions that have been opened to the daughters of educated men. In a section called "Government and Public Offices" he provides us with a plain statement of whom the Government employs professionally, and of what the Government pays those whom it employs. Since Whitaker adopts the alphabetical system, let us follow his lead and examine the first six letters of the alphabet. Under A there are the Admiralty, the Air Ministry, and Ministry of Agriculture. Under B there is the British Broadcasting Corporation; under C the Colonial Office and the Charity Commissioners; under D the Dominions Office and Development Commission; under E there are the Ecclesiastical Commissioners and the Board of Education; and so we come to the sixth letter F under which we find the Ministry of Fisheries, the Foreign Office, the Friendly Societies and the Fine Arts. These then are some of the professions which are now, as we are frequently reminded, open to both men and women equally. And the salaries paid to those employed in them come out of public money which is supplied by both sexes equally. And the income tax which supplies those salaries (among other things) now stands at about five shillings in the pound. We have all, therefore, an interest in asking how that money is spent, and upon whom. Let us look at the salary list of the Board of Education, since that is the class to which we both, Sir, though in very different degrees, have the honour to belong. The President, Whitaker says, of the Board of Education, gets £2,000; his principal Private Secretary gets from £847 to £1,058; his Assistant Private Secretary gets from £277 to £634. Then there is the Permanent Secretary of the Board of Education. He gets £3,000; his Private Secretary gets from £277 to £634. The Parliamentary Secretary gets £1,200; his Private Secretary gets from £277 to £634. The Deputy Secretary gets £2,200. The Permanent Secretary of the Welsh Department gets £1,650. And then there are Principal Assistant Secretaries and Assistant Secretaries, there are Directors of Establishments, Accountants-General, principal Finance Officers, Finance Officers, Legal Advisers, Assistant Legal Advisers—all these ladies and gentlemen, the impeccable and impartial Whitaker informs us, get incomes which run into four figures or over. Now an income which is over or about a thousand a year is a nice round sum when it is paid yearly and paid punctually; but when we consider that the work is a whole-time job and a skilled job we shall not grudge these ladies and gentlemen their salaries, even though our income tax does stand at five shillings in the pound, and our incomes are by no means paid punctually or paid annually. Men and women who spend every day and all day in an office from the age of about 23 to the age of 60 or so deserve every penny they get. Only, the reflection will intrude itself, if these ladies are drawing £1,000, £2,000 and £3,000 a year, not only in the Board of Education, but in all the other boards and offices which are now open to them, from the Admiralty at the beginning of the alphabet to the Board of Works at the end, the statement that "£250 is quite an achievement, even for a highly qualified woman with years of experience" must be, to put it plainly, an unmitigated lie. Why, we have only to walk down Whitehall; consider how many boards and offices are housed there; reflect that each is staffed and officered by a flock of secretaries and under-secretaries so many and so nicely graded that their very names make our heads spin; and remember that each has his or her own sufficient salary, to exclaim that the statement is impossible, inexplicable. How can we explain it? Only by putting on a stronger pair of glasses. Let us read down the list, further and further and further down. At last we come to a name to which the prefix "Miss" is attached. Can it be that all the names on top of hers, all the names to which the big salaries are attached, are the names of gentlemen? It seems so. So then it is not the salaries that are lacking; it is the daughters of educated men.

Now three good reasons for this curious deficiency or disparity lie upon the surface. Dr. Robson supplies us with the first— "The Administrative Class, which occupies all the controlling positions in the Home Civil Service, consists to an overwhelming extent of the fortunate few who can manage to get to Oxford and Cambridge; and the entrance examination has always been expressly designed for that purpose."[8] The fortunate few in our class, the daughters of educated men class, are very, very few. Oxford and Cambridge, as we have seen, strictly limit the number of educated men's daughters who are allowed to receive a university education. Secondly, many more daughters stay at home to look after old mothers than sons stay at home to look after old fathers. The private house, we must remember, is still a going concern. Hence fewer daughters than sons enter for the Civil Service Examination. In the third place, we may fairly assume that 60 years of examination passing are not so effective as 500. The Civil Service Examination is a stiff one; we may reasonably expect more sons to pass it than daughters. We have nevertheless to explain the curious fact that though a certain number of daughters enter for the examination and pass the examination those to whose names the word "Miss" is attached do not seem to enter the four-figure zone. The sex distinction seems, according to Whitaker, possessed of a curious leaden quality, liable to keep any name to which it is fastened circling in the lower spheres. Plainly the reason for this may lie not upon the surface, but within. It may be, to speak bluntly, that the daughters are in themselves deficient; that they have proved themselves untrustworthy; unsatisfactory; so lacking in the necessary ability that it is to the public interest to keep them to the lower grades where, if they are paid less, they have less chance of impeding the transaction of public business. This solution would be easy but, unfortunately, it is denied to us. It is denied to us by the Prime Minister himself. Women in the Civil Services are not untrustworthy, Mr. Baldwin* informed us the other day. "Many of them," he said, "are in positions in the course of their daily work to amass secret information. Secret information has a way of leaking very often, as we politicians know to our cost. I have never known a case of such a leakage being due to a woman, and I have known cases of leakage coming from men who should have known a great deal better." So they are not so loose-lipped and fond of gossip as the tradition would have it? A useful contribution in its way to psychology and a hint to novelists; but still there may be other objections to women's employment as Civil Servants.

---

*Since these words were written Mr. Baldwin has ceased to be Prime Minister and become an Earl.

Intellectually, they may not be so able as their brothers. But here again the Prime Minister will not help us out. "He was not prepared to say that any conclusion had been formed—or was even necessary—whether women were as good as, or better than, men, but he believed that women had worked in the Civil Service to their own content, and certainly to the complete satisfaction of everybody who had anything to do with them." Finally, as if to cap what must necessarily be an inconclusive statement by expressing a personal opinion which might rightly be more positive he said, "I should like to pay my personal tribute to the industry, capacity, ability and loyalty of the women I have come across in Civil Service positions." And he went on to express the hope that business men would make more use of those very valuable qualities.[9]

Now if anyone is in a position to know the facts it is the Prime Minister; and if anyone is able to speak the truth about them it is the same gentleman. Yet Mr. Baldwin says one thing; Mr. Whitaker says another. If Mr. Baldwin is well informed, so is Mr. Whitaker. Nevertheless, they contradict each other. The issue is joined; Mr. Baldwin says that women are first-class civil servants; Mr. Whitaker says that they are third-class civil servants. It is, in short, a case of *Baldwin* v. *Whitaker,* and since it is a very important case, for upon it depends the answer to many questions which puzzle us, not only about the poverty of educated men's daughters but about the psychology of educated men's sons, let us try the case of the *Prime Minister* v. *the Almanack.*

For such a trial you, Sir, have definite qualifications; as a barrister you have first-hand knowledge of one profession, and as an educated man second-hand knowledge of many more. And if it is true that the daughters of educated men who are of Mary Kingsley's persuasion have no direct knowledge, still through fathers and uncles, cousins and brothers they may claim some indirect knowledge of professional life—it is a photograph that they have often looked upon—and this indirect knowledge they can improve, if they have a mind, by peeping through doors, taking notes, and asking questions discreetly. If, then, we pool our first-hand, second-hand, direct and indirect knowledge of the professions with a view to trying the important case of *Baldwin* v. *Whitaker* we shall agree at the outset that professions are very queer things. It by no means follows that a clever man gets to the top or that a stupid man stays at the bottom. This rising and falling is by no means a cut-and-dried clear-cut rational process, we shall both agree. After all, as we both have reason to know, Judges are fathers; and Permanent Secretaries have sons. Judges require marshals; Permanent Secretaries, private secretaries. What is more natural than that a nephew should be a marshal or the son of an old school friend a private secretary? To have such perquisites in their gift is as much the due of the public servant as a cigar now and then or a cast-off dress here and there are perquisites of the private servant. But the giving of such perquisites, the exercise of such influence, queers the professions. Success is easier for some, harder for others, however equal the brain power may be, so that some rise unexpectedly; some fall unexpectedly; some remain strangely stationary; with the result that the professions are queered. Often indeed it is the public advantage that they should be queered. Since nobody, from the Master of Trinity downwards (bating, presumably, a few Head Mistresses), believes in the infallibility of examiners, a certain degree of elasticity is to the public advantage; since the impersonal is fallible, it is well that it should be supplemented by the personal. Happily for us all, therefore, we may conclude, a board is not made literally of oak, nor a division of iron. Both boards and divisions transmit human sympathies, and reflect human antipathies with the result that the imperfections of the examination system are rectified; the public interest is served; and the ties of blood and friendship are recognized. Thus it is quite possible that the name "Miss" transmits through the board or division some vibration which is not registered in the examination room. "Miss" transmits sex; and sex may carry with it an aroma. "Miss" may carry with it the swish of petticoats, the savour of scent or other odour perceptible to the nose on the further side of the partition and obnoxious to it. What charms and consoles in the private house may distract and exacerbate in the public office. The Archbishops' Commission assures us that this is so in the pulpit.[10] Whitehall may be equally susceptible. At any rate since Miss is a woman, Miss was not educated at Eton or Christchurch. Since Miss is a woman, Miss is not a son or a nephew. We are hazarding our way among imponderables. We can scarcely proceed too much on tiptoe. We are trying, remember, to discover what flavour attaches itself to sex in a public office; we are sniffing most delicately not facts but savours. And therefore it would be well not to depend on our own private noses, but to call in evidence from outside. Let us turn to the public press and see if we can discover from the opinions aired there any hint that will guide us in our attempt to decide the delicate and difficult question as to the aroma, the atmosphere that surrounds the word "Miss" in Whitehall. We will consult the newspapers.

First:

I think your correspondent . . . correctly sums up this discussion in the observation that woman has too much liberty. It is probable that this so-called liberty came with the war, when women assumed responsibilities so far unknown to them. They did splendid service during those days. Unfortunately, they were praised and petted out of all proportion to the value of their performances.[11]

That does very well for a beginning. But let us proceed:

I am of the opinion that a considerable amount of the distress which is prevalent in this section of the community [the clerical] could be relieved by the policy of employing men instead of women, wherever possible. There are today in Government offices, post offices, insurance companies, banks and other offices, thousands of women doing work which men could do. At the same time there are thousands of qualified men, young and middle-aged, who cannot get a job of any sort. There is a large demand for woman labour in the domestic arts, and in the process of re-grading a large number of women who have drifted into clerical service would become available for domestic service.[12]

The odour thickens, you will agree.
Then once more:

I am certain I voice the opinion of thousands of young men when I say that if men were doing the work that thousands of young women are now doing the men would be able to keep those same women in decent homes. Homes are the real places of the women who are now compelling men to be idle. It is time the Government insisted upon employers giving work to more men, thus enabling them to marry the women they cannot now approach.[13]

There! There can be no doubt of the odour now. The cat is out of the bag; and it is a Tom.

After considering the evidence contained in those three quotations, you will agree that there is good reason to think that the word "Miss," however delicious its scent in the private house, has a certain odour attached to it in Whitehall which is disagreeable to the noses on the other side of the partition; and that it is likely that a name to which "Miss" is attached will, because of this odour, circle in the lower spheres where the salaries are small rather than mount to the higher spheres where the salaries are substantial. As for "Mrs.," it is a contaminated word; an obscene word. The less said about that word the better. Such is the smell of it, so rank does it stink in the nostrils of Whitehall, that Whitehall excludes it entirely. In Whitehall, as in heaven, there is neither marrying nor giving in marriage.[14]

Odour then—or shall we call it "atmosphere"?—is a very important element in professional life; in spite of the fact that like other important elements it is impalpable. It can escape the noses of examiners in examination rooms, yet penetrate boards and divisions and affect the senses of those within. Its bearing upon the case before us is undeniable. For it allows us to decide in the case of *Baldwin* v. *Whitaker* that both the Prime Minister and the *Almanack* are telling the truth. It is true that women civil servants deserve to be paid as much as men; but it is also true that they are not paid as much as men. The discrepancy is due to atmosphere.

Atmosphere plainly is a very mighty power. Atmosphere not only changes the sizes and shapes of things; it affects solid bodies, like salaries, which might have been thought impervious to atmosphere. An epic poem might be written about atmosphere, or a novel in ten or fifteen volumes. But since this is only a letter, and you are pressed for time, let us confine ourselves to the plain statement that atmosphere is one of the most powerful, partly because it is one of the most impalpable, of the enemies with which the daughters of educated men have to fight. If you think that statement exaggerated, look once more at the samples of atmosphere contained in those three quotations. We shall find there not only the reason why the pay of the professional woman is still so small, but something more dangerous, something which, if it spreads, may poison both sexes equally. There, in those quotations, is the egg of the very same worm that we know under other names in other countries. There we have in embryo the creature, Dictator as we call him when he is Italian or German, who believes that he has the right, whether given by God, Nature, sex or race is immaterial, to dictate to other human beings how they shall live; what they shall do. Let us quote again: "Homes are the real places of the women who are now compelling men to be idle. It is time the Government insisted upon employers giving work to more men, thus enabling them to marry the women they cannot now approach." Place beside it another quotation: "There are two worlds in the life of the nation, the world of men and the world of women. Nature has done well to entrust the man with the care of his family and the nation. The woman's world is her family, her husband, her children, and her home." One is written in English, the other in German. But where is the difference? Are they not both saying the same thing? Are they not both the voices of Dictators, whether they speak English or German, and are we not all agreed that the dictator when we meet him abroad is a very dangerous as well as a very ugly animal? And he is here among us, raising his ugly head, spitting his poison, small still, curled up like a caterpillar on a leaf, but in the heart of England. Is it not from this egg, to quote Mr. Wells again, that "the practical obliteration of [our] freedom by Fascists or Nazis" will spring? And is not the woman who has to breathe that poison and to fight that insect, secretly and without arms, in her office, fighting the Fascist or the Nazi as surely as those who fight him with arms in the limelight of publicity? And must not that fight wear down her strength and exhaust her spirit? Should we not help her to crush him in our own country before we ask her to help us to crush him abroad? And what right have we, Sir, to trumpet our ideals of freedom and justice to other countries when we can shake out from our most respectable newspapers any day of the week eggs like these?

Here, rightly, you will check what has all the symptoms of becoming a peroration by pointing out that though the opinions expressed in these letters are not altogether agreeable to our national self-esteem they are the natural expression of a fear and a jealousy which we must understand before we condemn them. It is true, you will say, that these gentlemen seem a little unduly concerned with their own salaries and their own security, but that is comprehensible, given the traditions of their sex, and even compatible with a genuine love of freedom and a genuine hatred of dictatorship. For these gentlemen are, or wish to become, husbands and fathers, and in that case the support of the family will depend upon them. In other words, Sir, I take you to mean that the world as it is at present is divided into two services; one the public and the other the private. In one world the sons of educated men work as civil servants, judges, soldiers and are paid for that work; in the other world, the daughters of educated men work as wives, mothers, daughters—but are they not paid for that work? Is the work of a mother, of a wife, of a daughter, worth nothing to the nation in solid cash? That fact, if it be a fact, is so astonishing that we must confirm it by appealing once more to the impeccable Whitaker. Let us turn to his pages again. We may turn them, and turn them again. It seems incredible, yet it seems undeniable. Among all those offices there is no such office as a mother's; among all those salaries there is no such salary as a mother's. The work of an archbishop is worth £15,000 a year to the State; the work of a judge is worth £5,000 a year; the work of a permanent secretary is worth £3,000 a year; the work of an army captain, of a sea captain, of a sergeant of dragoons, of a policeman, of a postman—all these works are worth paying out of the taxes, but wives and mothers and daughters who work all day and every day, without whose work the State would collapse and fall to pieces, without whose work your sons, Sir, would cease to exist, are paid nothing whatever. Can it be possible? Or have we convicted Whitaker, the impeccable, of errata?

Ah, you will interpose, here is another misunderstanding. Husband and wife are not only one flesh; they are also one purse. The wife's salary is half the husband's income. The man is paid more than the woman for that very reason—because he has a wife to support. The bachelor then is paid at the same rate as the unmarried woman? It appears not—another queer effect of atmosphere, no doubt; but let it pass. Your statement that the wife's salary is half the husband's income seems to be an equitable arrangement, and no doubt, since it is equitable, it is confirmed by law. Your reply that the law leaves these private matters to be decided privately is less satisfactory, for it means that the wife's half-share of the common income is not paid legally into her hands, but into her husband's. But still a spiritual right may be as binding as a legal right; and if the wife of an educated man has a spiritual right to half her husband's income, then we may assume that the wife of an educated man has as much money to spend, once the common household bills are met, upon any cause that appeals to her as her husband. Now her husband, witness Whitaker, witness the wills in the daily paper, is often not merely well paid by his profession, but is master of a very considerable capital sum. Therefore this lady who asserts that £250 a year is all that a woman can earn today in the professions is evading the question; for the profession of marriage in the educated class is a highly paid one, since she has a right, a spiritual right, to half her husband's salary. The puzzle deepens; the mystery thickens. For if the wives of rich men are themselves rich women, how does it come about that the income of the W.S.P.U. was only £42,000 a year; how does it come about that the honorary treasurer of the college rebuilding fund is still asking for £100,000; how does it come about that the treasurer of a society for helping professional women to obtain employment is asking not merely for money to pay her rent but will be grateful for books, fruit or cast-off clothing? It stands to reason that if the wife has a spiritual right to half her husband's income because her own work as his wife is unpaid, then she must have as much money to spend upon such causes as appeal to her as he has. And since those causes are standing hat in hand a-begging we are forced to conclude that they are causes that do not take the fancy of the educated man's wife. The charge against her is a very serious one. For consider—there is the money—that surplus fund that can be devoted to education, to pleasure, to philanthropy when the household dues are met; she can spend her share as freely as her husband can spend his. She can spend it upon whatever causes she likes; and yet she will not spend it upon the causes that are dear to her own sex. There they are, hat in hand a-begging. That is a terrible charge to bring against her.

But let us pause for a moment before we decide that charge against her. Let us ask what are the causes, the pleasures, the philanthropies upon which the educated man's wife does in fact spend her share of the common surplus fund. And here we are confronted with facts which, whether we like them or not, we must face. The fact is that the tastes of the married woman in our class are markedly virile. She spends vast sums annually upon party funds; upon sport; upon grouse moors; upon cricket and football. She lavishes money upon clubs—Brooks', White's, the Travellers', the Reform, the Athenaeum—to mention only the most prominent. Her expenditure upon these causes, pleasures and philanthropies must run into many millions every year. And yet by far the greater part of this sum is spent upon pleasures which she does not share. She lays out thousands and thousands of pounds upon clubs to which her own sex is not admitted;[15] upon racecourses where she may not ride; upon colleges from which her own sex is excluded. She pays a huge bill annually for wine which she does not drink and for cigars which she does not smoke. In short, there are only two conclusions to which we can come about the educated man's wife — the first is that she is the most altruistic of beings who prefers to spend her share of the common fund upon his pleasures and causes; the second, and more probable, if less creditable, is not that she is the most altruistic of beings, but that her spiritual right to a share of half her husband's income peters out in practice to an actual right to board, lodging and a small annual allowance for pocket money and dress. Either of these conclusions is possible; the evidence of public institutions and subscription lists puts any other out of the question. For consider how nobly the educated man supports his old school, his old college; how splendidly he subscribes to party funds; how munificently he contributes to all those institutions and sports by which he and his sons educate their minds and develop their bodies — the daily papers bear daily witness to those indisputable facts. But the absence of her name from subscription lists, and the poverty of the institutions which educate her mind and her body seem to prove that there is something in the atmosphere of the private house which deflects the wife's spiritual share of the common income impalpably but irresistibly towards those causes which her husband approves and those pleasures which he enjoys. Whether creditable or discreditable, that is the fact. And that is the reason why those other causes stand a-begging.

With Whitaker's facts and the facts of the subscription lists before us, we seem to have arrived at three facts which are indisputable and must have great influence upon our enquiry how we can help you to prevent war. The first is that the daughters of educated men are paid very little from the public funds for their public services; the second is that they are paid nothing at all from the public funds for their private services; and the third is that their share of the husband's income is not a flesh-and-blood share but a spiritual or nominal share, which means that when both are clothed and fed the surplus fund that can be devoted to causes, pleasures or philanthropies gravitates mysteriously but indisputably towards those causes, pleasures and philanthropies which the husband enjoys, and of which the husband approves. It seems that the person to whom the salary is actually paid is the person who has the actual right to decide how that salary shall be spent.

These facts then bring us back in a chastened mood and with rather altered views to our starting point. For we were going, you may remember, to lay your appeal for help in the prevention of war before the women who earn their livings in the professions. It is to them, we said, to whom we must appeal, because it is they who have our new weapon, the influence of an independent opinion based upon an independent income, in their possession. But the facts once more are depressing. They make it clear in the first place that we must rule out, as possible helpers, that large group to whom marriage is a profession, because it is an unpaid profession, and because the spiritual share of half the husband's salary is not, facts seem to show, an actual share. Therefore, her disinterested influence founded upon an independent income is nil. If he is in favour of force, she too will be in favour of force. In the second place, facts seem to prove that the statement "To earn £250 a year is quite an achievement even for a highly qualified woman with years of experience" is not an unmitigated lie but a highly probable truth. Therefore, the influence which the daughters of educated men have at present from their money-earning power cannot be rated very highly. Yet since it has become more than ever obvious that it is to them that we must look for help, for they alone can help us, it is to them that we must appeal. This conclusion then brings us back to the letter from which we quoted above — the honorary treasurer's letter, the letter asking for a subscription to the society for helping the daughters of educated men to obtain employment in the professions. You will agree, Sir, that we have strong selfish motives for helping her — there can be no doubt about that. For to help women to earn their livings in the professions is to help them to possess that weapon of independent opinion which is still their most powerful weapon. It is to help them to have a mind of their own and a will of their own with which to help you to prevent war. But . . . — here again, in those dots, doubts and hesitations assert themselves. Can we, considering the facts given above, send her our guinea without laying down very stringent terms as to how that guinea shall be spent?

For the facts which we have discovered in checking her statement as to her financial position have raised questions which make us wonder whether we are wise to encourage people to enter the professions if we wish to prevent war. You will remember that we are using our psychological insight (for that is our only qualification) to decide what kind of qualities in human nature are likely to lead to war. And the facts disclosed above are of a kind to make us ask, before we write our cheque, whether if we encourage the daughters of educated men to enter the professions we shall not be encouraging the very qualities that we wish to prevent? Shall we not be doing our guinea's worth to ensure that in two or three centuries not only the educated men in the professions but the educated women in the professions will be asking — oh, of whom? as the poet says — the very question that you are asking us now: How can we prevent war? If we encourage the daughters to enter the professions without making any conditions as to the way in which the professions are to be practised shall we not be doing our best to stereotype the old tune which human nature, like a gramo-phone whose needle has stuck, is now grinding out with such disastrous unanimity? "Here we go round the mulberry tree, the mulberry tree, the mulberry tree. Give it all to me, give it all to me, all to me. Three hundred millions spent upon war." With that song, or something like it, ringing in our ears we cannot send our guinea to the honorary treasurer without warning her that she shall only have it on condition that she shall swear that the professions in future shall be practised so that they shall lead to a different song and a different conclusion. She shall only have it if she can satisfy us that our guinea shall be spent in the cause of peace. It is difficult to formulate such conditions; in our present psychological ignorance perhaps impossible. But the matter is so serious, war is so insupportable, so horrible, so inhuman, that an attempt must be made. Here then is another letter to the same lady.

"Your letter, Madam, has waited a long time for an answer, but we have been examining into certain charges made against you and making certain enquiries. We have acquitted you, Madam, you will be relieved to learn, of telling lies. It would seem to be true that you are poor. We have acquitted you fur-ther, of idleness, apathy and greed. The number of causes that you are championing, however secretly and ineffectively, is in your favour. If you prefer ice creams and peanuts to roast beef and beer the reason would seem to be economic rather than gustatory. It would seem probable that you have not much money to spend upon food or much leisure to spend upon eat-ing it in view of the circulars and leaflets you issue, the meetings you arrange, the bazaars you organize. Indeed, you would ap-pear to be working, without a salary too, rather longer hours than the Home Office would approve. But though we are will-ing to deplore your poverty and to commend your industry we are not going to send you a guinea to help you to help women to enter the professions unless you can assure us that they will practise those professions in such a way as to prevent war. That, you will say, is a vague statement, an impossible condition. Still, since guineas are rare and guineas are valuable, you will listen to the terms we wish to impose if, you intimate, they can be stated briefly. Well then, Madam, since you are pressed for time, what with the Pensions Bill, what with shepherding the Peers into the House of Lords so that they may vote on it as instructed by you, what with reading Hansard and the newspapers—though that should not take much time; you will find no mention of your activities there;[16] a conspiracy of silence seems to be the rule; what with plotting still for equal pay for equal work in the Civil Service, while at the same time you are arranging hares and old coffee-pots so as to seduce people into paying more for them than they are strictly worth at a bazaar—since, in one word, it is obvious that you are busy, let us be quick; make a rapid survey; discuss a few passages in the books in your library; in the papers on your table, and then see if we can make the statement less vague, the conditions more clear.

"Let us then begin by looking at the outside of things, at the general aspect. Things have outsides let us remember as well as insides. Close at hand is a bridge over the Thames, an admirable vantage ground for such a survey. The river flows beneath; barges pass, laden with timber, bursting with corn; there on one side are the domes and spires of the city; on the other, Westminster and the Houses of Parliament. It is a place to stand on by the hour, dreaming. But not now. Now we are pressed for time. Now we are here to consider facts; now we must fix our eyes upon the procession—the procession of the sons of educated men.

"There they go, our brothers who have been educated at public schools and universities, mounting those steps, passing in and out of those doors, ascending those pulpits, preaching, teaching, administering justice, practising medicine, transacting business, making money. It is a solemn sight always—a procession, like a caravanserai crossing a desert. Great-grandfathers, grandfathers, fathers, uncles—they all went that way, wearing their gowns, wearing their wigs, some with ribbons across their breasts, others without. One was a bishop. Another a judge. One was an admiral. Another a general. One was a professor. Another a doctor. And some left the procession and were last heard of doing nothing in Tasmania; were seen, rather shabbily dressed, selling newspapers at Charing Cross. But most of them kept in step, walked according to rule, and by hook or by crook made enough to keep the family house, somewhere, roughly speaking, in the West End, supplied with beef and mutton for all, and with education for Arthur. It is a solemn sight, this procession, a sight that has often caused us, you may remember, looking at it sidelong from an upper window, to ask ourselves certain questions. But now, for the past twenty years or so, it is no longer a sight merely, a photograph, or fresco scrawled upon the walls of time, at which we can look with merely an esthetic appreciation. For there, trapesing along at the tail end of the procession, we go ourselves. And that makes a difference. We who have looked so long at the pageant in books, or from a curtained window watched educated men leaving the house at about nine-thirty to go to an office, returning to the house at about six-thirty from an office, need look passively no longer. We too can leave the house, can mount those steps, pass in and out of those doors, wear wigs and gowns, make money, administer justice. Think—one of these days, you may wear a judge's wig on your head, an ermine cape on your shoulders; sit under the lion and the unicorn; draw a salary of five thousand a year with a pension on retiring. We who now agitate these humble pens may in another century or two speak from a pulpit. Nobody will dare contradict us then; we shall be the mouthpieces

of the divine spirit—a solemn thought, is it not? Who can say whether, as time goes on, we may not dress in military uniform, with gold lace on our breasts, swords at our sides, and something like the old family coal-scuttle on our heads, save that that venerable object was never decorated with plumes of white horsehair. You laugh—indeed the shadow of the private house still makes those dresses look a little queer. We have worn private clothes so long—the veil that St. Paul recommended. But we have not come here to laugh, or to talk of fashions—men's and women's. We are here, on the bridge, to ask ourselves certain questions. And they are very important questions; and we have very little time in which to answer them. The questions that we have to ask and to answer about that procession during this moment of transition are so important that they may well change the lives of all men and women for ever. For we have to ask ourselves, here and now, do we wish to join that procession, or don't we? On what terms shall we join that procession? Above all, where is it leading us, the procession of educated men? The moment is short; it may last five years; ten years, or perhaps only a matter of a few months longer. But the questions must be answered; and they are so important that if all the daughters of educated men did nothing, from morning to night, but consider that procession, from every angle, if they did nothing but ponder it and analyse it, and think about it and read about it and pool their thinking and reading, and what they see and what they guess, their time would be better spent than in any other activity now open to them. But, you will object, you have no time to think; you have your battles to fight, your rent to pay, your bazaars to organize. That excuse shall not serve you, Madam. As you know from your own experience, and there are facts that prove it, the daughters of educated men have always done their thinking from hand to mouth; not under green lamps at study tables in the cloisters of secluded colleges. They have thought while they stirred the pot, while they rocked the cradle. It was thus that they won us the right to our brand-new sixpence. It falls to us now to go on thinking; how are we to spend that sixpence? Think we must. Let us think in offices; in omnibuses; while we are standing in the crowd watching Coronations and Lord Mayor's Shows; let us think as we pass the Cenotaph; and in Whitehall; in the gallery of the House of Commons; in the Law Courts; let us think at baptisms and marriages and funerals. Let us never cease from thinking—what is this 'civilization' in which we find ourselves? What are these ceremonies and why should we take part in them? What are these professions and why should we make money out of them? Where in short is it leading us, the procession of the sons of educated men?

"But you are busy; let us return to facts. Come indoors then, and open the books on your library shelves. For you have a library, and a good one. A working library, a living library; a library where nothing is chained down and nothing is locked up; a library where the songs of the singers rise naturally from the lives of the livers. There are the poems, here the biographies. And what light do they throw upon the professions, these biographies? How far do they encourage us to think that if we help the daughters to become professional women we shall discourage war? The answer to that question is scattered all about these volumes; and is legible to anyone who can read plain English. And the answer, one must admit, is extremely queer. For almost every biography we read of professional men in the nineteenth century, to limit ourselves to that not distant and fully documented age, is largely concerned with war. They were great fighters, it seems, the professional men in the age of Queen Victoria. There was the battle of Westminster. There was the battle of the universities. There was the battle of Whitehall. There was the battle of Harley Street. There was the battle of the Royal

Academy. Some of these battles, as you can testify, are still in progress. In fact the only profession which does not seem to have fought a fierce battle during the nineteenth century is the profession of literature. All the other professions, according to the testimony of biography, seem to be as bloodthirsty as the profession of arms itself. It is true that the combatants did not inflict flesh wounds;[17] chivalry forbade; but you will agree that a battle that wastes time is as deadly as a battle that wastes blood. You will agree that a battle that costs money is as deadly as a battle that costs a leg or an arm. You will agree that a battle that forces youth to spend its strength haggling in committee rooms, soliciting favours, assuming a mask of reverence to cloak its ridicule, inflicts wounds upon the human spirit which no surgery can heal. Even the battle of equal pay for equal work is not without its timeshed, its spiritshed, as you yourself, were you not unaccountably reticent on certain matters, might agree. Now the books in your library record so many of these battles that it is impossible to go into them all; but as they all seem to have been fought on much the same plan, and by the same combatants, that is by professional men *v.* their sisters and daughters, let us, since time presses, glance at one of these campaigns only and examine the battle of Harley Street, in order that we may understand what effect the professions have upon those who practise them.

"The campaign was opened in the year 1869 under the leadership of Sophia Jex-Blake. Her case is so typical an instance of the great Victorian fight between the victims of the patriarchal system and the patriarchs, of the daughters against the fathers, that it deserves a moment's examination. Sophia's father was an admirable specimen of the Victorian educated man, kindly, cultivated and well-to-do. He was a proctor of Doctors' Commons. He could afford to keep six servants, horses and carriages, and could provide his daughter not only with food and lodging but with 'handsome furniture' and 'a cosy fire' in her bedroom. For salary, 'for dress and private money,' he gave her £40 a year. For some reason she found this sum insufficient. In 1859, in view of the fact that she had only nine shillings and ninepence left to last her till next quarter, she wished to earn money herself. And she was offered a tutorship with the pay of five shillings an hour. She told her father of the offer. He replied, 'Dearest, I have only this moment heard that you contemplate being *paid* for the tutorship. It would be quite beneath you, darling, and *I cannot consent to it.*' She argued: 'Why should I not take it? You as a man did your work and received your payment, and no one thought it any degradation, but a fair exchange. . . . Tom is doing on a large scale what I am doing on a small one.' He replied: 'The cases you cite, darling, are not to the point. . . . T. W. . . . feels bound as a *man* . . . to support his wife and family, and his position is a high one, which can only be filled by a first-class man of character, and yielding him nearer two than one thousand a year. . . . How entirely different is my darling's case! You want for nothing, and know that (humanly speaking) you will want for nothing. If you married tomorrow—to my liking—and I don't believe you would ever marry otherwise—I should give you a good fortune.' Upon which her comment, in a private diary, was: 'Like a fool I have consented to give up the fees for this term only—though I am miserably poor. It was foolish. It only defers the struggle.'[18]

"There she was right. The struggle with her own father was over. But the struggle with fathers in general, with the patriarchy itself, was deferred to another place and another time. The second fight was at Edinburgh in 1869. She had applied for admission to the Royal College of Surgeons. Here is a newspaper account of the first skirmish. 'A disturbance of a very unbecoming nature took place yesterday afternoon in front of the Royal College of Surgeons. . . . Shortly before four o'clock . . . nearly

200 students assembled in front of the gate leading to the building. . . .' The medical students howled and sang songs. 'The gate
was closed in their [the women's] faces. . . . Dr. Handyside found
it utterly impossible to begin his demonstration . . . a pet sheep
was introduced into the room' and so on. The methods were
much the same as those that were employed at Cambridge during the battle of the Degree. And again, as on that occasion, the
authorities deplored those downright methods and employed
others, more astute and more effective, of their own. Nothing
would induce the authorities encamped within the sacred gates
to allow the women to enter. They said that God was on their
side, Nature was on their side, Law was on their side, and Property was on their side. The college was founded for the benefit
of men only; men only were entitled by law to benefit from its
endowments. The usual committees were formed. The usual
petitions were signed. The usual humble appeals were made.
The usual bazaars were held. The usual questions of tactics were
debated. As usual it was asked, ought we to attack now, or is it
wiser to wait? Who are our friends and who are our enemies?
There were the usual differences of opinion, the usual divisions
among the counsellors. But why particularize? The whole pro-
ceeding is so familiar that the battle of Harley Street in the year
1869 might well be the battle of Cambridge University at the
present moment. On both occasions there is the same waste of
strength, waste of temper, waste of time, and waste of money.
Almost the same daughters ask almost the same brothers for almost the same privileges. Almost the same gentlemen intone almost the same refusals for almost the same reasons. It seems as
if there were no progress in the human race, but only repetition.
We can almost hear them, if we listen, singing the same old
song, 'Here we go round the mulberry tree, the mulberry tree,
the mulberry tree,' and if we add, 'of property, of property, of

property,' we shall fill in the rhyme without doing violence to the facts.

"But we are not here to sing old songs or to fill in missing rhymes. We are here to consider facts. And the facts which we have just extracted from biography seem to prove that the professions have a certain undeniable effect upon the professors. They make the people who practise them possessive, jealous of any infringement of their rights, and highly combative if anyone dares dispute them. Are we not right then in thinking that if we enter the same professions we shall acquire the same qualities? And do not such qualities lead to war? In another century or so if we practise the professions in the same way, shall we not be just as possessive, just as jealous, just as pugnacious, just as positive as to the verdict of God, Nature, Law and Property as these gentlemen are now? Therefore this guinea, which is to help you to help women to enter the professions, has this condition as a first condition attached to it. You shall swear that you will do all in your power to insist that any woman who enters any profession shall in no way hinder any other human being, whether man or woman, white or black, provided that he or she is qualified to enter that profession, from entering it; but shall do all in her power to help them.

"You are ready to put your hand to that, here and now, you say, and at the same time stretch out that hand for the guinea. But wait. Other conditions are attached to it before it is yours. For consider once more the procession of the sons of educated men; ask yourself once more, where is it leading us? One answer suggests itself instantly. To incomes, it is obvious, that seem, to us at least, extremely handsome. Whitaker puts that beyond a doubt. And besides the evidence of Whitaker, there is the evidence of the daily paper—the evidence of the wills, of the subscription lists that we have considered already. In one issue of one paper, for example, it is stated that three educated men died; and one left £1,193,251; another £1,010,288; another £1,404,132. These are large sums for private people to amass, you will admit. And why should we not amass them too in course of time? Now that the Civil Service is open to us we may well earn from one thousand to three thousand a year; now that the Bar is open to us we may well earn £5,000 a year as judges, and any sum up to forty or fifty thousand a year as barristers. When the Church is open to us we may draw salaries of fifteen thousand, five thousand, three thousand yearly, with palaces and deaneries attached. When the Stock Exchange is open to us we may die worth as many millions as Pierpont Morgan, or as Rockefeller himself. As doctors we may make anything from two thousand to fifty thousand a year. As editors even we may earn salaries that are by no means despicable. One has a thousand a year; another two thousand; it is rumoured that the editor of a great daily paper has a salary of five thousand yearly. All this wealth may in the course of time come our way if we follow the professions. In short, we may change our position from being the victims of the patriarchal system, paid on the truck system, with £30 or £40 a year in cash and board and lodging thrown in, to being the champions of the capitalist system, with a yearly income in our own possession of many thousands which, by judicious investment, may leave us when we die possessed of a capital sum of more millions than we can count.

"It is a thought not without its glamour. Consider what it would mean if among us there were now a woman motor-car manufacturer who, with a stroke of her pen, could endow the women's colleges with two or three hundred thousand pounds apiece. The honorary treasurer of the rebuilding fund, your sister at Cambridge, would have her labours considerably lightened then. There would be no need of appeals and committees, of bazaars and strawberries and cream. And suppose that there were not merely one rich woman, but that rich women were as common as rich men. What could you not do? You could shut up your office at once. You could finance a woman's party in the House of Commons. You could run a daily newspaper committed to a conspiracy, not of silence, but of speech. You could get pensions for spinsters; those victims of the patriarchal system, whose allowance is insufficient and whose board and lodging are no longer thrown in. You could get equal pay for equal work. You could provide every mother with chloroform when her child is born;[19] you could bring down the maternal death-rate from four in every thousand to none at all, perhaps. In one session you could pass Bills that will now take you perhaps a hundred years of hard and continuous labour to get through the House of Commons. There seems at first sight nothing that you could not do, if you had the same capital at your disposal that your brothers have at theirs. Why not, then, you exclaim, help us to take the first step towards possessing it? The professions are the only way in which we can earn money. Money is the only means by which we can achieve objects that are immensely desirable. Yet here you are, you seem to protest, haggling and bargaining over conditions. But consider this letter from a professional man asking us to help him to prevent war. Look also at the photographs of dead bodies and ruined houses that the Spanish Government sends almost weekly. That is why it is necessary to haggle and to bargain over conditions.

"For the evidence of the letter and of the photographs when combined with the facts with which history and biography provide us about the professions seem together to throw a certain light, a red light, shall we say, upon those same professions. You make money in them; that is true; but how far is money in view of those facts in itself a desirable possession? A great authority upon human life, you will remember, held over two thousand years ago that great possessions were undesirable.

To which you reply, and with some heat as if you suspected another excuse for keeping the purse-string tied, that Christ's words about the rich and the Kingdom of Heaven are no longer helpful to those who have to face different facts in a different world. You argue that as things are now in England extreme poverty is less desirable than extreme wealth. The poverty of the Christian who should give away all his possessions produces, as we have daily and abundant proof, the crippled in body, the feeble in mind. The unemployed, to take the obvious example, are not a source of spiritual or intellectual wealth to their country. These are weighty arguments; but consider for a moment the life of Pierpont Morgan. Do you not agree with that evidence before us that extreme wealth is equally undesirable, and for the same reasons? If extreme wealth is undesirable and extreme poverty is undesirable, it is arguable that there is some mean between the two which is desirable. What then is that mean—how much money is needed to live upon in England today? And how should that money be spent? What is the kind of life, the kind of human being, you propose to aim at if you succeed in extracting this guinea? Those, Madam, are the questions that I am asking you to consider and you cannot deny that those are questions of the utmost importance. But alas, they are questions that would lead us far beyond the solid world of actual fact to which we are here confined. So let us shut the New Testament, Shakespeare, Shelley, Tolstoy and the rest, and face the fact that stares us in the face at this moment of transition—the fact of the procession; the fact that we are trapesing along somewhere in the rear and must consider that fact before we can fix our eyes upon the vision on the horizon.

"There it is then, before our eyes, the procession of the sons of educated men, ascending those pulpits, mounting those steps, passing in and out of those doors, preaching, teaching, administering justice, practising medicine, making money. And it is obvious that if you are going to make the same incomes from the same professions that those men make you will have to accept the same conditions that they accept. Even from an upper window and from books we know or can guess what those conditions are. You will have to leave the house at nine and come back to it at six. That leaves very little time for fathers to know their children. You will have to do this daily from the age of twenty-one or so to the age of about sixty-five. That leaves very little time for friendship, travel or art. You will have to perform some duties that are very arduous, others that are very barbarous. You will have to wear certain uniforms and profess certain loyalties. If you succeed in those professions the words 'For God and the Empire' will very likely be written, like the address on a dog-collar, round your neck.[20] And if words have meaning, as words perhaps should have meaning, you will have to accept that meaning and do what you can to enforce it. In short, you will have to lead the same lives and profess the same loyalties that professional men have professed for many centuries. There can be no doubt of that.

"If you retaliate, what harm is there in that? Why should we hesitate to do what our fathers and grandfathers have done before us? let us go into greater detail and consult the facts which are nowadays open to the inspection of all who can read their mother tongue in biography. There they are, those innumerable and invaluable works upon the shelves of your own library. Let us glance again rapidly at the lives of professional men who have succeeded in their professions. Here is an extract from the life of a great lawyer. 'He went to his chambers about half-past nine. . . . He took briefs home with him . . . so that he was lucky if he got to bed about one or two o'clock in the morning.'[21] That explains why most successful barristers are hardly worth sitting next at dinner—they yawn so. Next, here is a quotation from a famous politician's speech. '. . . since 1914 I have never seen the pageant of the blossom from the first damson to the last apple—never once have I seen that in Worcestershire since 1914, and if that is not a sacrifice I do not know what is.'[22] A sacrifice indeed, and one that explains the perennial indifference of the Government to art—why, these unfortunate gentlemen must be as blind as bats. Take the religious profession next. Here is a quotation from the life of a great bishop. 'This is an awful mind- and soul-destroying life. I really do not know how to live it. The arrears of important work accumulate and crush.'[23] That bears out what so many people are saying now about the Church and the nation. Our bishops and deans seem to have no soul with which to preach and no mind with which to write. Listen to any sermon in any church; read the journalism of Dean Alington or Dean Inge in any newspaper. Take the doctor's profession next. 'I have taken a good deal over £13,000 during the year, but this cannot possibly be maintained, and while it lasts it is slavery. What I feel most is being away from Eliza and the children so frequently on Sundays, and again at Christmas.'[24] That is the complaint of a great doctor; and his patient might well echo it, for what Harley Street specialist has time to understand the body, let alone the mind or both in combination, when he is a slave to thirteen thousand a year? But is the life of a professional writer any better? Here is a sample taken from the life of a highly successful journalist. 'On another day at this time he wrote a 1,600 words article on Nietzsche, a leader of equal length on the railway strike for the *Standard,* 600 words for the *Tribune* and in the evening was at Shoe Lane.'[25] That explains among other things why the public reads its politics with cynicism, and authors read their reviews with foot-rules—it is the advertisement that counts; praise or blame have ceased to have any meaning. And with one more glance at the politician's life, for his profession after all is the most important practically, let us have done. 'Lord Hugh *loitered in the lobby*. . . . The Bill [the Deceased Wife's Sister Bill] was in consequence dead, and the further chances of the cause were relegated to the chances and mischances of another year.'[26] That not only serves to explain a certain prevalent distrust of politicians, but also reminds us that since you have the Pensions Bill to steer through the lobbies of so just and humane an institution as the House of Commons, we must not loiter too long ourselves among these delightful biographies, but must try to sum up the information which we have gained from them.

"What then do these quotations from the lives of successful professional men prove, you ask? They prove, as Whitaker proves things, nothing whatever. If Whitaker, that is, says that a bishop is paid five thousand a year, that is a fact; it can be checked and verified. But if Bishop Gore says that the life of a bishop is 'an awful mind- and soul-destroying life' he is merely giving us his opinion; the next bishop on the bench may flatly contradict him. These quotations then prove nothing that can be checked and verified; they merely cause us to hold opinions. And those opinions cause us to doubt and criticize and question the value of professional life—not its cash value; that is great; but its spiritual, its moral, its intellectual value. They make us of the opinion that if people are highly successful in their professions they lose their senses. Sight goes. They have no time to look at pictures. Sound goes. They have no time to listen to music. Speech goes. They have no time for conversation. They lose their sense of proportion—the relations between one thing and another. Humanity goes. Money making becomes so important that they must work by night as well as by day. Health goes. And so competitive do they become that they will not share their work with others though they have more than they can do themselves. What then remains of a human being who has lost sight, and sound, and sense of proportion? Only a cripple in a cave.

"That of course is a figure, and fanciful; but that it has some connection with figures that are statistical and not fanciful—with the three hundred millions spent upon arms—seems possible. Such at any rate would seem to be the opinion of disinterested observers whose position gives them every opportunity for judging widely, and for judging fairly. Let us examine two such opinions only. The Marquess of Londonderry said:

> 'We seem to hear a babel of voices among which direction and guidance are lacking, and the world appears to be marking time. . . . During the last century gigantic forces of scientific discovery had been unloosed, while at the same time we could discern no corresponding advance in literary or scientific achievement. . . . The question we are asking ourselves is whether man is capable of enjoying these new fruits of scientific knowledge and discovery, or whether by their misuse he will bring about the destruction of himself and the edifice of civilization.'[27]

"Mr. Churchill said:

> 'Certain it is that while men are gathering knowledge and power with ever-increasing and measureless speed, their virtues and their wisdom have not shown any notable improvement as the centuries have rolled. The brain of a modern man does not differ in essentials from that of the human beings who fought and loved here millions of years ago. The nature of man has remained hitherto practically unchanged. Under sufficient stress—starvation,

terror, warlike passion, or even cold intellectual frenzy—
the modern man we know so well will do the most terrible
deeds, and his modern woman will back him up.'[28]

"Those are two quotations only from a great number to the
same effect. And to them let us add another, from a less impressive source but worth your reading since it too bears upon our
problem, from Mr. Cyril Chaventry of North Wembley.

'"A woman's sense of values," he writes, "is indisputably
different from that of a man. Obviously therefore a
woman is at a disadvantage and under suspicion when in
competition in a man-created sphere of activity. More
than ever today women have the opportunity to build a
new and better world, but in this slavish imitation of men
they are wasting their chance."'[29]

"That opinion, too, is a representative opinion, one from a
great number to the same effect provided by the daily papers.
And the three quotations taken together are highly instructive.
The two first seem to prove that the enormous professional
competence of the educated man has not brought about an altogether desirable state of things in the civilized world; and the
last, which calls upon professional women to use 'their different sense of values' to 'build a new and better world' not only
implies that those who have built that world are dissatisfied with
the results, but, by calling upon the other sex to remedy the evil
imposes a great responsibility and implies a great compliment.
For if Mr. Chaventry and the gentlemen who agree with him believe that 'at a disadvantage and under suspicion' as she is, with
little or no political or professional training and upon a salary of
about £250 a year, the professional woman can yet 'build a new

and better world,' they must credit her with powers that might almost be called divine. They must agree with Goethe:

> 'The things that must pass
> Are only symbols;
> Here shall all failure
> Grow to achievement,
> Here, the Untellable
> Work all fulfilment,
> The woman in woman
> Lead forward for ever.'[30]

—another very great compliment, and from a very great poet you will agree.

"But you do not want compliments; you are pondering quotations. And since your expression is decidedly downcast, it seems as if these quotations about the nature of professional life have brought you to some melancholy conclusion. What can it be? Simply, you reply, that we, daughters of educated men, are between the devil and the deep sea. Behind us lies the patriarchal system; the private house, with its nullity, its immorality, its hypocrisy, its servility. Before us lies the public world, the professional system, with its possessiveness, its jealousy, its pugnacity, its greed. The one shuts us up like slaves in a harem; the other forces us to circle, like caterpillars head to tail, round and round the mulberry tree, the sacred tree, of property. It is a choice of evils. Each is bad. Had we not better plunge off the bridge into the river; give up the game; declare that the whole of human life is a mistake and so end it?

"But before you take that step, Madam, a decisive one, unless you share the opinion of the professors of the Church of England that death is the gate of life—*Mors Janua Vitae* is written upon an arch in St. Paul's—in which case there is, of course, much to recommend it, let us see if another answer is not possible.

"Another answer may be staring us in the face on the shelves of your own library, once more in the biographies. Is it not possible that by considering the experiments that the dead have made with their lives in the past we may find some help in answering the very difficult question that is now forced upon us? At any rate, let us try. The question that we will now put to biography is this: For reasons given above we are agreed that we must earn money in the professions. For reasons given above those professions seem to us highly undesirable. The question we put to you, lives of the dead, is how can we enter the professions and yet remain civilized human beings; human beings, that is, who wish to prevent war?

"This time let us turn to the lives not of men but of women in the nineteenth century—to the lives of professional women. But there would seem to be a gap in your library, Madam. There are no lives of professional women in the nineteenth century. A Mrs. Tomlinson, the wife of a Mr. Tomlinson, F.R.S., F.C.S., explains the reason. This lady, who wrote a book 'advocating the employment of young ladies as nurses for children,' says: '. . . it seemed as if there were no way in which an unmarried lady could earn a living but by taking a situation as governess, for which post she was often unfit by nature and education, or want of education.'[31] That was written in 1859—less than 100 years ago. That explains the gap on your shelves. There were no professional women, except governesses, to have lives written of them. And the lives of governesses, that is the written lives, can be counted on the fingers of one hand. What then can we learn about the lives of professional women from studying the lives of governesses? Happily old boxes are beginning to give up their old secrets. Out the other day crept one such document written about the year 1811. There was, it appears, an obscure

Miss Weeton, who used to scribble down her thoughts upon professional life among other things when her pupils were in bed. Here is one such thought. 'Oh! how I have burned to learn Latin, French, the Arts, the Sciences, anything rather than the dog trot way of sewing, teaching, writing copies, and washing dishes every day. . . . Why are not females permitted to study physics, divinity, astronomy, etc., etc., with their attendants, chemistry, botany, logic, mathematics, &c.?'[32] That comment upon the lives of governesses, that question from the lips of governesses, reaches us from the darkness. It is illuminating, too. But let us go on groping; let us pick up a hint here and a hint there as to the professions as they were practised by women in the nineteenth century. Next we find Anne Clough, the sister of Arthur Clough, pupil of Dr. Arnold, Fellow of Oriel, who, though she served without a salary, was the first principal of Newnham, and thus may be called a professional woman in embryo—we find her training for her profession by 'doing much of the housework' . . . 'earning money to pay off what had been lent by their friends,' 'pressing for leave to keep a small school,' reading books her brother lent her, and exclaiming, 'If I were a man, I would not work for riches, to make myself a name or to leave a wealthy family behind me. No, I think I would work for my country, and make its people my heirs.'[33] The nineteenth-century women were not without ambition it seems. Next we find Josephine Butler, who, though not strictly speaking a professional woman, led the campaign against the Contagious Diseases Act to victory, and then the campaign against the sale and purchase of children 'for infamous purposes'—we find Josephine Butler refusing to have a life of herself written, and saying of the women who helped her in those campaigns: 'The utter absence in them of any desire for recognition, of any vestige of egotism in any form, is worthy of remark. In the purity of their motives they shine out "clear as crystal."'[34] That, then,

was one of the qualities that the Victorian woman praised and
practised—a negative one, it is true; not to be recognized; not
to be egotistical; to do the work for the sake of doing the
work.[35] An interesting contribution to psychology in its way.
And then we come closer to our own time; we find Gertrude
Bell, who, though the diplomatic service was and is shut to
women, occupied a post in the East which almost entitled her
to be called a pseudo-diplomat—we find rather to our surprise
that 'Gertrude could never go out in London without a female
friend or, failing that, a maid.[36] . . . When it seemed unavoidable
for Gertrude to drive in a hansom with a young man from one
tea party to another, she feels obliged to write and confess it
to my mother.'[37] So they were chaste, the women pseudo-
diplomats of the Victorian Age?[38] And not merely in body; in
mind also. Gertrude 'was not allowed to read Bourget's *The Disciple*' for fear of contracting whatever disease that book may dis-
seminate. Dissatisfied but ambitious, ambitious but austere,
chaste yet adventurous—such are some of the qualities that we
have discovered. But let us go on looking—if not at the lines,
then between the lines of biography. And we find, between the
lines of their husbands' biographies, so many women practising—but what are we to call the profession that consists in
bringing nine or ten children into the world, the profession
which consists in running a house, nursing an invalid, visiting
the poor and the sick, tending here an old father, there an old
mother?—there is no name and there is no pay for that profession; but we find so many mothers, sisters and daughters of educated men practising it in the nineteenth century that we must
lump them and their lives together behind their husbands' and
brothers', and leave them to deliver their message to those who
have the time to extract it and the imagination with which to de-
cipher it. Let us ourselves, who as you hint are pressed for time,
sum up these random hints and reflections upon the professional

life of women in the nineteenth century by quoting once more the highly significant words of a woman who was not a professional woman in the strict sense of the word, but had some nondescript reputation as a traveller nevertheless—Mary Kingsley:

'I don't know if I ever revealed the fact to you that being allowed to learn German was *all* the paid-for education I ever had. £2,000 was spent on my brother's. I still hope not in vain.'

"That statement is so suggestive that it may save us the bother of groping and searching between the lines of professional men's lives for the lives of their sisters. If we develop the suggestions we find in that statement, and connect it with the other hints and fragments that we have uncovered, we may arrive at some theory or point of view that may help us to answer the very difficult question, which now confronts us. For when Mary Kingsley says, '. . . being allowed to learn German was *all* the paid-for education I ever had,' she suggests that she had an unpaid-for education. The other lives that we have been examining corroborate that suggestion. What then was the nature of that 'unpaid-for education' which, whether for good or for evil, has been ours for so many centuries? If we mass the lives of the obscure behind four lives that were not obscure, but were so successful and distinguished that they were actually written, the lives of Florence Nightingale, Miss Clough, Mary Kingsley and Gertrude Bell, it seems undeniable that they were all educated by the same teachers. And those teachers, biography indicates, obliquely, and indirectly, but emphatically and indisputably none the less, were poverty, chastity, derision, and—what word however covers 'lack of rights and privileges'? Shall we press the old word 'freedom' once more into service? 'Freedom from unreal loyalties,' then, was the fourth of their teachers; that freedom

from loyalty to old schools, old colleges, old churches, old ceremonies, old countries which all those women enjoyed, and which,
to a great extent, we still enjoy by the law and custom of England.
We have no time to coin new words, greatly though the language
is in need of them. Let 'freedom from unreal loyalties' then stand
as the fourth great teacher of the daughters of educated men.

"Biography thus provides us with the fact that the daughters of educated men received an unpaid-for education at the
hands of poverty, chastity, derision and freedom from unreal
loyalties. It was this unpaid-for education, biography informs
us, that fitted them, aptly enough, for the unpaid-for professions. And biography also informs us that those unpaid-for professions had their laws, traditions, and labours no less certainly
than the paid-for professions. Further, the student of biography
cannot possibly doubt from the evidence of biography that this
education and these professions were in many ways bad in the
extreme, both for the unpaid themselves and for their descen-
dants. The intensive childbirth of the unpaid wife, the intensive
money-making of the paid husband in the Victorian age had terrible results, we cannot doubt, upon the mind and body of the
present age. To prove it we need not quote once more the famous passage in which Florence Nightingale denounced that
education and its results; nor stress the natural delight with
which she greeted the Crimean war; nor illustrate from other
sources—they are, alas, innumerable—the inanity, the petti-
ness, the spite, the tyranny, the hypocrisy, the immorality which
it engendered as the lives of both sexes so abundantly testify.
Final proof of its harshness upon one sex at any rate can be
found in the annals of our 'great war,' when hospitals, harvest
fields and munition works were largely staffed by refugees flying from its horrors to their comparative amenity.

"But biography is many-sided; biography never returns a
single and simple answer to any question that is asked of it.

Thus the biographies of those who had biographies—say Florence Nightingale, Anne Clough, Emily Brontë, Christina Rossetti, Mary Kingsley—prove beyond a doubt that this same education, the unpaid for, must have had great virtues as well as great defects, for we cannot deny that these, if not educated, still were civilized women. We cannot, when we consider the lives of our uneducated mothers and grandmothers, judge education simply by its power to 'obtain appointments,' to win honour, to make money. We must, if we are honest, admit that some who had no paid-for education, no salaries and no appointments were civilized human beings—whether or not they can rightly be called 'English' women is matter for dispute; and thus admit that we should be extremely foolish if we threw away the results of that education or gave up the knowledge that we have obtained from it for any bribe or decoration whatsoever. Thus biography, when asked the question we have put to it—how can we enter the professions and yet remain civilized human beings, human beings who discourage war, would seem to reply: If you refuse to be separated from the four great teachers of the daughters of educated men—poverty, chastity, derision and freedom from unreal loyalties—but combine them with some wealth, some knowledge, and some service to real loyalties then you can enter the professions and escape the risks that make them undesirable.

"Such being the answer of the oracle, such are the conditions attached to this guinea. You shall have it, to recapitulate, on condition that you help all properly qualified people, of whatever sex, class or colour, to enter your profession; and further on condition that in the practise of your profession you refuse to be separated from poverty, chastity, derision and freedom from unreal loyalties. Is the statement now more positive, have the conditions been made more clear and do you agree to the terms? You hesitate. Some of the conditions, you seem to suggest, need further discussion. Let us take them, then, in order. By poverty is meant enough money to live upon. That is, you must earn enough to be independent of any other human being and to buy that modicum of health, leisure, knowledge and so on that is needed for the full development of body and mind. But no more. Not a penny more.

"By chastity is meant that when you have made enough to live on by your profession you must refuse to sell your brain for the sake of money. That is you must cease to practise your profession, or practise it for the sake of research and experiment; or, if you are an artist, for the sake of the art; or give the knowledge acquired professionally to those who need it for nothing. But directly the mulberry tree begins to make you circle, break off. Pelt the tree with laughter.

"By derision—a bad word, but once again the English language is much in need of new words—is meant that you must refuse all methods of advertising merit, and hold that ridicule, obscurity and censure are preferable, for psychological reasons, to fame and praise. Directly badges, orders, or degrees are offered you, fling them back in the giver's face.

"By freedom from unreal loyalties is meant that you must rid yourself of pride of nationality in the first place; also of religious pride, college pride, school pride, family pride, sex pride and those unreal loyalties that spring from them. Directly the seducers come with their seductions to bribe you into captivity, tear up the parchments; refuse to fill up the forms.

"And if you still object that these definitions are both too arbitrary and too general, and ask how anybody can tell how much money and how much knowledge are needed for the full development of body and mind, and which are the real loyalties which we must serve and which the unreal which we must despise, I can only refer you—time presses—to two authorities. One is familiar enough. It is the psychometer that you carry on your wrist, the little instrument upon which you depend in all personal relationships. If it were visible it would look something like a thermometer. It has a vein of quicksilver in it which is affected by any body or soul, house or society in whose presence it is exposed. If you want to find out how much wealth is desirable, expose it in a rich man's presence; how much learning is desirable expose it in a learned man's presence. So with patriotism, religion and the rest. The conversation need not be interrupted while you consult it; nor its amenity disturbed. But if you object that this is too personal and fallible a method to employ without risk of mistake, witness the fact that the private psychometer has led to many unfortunate marriages and broken friendships, then there is the other authority now easily within the reach even of the poorest of the daughters of educated men. Go to the public galleries and look at pictures; turn on the wireless and rake down music from the air; enter any of the public libraries which are now free to all. There you will be able to consult the findings of the public psychometer for yourself. To take one example, since we are pressed for time. The *Antigone* of Sophocles has been done into English prose or verse by a man whose name is immaterial.[39] Consider the character of Creon. There you have a most profound analysis by a poet, who is a psychologist in action, of the effect of power and wealth upon the soul. Consider Creon's claim to absolute rule over his subjects. That is a far more instructive analysis of tyranny than any our politicians can offer us. You want to know which are the unreal loyalties which we must despise, which are the real loyalties which we must honour? Consider Antigone's distinction between the laws and the Law. That is a far more profound statement of the duties of the individual to society than any our sociologists can offer us. Lame as the English rendering is, Antigone's five words are worth all the sermons of all the archbishops.[40] But to enlarge would be impertinent. Private judgment is still free in private; and that freedom is the essence of freedom.

"For the rest, though the conditions may seem many and the guinea, alas, is single, they are not for the most part as things are at present very difficult of fulfilment. With the exception of the first—that we must earn enough money to live upon—they are largely ensured us by the laws of England. The law of England sees to it that we do not inherit great possessions; the law of England denies us, and let us hope will long continue to deny us, the full stigma of nationality. Then we can scarcely doubt that our brothers will provide us for many centuries to come, as they have done for many centuries past, with what is so essential for sanity, and so invaluable in preventing the great modern sins of vanity, egotism, megalomania—that is to say ridicule, censure and contempt.[41] And so long as the Church of England refuses our services—long may she exclude us!—and the ancient schools and colleges refuse to admit us to a share of their endowments and privileges we shall be immune without any trouble on our part from the particular loyalties and fealties which such endowments and privileges engender. Further, Madam, the traditions of the private house, that ancestral memory which lies behind the present moment, are there to help you. We have seen in the quotations given above how great a part chastity, bodily chastity, has played in the unpaid education of our sex. It should not be difficult to transmute the old ideal of bodily chastity into the new ideal of mental chastity—to hold that if it was wrong to sell the body for money it is much more wrong to sell the mind for money, since the mind, people say, is nobler than the body. Then again, are we not greatly fortified in resisting the seductions of the most powerful of all seducers—money—by those same traditions? For how many centuries have we not enjoyed the right of working all day and every day for £40 a year with board and lodging thrown in? And does not Whitaker prove that half the work of educated men's daughters is still unpaid-for work? Finally, honour, fame, consequence—is it not easy for us to resist that seduction, we who have worked for centuries without other honour than that which is reflected from the coronets and badges on our father's or husband's brows and breasts?

"Thus, with law on our side, and property on our side, and ancestral memory to guide us, there is no need of further argument; you will agree that the conditions upon which this guinea is yours are, with the exception of the first, comparatively easy to fulfil. They merely require that you should develop, modify and direct by the findings of the two psychometers the traditions and the education of the private house which have been in existence these 2,000 years. And if you will agree to do that, there can be an end of bargaining between us. Then the guinea with which to pay the rent of your house is yours—would that it were a thousand! For if you agree to these terms then you can join the professions and yet remain uncontaminated by them; you can rid them of their possessiveness, their jealousy, their pugnacity, their greed. You can use them to have a mind of your own and a will of your own. And you can use that mind and will to abolish the inhumanity, the beastliness, the horror, the folly of war. Take this guinea then and use it, not to burn the house down, but to make its windows blaze. And let the daughters of uneducated women dance round the new house, the poor house, the house that stands in a narrow street where omnibuses pass and the street hawkers cry their wares, and let them sing, 'We have done with war! We have done with tyranny!' And their mothers will laugh from their graves, 'It was for this that we suffered obloquy and contempt! Light up the windows of the new house, daughters! Let them blaze!'

"Those then are the terms upon which I give you this guinea with which to help the daughters of uneducated women to enter the professions. And by cutting short the peroration let us hope that you will be able to give the finishing touches to your bazaar, arrange the hare and the coffee-pot, and receive the Right Honourable Sir Sampson Legend, O.M., K.C.B., LL.D., D.C.L., P.C., etc., etc., with that air of smiling deference which befits the daughter of an educated man in the presence of her brother."

Such then, Sir, was the letter finally sent to the honorary treasurer of the society for helping the daughters of educated men to enter the professions. In it such influence as a guinea can exert has been framed so far as our psychological competence allows to ensure that she shall do all that is in her power to help you to prevent war. Whether the terms have been rightly defined it is impossible to say. But as you will see, it was necessary to answer her letter and the letter from the honorary treasurer of the college rebuilding fund, and to send them both guineas before answering your letter, because unless they are helped, first to educate the daughters of educated men, and then to earn their livings in the professions, those daughters cannot possess an independent and disinterested influence with which to help you to prevent war. The causes it seems are connected. But having shown this to the best of our ability, let us return to your own letter and to your request for a subscription to your own society.

THREE

HERE THEN is your own letter. In that, as we have seen, after asking for an opinion as to how to prevent war, you go on to suggest certain practical measures by which we can help you to prevent it. These are it appears that we should sign a manifesto, pledging ourselves "to protect culture and intellectual liberty";[1] that we should join a certain society, devoted to certain measures whose aim is to preserve peace; and, finally, that we should subscribe to that society which like the others is in need of funds.

First, then, let us consider how we can help you to prevent war by protecting culture and intellectual liberty, since you assure us that there is a connection between those rather abstract words and these very positive photographs—the photographs of dead bodies and ruined houses.

But if it was surprising to be asked for an opinion how to prevent war, it is still more surprising to be asked to help you in the rather abstract terms of your manifesto to protect culture and intellectual liberty. Consider, Sir, in the light of the facts given above, what this request of yours means. It means that in the year 1938 the sons of educated men are asking the daughters to help them to protect culture and intellectual liberty. And why, you may ask, is that so surprising? Suppose that the Duke of Devonshire, in his star and garter, stepped down into the kitchen and said to the maid who was peeling potatoes with a smudge on her cheek: "Stop your potato peeling, Mary, and help me to construe this rather difficult passage in Pindar," would not Mary be surprised and run screaming to Louisa the cook, "Lawks, Louie, Master must be mad!" That, or something like it, is the cry that rises to our lips when the sons of educated men ask us, their sisters, to protect intellectual liberty and culture. But let us try to translate the kitchenmaid's cry into the language of educated people.

Once more we must beg you, Sir, to look from our angle, from our point of view, at Arthur's Education Fund. Try once more, difficult though it is to twist your head in that direction, to understand what it has meant to us to keep that receptacle filled all these centuries so that some 10,000 of our brothers may be educated every year at Oxford and Cambridge. It has meant that we have already contributed to the cause of culture and intellectual liberty more than any other class in the community. For have not the daughters of educated men paid into Arthur's Education Fund from the year 1262 to the year 1870 all the money that was needed to educate themselves, bating such miserable sums as went to pay the governess, the German teacher, and the dancing master? Have they not paid with their own education for Eton and Harrow, Oxford and Cambridge, and all the great schools and universities on the continent—the Sorbonne and Heidelberg, Salamanca and Padua and Rome? Have they not paid so generously and lavishly if so indirectly, that when at last, in the nineteenth century, they won the right to some paid-for education for themselves, there was not a single woman who had received enough paid-for education to be able to teach them?[2] And now, out of the blue, just as they were hoping that they might filch not only a little of that same university education for themselves but some of the trimmings—travel, pleasure, liberty—for themselves, here is your letter informing them that the whole of that vast, that fabulous sum—for whether counted directly in cash, or indirectly in things done without, the sum that filled Arthur's Education Fund is vast— has been wasted or wrongly applied. With what other purpose were the universities of Oxford and Cambridge founded, save to protect culture and intellectual liberty? For what other object did your sisters go without teaching or travel or luxuries them- selves except that with the money so saved their brothers should go to schools and universities and there learn to protect culture and intellectual liberty? But now since you proclaim them in danger and ask us to add our voice to yours, and our sixpence to your guinea, we must assume that the money so spent was wasted and that those societies have failed. Yet, the reflection must intrude, if the public schools and universities with their elaborate machinery for mind-training and body-training have failed, what reason is there to think that your society, sponsored though it is by distinguished names, is going to succeed, or that your manifesto, signed though it is by still more distinguished names, is going to convert? Ought you not, before you lease an office, hire a secretary, elect a committee and appeal for funds, to consider why those schools and universities have failed?

That, however, is a question for you to answer. The ques- tion which concerns us is what possible help we can give you in protecting culture and intellectual liberty—we who have been shut out from the universities so repeatedly, and are only now admitted so restrictedly; we who have received no paid-for ed- ucation whatsoever, or so little that we can only read our own tongue and write our own language, we who are, in fact, mem- bers not of the intelligentsia but of the ignorantsia? To confirm us in our modest estimate of our own culture and to prove that you in fact share it there is Whitaker with his facts. Not a single educated man's daughter, Whitaker says, is thought capable of teaching the literature of her own language at either university.

Nor is her opinion worth asking, Whitaker informs us, when it comes to buying a picture for the National Gallery, a portrait for the Portrait Gallery, or a mummy for the British Museum. How then can it be worth your while to ask us to protect culture and intellectual liberty when, as Whitaker proves with his cold facts, you have no belief that our advice is worth having when it comes to spending the money, to which we have contributed, in buying culture and intellectual liberty for the State? Do you wonder that the unexpected compliment takes us by surprise? Still, there is your letter. There are facts in that letter, too. In it you say that war is imminent; and you go on to say, in more languages than one—here is the French version: *Seule la culture désintéressée peut garder le monde de sa ruine*[3]—you go on to say that by protecting intellectual liberty and our inheritance of culture we can help you to prevent war. And since the first statement at least is indisputable and any kitchenmaid even if her French is defective can read and understand the meaning of "Air Raid Precautions" when written in large letters upon a blank wall, we cannot ignore your request on the plea of ignorance or remain silent on the plea of modesty. Just as any kitchenmaid would attempt to construe a passage in Pindar if told that her life depended on it, so the daughters of educated men, however little their training qualifies them, must consider what they can do to protect culture and intellectual liberty if by so doing they can help you to prevent war. So let us by all means in our power examine this further method of helping you, and see, before we consider your request that we should join your society, whether we can sign this manifesto in favour of culture and intellectual liberty with some intention of keeping our word.

What, then, is the meaning of those rather abstract words? If we are to help you to protect them it would be well to define them in the first place. But like all honorary treasurers you are pressed for time, and to ramble through English literature in search of a definition, though a delightful pastime in its way, might well lead us far. Let us agree, then, for the present, that we know what they are, and concentrate upon the practical question how we can help you to protect them. Now the daily paper with its provision of facts lies on the table; and a single quotation from it may save time and limit our enquiry. "It was decided yesterday at a conference of head masters that women were not fit teachers for boys over the age of fourteen." That fact is of instant help to us here, for it proves that certain kinds of help are beyond our reach. For us to attempt to reform the education of our brothers at public schools and universities would be to invite a shower of dead cats, rotten eggs and bro-ken gates from which only street scavengers and locksmiths would benefit, while the gentlemen in authority, history assures us, would survey the tumult from their study windows without taking the cigars from their lips or ceasing to sip, slowly as its bouquet deserves, their admirable claret.[4] The teaching of his-tory, then, reinforced by the teaching of the daily paper, drives us to a more restricted position. We can only help you to defend culture and intellectual liberty by defending our own culture and our own intellectual liberty. That is to say, we can hint, if the treasurer of one of the women's colleges asks us for a subscrip-tion, that some change might be made in that satellite body when it ceases to be satellite; or again, if the treasurer of some society for obtaining professional employment for women asks us for a subscription, suggest that some change might be desir-able, in the interests of culture and intellectual liberty, in the practice of the professions. But as paid-for education is still raw and young, and as the number of those allowed to enjoy it at Oxford and Cambridge is still strictly limited, culture for the great majority of educated men's daughters must still be that which is acquired outside the sacred gates, in public libraries or in private libraries, whose doors by some unaccountable oversight have been left unlocked. It must still, in the year 1938, largely consist in reading and writing our own tongue. The question thus becomes more manageable. Shorn of its glory it is easier to deal with. What we have to do now, then, Sir, is to lay your request before the daughters of educated men and to ask them to help you to prevent war, not by advising their brothers how they shall protect culture and intellectual liberty, but simply by reading and writing their own tongue in such a way as to protect those rather abstract goddesses themselves.

This would seem, on the face of it, a simple matter, and one that needs neither argument nor rhetoric. But we are met at the outset by a new difficulty. We have already noted the fact that the profession of literature, to give it a simple name, is the only profession which did not fight a series of battles in the nineteenth century. There has been no battle of Grub Street. That profession has never been shut to the daughters of educated men. This was due of course to the extreme cheapness of its professional requirements. Books, pens and paper are so cheap, reading and writing have been, since the eighteenth century at least, so universally taught in our class, that it was impossible for any body of men to corner the necessary knowledge or to refuse admittance, except on their own terms, to those who wished to read books or to write them. But it follows, since the profession of literature is open to the daughters of educated men, that there is no honorary treasurer of the profession in such need of a guinea with which to prosecute her battle that she will listen to our terms, and promise to do what she can to observe them. This places us, you will agree, in an awkward predicament. For how then can we bring pressure upon them— what can we do to persuade them to help us? The profession of literature differs, it would seem, from all the other professions. There is no head of the profession; no Lord Chancellor as in your own case: no official body with the power to lay down rules and enforce them.[5] We cannot debar women from the use of libraries;[6] or forbid them to buy ink and paper; or rule that metaphors shall only be used by one sex, as the male only in art schools was allowed to study from the nude; or rule that rhyme shall be used by one sex only as the male only in Academies of music was allowed to play in orchestras. Such is the inconceivable licence of the profession of letters that any daughter of an educated man may use a man's name — say George Eliot or George Sand — with the result that an editor or a publisher, unlike the authorities in Whitehall, can detect no difference in the scent or savour of a manuscript, or even know for certain whether the writer is married or not.

Thus, since we have very little power over those who earn their livings by reading and writing, we must go to them humbly without bribes or penalties. We must go to them cap in hand, like beggars, and ask them of their goodness to spare time to listen to our request that they shall practise the profession of reading and writing in the interests of culture and intellectual liberty.

And now, clearly, some further definition of "culture and intellectual liberty" would be useful. Fortunately, it need not be, for our purposes, exhaustive or elaborate. We need not consult Milton, Goethe, or Matthew Arnold; for their definition would apply to paid-for culture — the culture which, in Miss Weeton's definition, includes physics, divinity, astronomy, chemistry, botany, logic and mathematics, as well as Latin, Greek and French. We are appealing in the main to those whose culture is the unpaid-for culture, that which consists in being able to read and write their own tongue. Happily your manifesto is at hand to help us to define the terms further; "disinterested" is the word you use. Therefore let us define culture for our purposes as the disinterested pursuit of reading and writing the English language. And intellectual liberty may be defined for our purposes as the right to say or write what you think in your own words, and in your own way. These are very crude definitions, but they must serve. Our appeal then might begin: "Oh, daughters of educated men, this gentleman, whom we all respect, says that war is imminent; by protecting culture and intellectual liberty he says that we can help him to prevent war. We entreat you, therefore, who earn your livings by reading and writing . . ." But here the words falter on our lips, and the prayer peters out into three separate dots because of facts again—because of facts in books, facts in biographies, facts which make it difficult, perhaps impossible, to go on.

What are those facts then? Once more we must interrupt our appeal in order to examine them. And there is no difficulty in finding them. Here, for example, is an illuminating document before us, a most genuine and indeed moving piece of work, the autobiography of Mrs. Oliphant, which is full of facts. She was an educated man's daughter who earned her living by reading and writing. She wrote books of all kinds. Novels, biographies, histories, handbooks of Florence and Rome, reviews, newspaper articles innumerable came from her pen. With the proceeds she earned her living and educated her children. But how far did she protect culture and intellectual liberty? That you can judge for yourself by reading first a few of her novels: *The Duke's Daughter, Diana Trelawny, Harry Joscelyn,* say; continue with the lives of Sheridan and Cervantes; go on to the *Makers of Florence and Rome;* conclude by sousing yourself in the innumerable faded articles, reviews, sketches of one kind and another which she contributed to literary papers. When you have done, examine the state of your own mind, and ask yourself whether that reading has led you to respect disinterested culture and intellectual liberty. Has it not on the contrary smeared your mind and dejected your imagination, and led you to deplore the fact that Mrs. Oliphant sold her brain, her very admirable brain, prostituted her culture and enslaved her intellectual liberty in order that she might earn her living and educate her children?[7] Inevitably, considering the damage that poverty inflicts upon mind and body, the necessity that is laid upon those who have children to see that they are fed and clothed, nursed and educated, we have to applaud her choice and to admire her courage. But if we applaud the choice and admire the courage of those who do what she did, we can spare ourselves the trouble of addressing our appeal to them, for they will no more be able to protect disinterested culture and intellectual liberty than she was. To ask them to sign your manifesto would be to ask a publican to sign a manifesto in favour of temperance. He may himself be a total abstainer; but since his wife and children depend upon the sale of beer, he must continue to sell beer, and his signature to the manifesto would be of no value to the cause of temperance because directly he had signed it he must be at the counter inducing his customers to drink more beer. So to ask the daughters of educated men who have to earn their livings by reading and writing to sign your manifesto would be of no value to the cause of disinterested culture and intellectual liberty, because directly they had signed it they must be at the desk writing those books, lectures and articles by which culture is prostituted and intellectual liberty is sold into slavery. As an expression of opinion it may have value; but if what you need is not merely an expression of opinion but positive help, you must frame your request rather differently. Then you will have to ask them to pledge themselves not to write anything that defiles culture, or to sign any contract that infringes intellectual liberty. And to that the answer given us by biography would be short but sufficient: Have I not to earn my living?

Thus, Sir, it becomes clear that we must make our appeal only to those daughters of educated men who have enough to live upon. To them we might address ourselves in this wise: "Daughters of educated men who have enough to live upon . . ."

But again the voice falters: again the prayer peters out into separate dots. For how many of them are there? Dare we assume in the face of Whitaker, of the laws of property, of the wills in the newspapers, of facts in short, that 1,000, 500, or even 250 will answer when thus addressed? However that may be, let the plural stand and continue: "Daughters of educated men who have enough to live upon, and read and write your own language for your own pleasure, may we very humbly entreat you to sign this gentleman's manifesto with some intention of putting your promise into practice?"

Here, if indeed they consent to listen, they might very reasonably ask us to be more explicit—not indeed to define culture and intellectual liberty, for they have books and leisure and can define the words for themselves. But what, they may well ask, is meant by this gentleman's "disinterested" culture, and how are we to protect that and intellectual liberty in practice? Now as they are daughters, not sons, we may begin by reminding them of a compliment once paid them by a great historian. "Mary's conduct," says Macaulay, "was really a signal instance of that perfect disinterestedness and self-devotion of which man seems to be incapable, but which is sometimes found in women."[8] Compliments, when you are asking a favour, never come amiss. Next let us refer them to the tradition which has long been honoured in the private house—the tradition of chastity. "Just as for many centuries, Madam," we might plead, "it was thought vile for a woman to sell her body without love, but right to give it to the husband whom she loved, so it is wrong, you will agree, to sell your mind without love, but right to give it to the art which you love." "But what," she may ask, "is meant by 'selling your mind without love'?" "Briefly," we might reply, "to write at the command of another person what you do not want to write for the sake of money. But to sell a brain is worse than to sell a body, for when the body seller has sold her momentary pleasure she takes good care that the matter shall end there. But when a brain seller has sold her brain, its anaemic, vicious and diseased progeny are let loose upon the world to infect and corrupt and sow the seeds of disease in others. Thus we are asking you, Madam, to pledge yourself not to commit adultery of the brain because it is a much more serious offence than the other." "Adultery of the brain," she may reply, "means writing what I do not want to write for the sake of money. Therefore you ask me to refuse all publishers, editors, lecture agents and so on who bribe me to write or to speak what I do not want to write or to speak for the sake of money?" "That is so, Madam; and we further ask that if you should receive proposals for such sales you will resent them and expose them as you would resent and expose such proposals for selling your body, both for your own sake and for the sake of others. But we would have you observe that the verb 'to adulterate' means, according to the dictionary, 'to falsify by admixture of baser ingredients.' Money is not the only baser ingredient. Advertisement and publicity are also adulterers. Thus, culture mixed with personal charm, or culture mixed with advertisement and publicity, are also adulterated forms of culture. We must ask you to abjure them; not to appear on public platforms; not to lecture; not to allow your private face to be published, or details of your private life; not to avail yourself, in short, of any of the forms of brain prostitution which are so insidiously suggested by the pimps and panders of the brain-selling trade; or to accept any of those baubles and labels by which brain merit is advertised and certified—medals, honours, degrees—we must ask you to refuse them absolutely, since they are all tokens that culture has been prostituted and intellectual liberty sold into captivity."

Upon hearing this definition, mild and imperfect as it is, of what it means, not merely to sign your manifesto in favour of culture and intellectual liberty, but to put that opinion into practice, even those daughters of educated men who have enough to live upon may object that the terms are too hard for them to keep. For they would mean loss of money which is desirable, loss of fame which is universally held to be agreeable, and censure and ridicule which are by no means negligible. Each would be the butt of all who have an interest to serve or money to make from the sale of brains. And for what reward? Only, in the rather abstract terms of your manifesto, that they would thus "protect culture and intellectual liberty," not by their opinion but by their practice.

Since the terms are so hard, and there is no body in existence whose ruling they need respect or obey, let us consider what other method of persuasion is left to us. Only, it would seem, to point to the photographs—the photographs of dead bodies and ruined houses. Can we bring out the connection between them and prostituted culture and intellectual slavery and make it so clear that the one implies the other, that the daughters of educated men will prefer to refuse money and fame, and to be the objects of scorn and ridicule rather than suffer themselves, or allow others to suffer, the penalties there made visible? It is difficult in the short time at our disposal, and with the weak weapons in our possession, to make that connection clear, but if what you, Sir, say is true, and there is a connection and a very real one between them, we must try to prove it.

Let us then begin by summoning, if only from the world of imagination, some daughter of an educated man who has enough to live upon and can read and write for her own pleasure and, taking her to be the representative of what may in fact be no class at all, let us ask her to examine the products of that reading and writing which lie upon her own table. "Look, Madam," we might begin, "at the newspapers on your table. Why, may we ask, do you take in three dailies, and three weeklies?" "Because," she replies, "I am interested in politics, and wish to know the facts." "An admirable desire, Madam. But why three? Do they differ then about facts, and if so, why?" To which she replies, with some irony, "You call yourself an educated man's daughter, and yet pretend not to know the facts—roughly that each paper is financed by a board; that each board has a policy; that each board employs writers to expound that policy, and if the writers do not agree with that policy, the writers, as you may remember after a moment's reflection, find themselves unemployed in the street. Therefore if you want to know any fact about politics you must read at least three different papers, compare at least three different versions of the same fact, and come in the end to your own conclusion. Hence the three daily papers on my table." Now that we have discussed, very briefly, what may be called the literature of fact, let us turn to what may be called the literature of fiction. "There are such things, Madam," we may remind her, "as pictures, plays, music and books. Do you pursue the same rather extravagant policy there—glance at three daily papers and three weekly papers if you want to know the facts about pictures, plays, music and books, because those who write about art are in the pay of an editor, who is in the pay of a board, which has a policy to pursue, so that each paper takes a different view, so that it is only by comparing three different views that you can come to your own conclusion—what pictures to see, what play or concert to go to, which book to order from the library?" And to that she replies, "Since I am an educated man's daughter, with a smattering of culture picked up from reading, I should no more dream, given the conditions of journalism at present, of taking my opinions of pictures, plays, music or books from the newspapers than I would take my opinion of politics from the newspapers. Compare the views, make allowance for the distortions, and then judge for yourself. That is the only way. Hence the many newspapers on my table."[9]

So then the literature of fact and the literature of opinion, to make a crude distinction, are not pure fact, or pure opinion, but adulterated fact and adulterated opinion, that is fact and opinion "adulterated by the admixture of baser ingredients" as the dictionary has it. In other words you have to strip each statement of its money motive, of its power motive, of its advertisement motive, of its publicity motive, of its vanity motive, let alone of all the other motives which, as an educated man's daughter, are familiar to you, before you make up your mind which fact about politics to believe, or even which opinion about art? "That is so," she agrees. But if you were told by somebody who had none of those motives for wrapping up truth that the fact was in his or her opinion this or that, you would believe him or her, always allowing of course for the fallibility of human judgment which, in judging works of art, must be considerable? "Naturally," she agrees. If such a person said that war was bad, you would believe him; or if such a person said that some picture, symphony, play or poem were good you would believe him? "Allowing for human fallibility, yes." Now suppose, Madam, that there were 250, or 50, or 25 such people in existence, people pledged not to commit adultery of the brain, so that it was unnecessary to strip what they said of its money motive, power motive, advertisement motive, publicity motive, vanity motive and so on, before we unwrapped the grain of truth, might not two very remarkable consequences follow? Is it not possible that if we knew the truth about war, the glory of war would be scotched and crushed where it lies curled up in the rotten cabbage leaves of our prostituted fact-purveyors; and if we knew the truth about art instead of shuffling and shambling through the smeared and dejected pages of those who must live by prostituting culture, the enjoyment and practice of art would become so desirable that by comparison the pursuit of war would be a tedious game for elderly dilettantes in search of a mildly sanitary amusement—the tossing of bombs instead of balls over frontiers instead of nets? In short, if newspapers were written by people whose sole object in writing was to tell the truth about politics and the truth about art we should not believe in war, and we should believe in art.

Hence there is a very clear connection between culture and intellectual liberty and those photographs of dead bodies and ruined houses. And to ask the daughters of educated men who have enough to live upon to commit adultery of the brain is to ask them to help in the most positive way now open to them—since the profession of literature is still that which stands widest open to them—to prevent war.

Thus, Sir, we might address this lady, crudely, briefly it is true; but time presses and we cannot define further. And to this appeal she might well reply, if indeed she exists: "What you say is obvious; so obvious that every educated man's daughter already knows it for herself, or if she does not, has only to read the newspapers to be sure of it. But suppose she were well enough off not merely to sign this manifesto in favour of disinterested culture and intellectual liberty but to put her opinion into practice, how could she set about it? And do not," she may reasonably add, "dream dreams about ideal worlds behind the stars; consider actual facts in the actual world." Indeed, the actual world is much more difficult to deal with than the dream world. Still, Madam, the private printing press is an actual fact, and not beyond the reach of a moderate income. Typewriters and duplicators are actual facts and even cheaper. By using these cheap and so far unforbidden instruments you can at once rid yourself of the pressure of boards, policies and editors. They will speak your own mind, in your own words, at your own time, at your own length, at your own bidding. And that, we are agreed, is our definition of "intellectual liberty." "But," she may say, "'the public'? How can that be reached without putting my own mind through the mincing machine and turning it into sausage?" "'The public,' Madam," we may assure her, "is very like ourselves; it lives in rooms; it walks in streets, and is said moreover to be tired of sausage. Fling leaflets down basements; expose them on stalls; trundle them along streets on barrows to be sold for a penny or given away. Find out new ways of approaching 'the public'; single it into separate people instead of massing it into one monster, gross in body, feeble in mind. And then reflect—since you have enough to live on, you have a room, not necessarily 'cosy' or 'handsome' but still silent, private; a room where safe from publicity and its poison you could, even asking a reasonable fee for the service, speak the truth to artists, about pictures, music, books, without fear of affecting their sales, which are exiguous, or wounding their vanity, which is prodigious.[10] Such at least was the criticism that Ben Jonson gave Shakespeare at the Mermaid and there is no reason to suppose, with *Hamlet* as evidence, that literature suffered in consequence. Are not the best critics private people, and is not the only criticism worth having spoken criticism? Those then are some of the active ways in which you, as a writer of your own tongue, can put your opinion into practice. But if you are passive, a reader, not a writer, then you must adopt not active but passive methods of protecting culture and intellectual liberty." "And what may they be?" she will ask. "To abstain, obviously. Not to subscribe to papers that encourage intellectual slavery; not to attend lectures that prostitute culture; for we are agreed that to write at the command of another what you do not want to write is to be enslaved, and to mix culture with personal charm or advertisement is to prostitute culture. By these active and passive measures you would do all in your power to break the ring, the vicious circle, the dance round and round the mulberry tree, the poison tree of intellectual harlotry. The ring once broken, the captives would be freed. For who can doubt that once writers had the chance of writing what they enjoy writing they would find it so much more pleasurable that they would refuse to write on any other terms; or that readers once they had the chance of reading what writers enjoy writing, would find it so much more nourishing than what is written for money that they would refuse to be palmed off with the stale substitute any longer? Thus the slaves who are now kept hard at work piling words into books, piling words into articles, as the old slaves piled stones into pyramids, would shake the manacles from their wrists and give up their loathsome labour. And 'culture,' that amorphous bundle, swaddled up as she now is in insincerity, emitting half truths from her timid lips, sweetening and diluting her message with whatever sugar or water serves to swell the writer's fame or his master's purse, would regain her shape and become, as Milton, Keats and other great writers assure us that she is in reality, muscular, adventurous, free. Whereas now, Madam, at the very mention of culture the head aches, the eyes close, the doors shut, the air thickens; we are in a lecture room, rank with the fumes of stale print, listening to a gentleman who is forced to lecture or to write every Wednesday, every Sunday, about Milton or about Keats, while the lilac shakes its branches in the garden free, and the gulls, swirling and swooping, suggest with wild laughter that such stale fish might with advantage be tossed to them. That is our plea to you, Madam; those are our reasons for urging it. Do not merely sign this manifesto in favour of culture and intellectual liberty; attempt at least to put your promise into practice."

WHETHER THE daughters of educated men who have enough to live upon and read and write their own tongue for their own pleasure will listen to this request or not, we cannot say, Sir. But if culture and intellectual liberty are to be protected, not by opinions merely but by practice, this would seem to be the way.

It is not an easy way, it is true. Nevertheless, such as it is, there are reasons for thinking that the way is easier for them than for their brothers. They are immune, through no merit of their own, from certain compulsions. To protect culture and intellectual liberty in practice would mean, as we have said, ridicule and chastity, loss of publicity and poverty. But those, as we have seen, are their familiar teachers. Further, Whitaker with his facts is at hand to help them; for since he proves that all the fruits of professional culture—such as directorships of art galleries and museums, professorships and lectureships and editorships are still beyond their reach, they should be able to take a more purely disinterested view of culture than their brothers, without for a moment claiming, as Macaulay asserts, that they are by nature more disinterested. Thus helped by tradition and by facts as they are, we have not only some right to ask them to help us to break the circle, the vicious circle of prostituted culture, but some hope that if such people exist they will help us. To return then to your manifesto: we will sign it if we can keep these terms; if we cannot keep them, we will not sign it.

Now that we have tried to see how we can help you to prevent war by attempting to define what is meant by protecting culture and intellectual liberty let us consider your next and inevitable request: that we should subscribe to the funds of your society. For you, too, are an honorary treasurer, and like the other honorary treasurers in need of money. Since you, too, are asking for money it might be possible to ask you, also, to define your aims, and to bargain and to impose terms as with the other honorary treasurers. What then are the aims of your society? To prevent war, of course. And by what means? Broadly speaking, by protecting the rights of the individual; by opposing dictatorship; by ensuring the democratic ideals of equal opportunity for all. Those are the chief means by which as you say, "the lasting peace of the world can be assured." Then, Sir, there is no need to bargain or to haggle. If those are your aims, and if, as it is impossible to doubt, you mean to do all in your power to achieve them, the guinea is yours—would that it were a million! The guinea is yours; and the guinea is a free gift, given freely.

But the word "free" is used so often, and has come, like used words, to mean so little, that it may be well to explain exactly, even pedantically, what the word "free" means in this context. It means here that no right or privilege is asked in return. The giver is not asking you to admit her to the priesthood of the Church of England; or to the Stock Exchange; or to the Diplomatic Service. The giver has no wish to be "English" on the same terms that you yourself are "English." The giver does not claim in return for the gift admission to any profession; any honour, title, or medal; any professorship or lectureship; any seat upon any society, committee or board. The gift is free from all such conditions because the one right of paramount importance to all human beings is already won. You cannot take away her right to earn a living. Now then for the first time in English history an educated man's daughter can give her brother one guinea of her own making at his request for the purpose specified above without asking for anything in return. It is a free gift, given without fear, without flattery, and without conditions. That, Sir, is so momentous an occasion in the history of civilization that some celebration seems called for. But let us have done with the old ceremonies—the Lord Mayor, with turtles and sheriffs in attendance, tapping nine times with his mace upon a stone while the Archbishop of Canterbury in full canonicals invokes a blessing. Let us invent a new ceremony for this new occasion. What more fitting than to destroy an old word, a vicious and corrupt word that has done much harm in its day and is now obsolete? The word "feminist" is the word indicated. That word, according to the dictionary, means "one who champions the rights of women." Since the only right, the right to earn a living, has been won, the word no longer has a meaning. And a word without a meaning is a dead word, a corrupt word. Let us therefore celebrate this occasion by cremating the corpse. Let us write that word in large black letters on a sheet of foolscap; then solemnly apply a match to the paper. Look, how it burns! What a light dances over the world! Now let us bray the ashes in a mortar with a goose-feather pen, and declare in unison singing together that anyone who uses that word in future is a ring-the-bell-and-run-away-man,[11] a mischief maker, a groper among old bones, the proof of whose defilement is written in a smudge of dirty water upon his face. The smoke has died down; the word is destroyed. Observe, Sir, what has happened as the result of our celebration. The word "feminist" is destroyed; the air is cleared; and in that clearer air what do we see? Men and women working together for the same cause. The cloud has lifted from the past too. What were they working for in the nineteenth century—those queer dead women in their poke bonnets and shawls? The very same cause for which we are working now. "Our claim was no claim of women's rights only;"—it is Josephine Butler who speaks—"it was larger and deeper; it was a claim for the rights of all—all men and women—to the respect in their persons of the great principles of Justice and Equality and Liberty." The words are the same as yours; the claim is the same as yours. The daughters of educated men who were called, to their resentment, "feminists" were in fact the advance guard of your own movement. They were fighting the same enemy that you are fighting and for the same reasons. They were fighting the tyranny of the patriarchal state as you are fighting the tyranny of the Fascist state. Thus we are merely carrying on the same fight that our mothers and grandmothers fought; their words prove it; your words prove it. But now with your letter before us we have your assurance that you are fighting with us, not against us. That fact is so inspiring that another celebration seems called for. What could be more fitting than to write more dead words, more corrupt words, upon more sheets of paper and burn them—the words, Tyrant, Dictator, for example? But, alas, those words are not yet obsolete. We can still shake out eggs from newspapers; still smell a peculiar and unmistakable odour in the region of Whitehall and Westminster. And abroad the monster has come more openly to the surface. There is no mistaking him there. He has widened his scope. He is interfering now with your liberty; he is dictating how you shall live; he is making distinctions not merely between the sexes, but between the races. You are feeling in your own persons what your mothers felt when they were shut out, when they were shut up, because they were women. Now you are being shut out, you are being shut up, because you are Jews, because you are democrats, because of race, because of religion. It is not a photograph that you look upon any longer; there you go, trapesing along in the procession yourselves. And that makes a difference. The whole iniquity of dictatorship, whether in Oxford or Cambridge, in Whitehall or Downing Street, against Jews or against women, in England, or in Germany, in Italy or in Spain is now apparent to you. But now we are fighting together. The daughters and sons of educated men are fighting side by side. That fact is so inspiring, even if no celebration is yet possible, that if this one guinea could be multiplied a million times all those guineas should be at your service without any other conditions than those that you have imposed upon yourself. Take this one guinea then and use it to assert "the rights of all—all men and women—to the respect in their persons of the great principles of Justice and Equality and Liberty." Put this penny candle in the window of your new society, and may we live to see the day when in the blaze of our common freedom the words tyrant and dictator shall be burnt to ashes, because the words tyrant and dictator shall be obsolete.

That request then for a guinea answered, and the cheque signed, only one further request of yours remains to be considered—it is that we should fill up a form and become members of your society. On the face of it that seems a simple request, easily granted. For what can be simpler than to join the society to which this guinea has just been contributed? On the face of it, how easy, how simple; but in the depths, how difficult, how complicated. . . . What possible doubts, what possible hesitations can those dots stand for? What reason or what emotion can make us hesitate to become members of a society whose aims we approve, to whose funds we have contributed? It may be neither reason nor emotion, but something more profound and fundamental than either. It may be difference. Different we are, as facts have proved, both in sex and in education. And it is from that difference, as we have already said, that our help can come, if help we can, to protect liberty, to prevent war. But if we sign this form which implies a promise to become active members of your society, it would seem that we must lose that difference and therefore sacrifice that help. To explain why this is so is not easy, even though the gift of a guinea has made it possible (so we have boasted) to speak freely without fear or flattery. Let us then keep the form unsigned on the table before us while we discuss, so far as we are able, the reasons and the emotions which make us hesitate to sign it. For those reasons and emotions have their origin deep in the darkness of ancestral memory; they have grown together in some confusion; it is very difficult to untwist them in the light.

To begin with an elementary distinction: a society is a conglomeration of people joined together for certain aims; while you, who write in your own person with your own hand are single. You the individual are a man whom we have reason to respect; a man of the brotherhood, to which, as biography proves, many brothers have belonged. Thus Anne Clough, describing

her brother, says: "Arthur is my best friend and adviser. . . .
Arthur is the comfort and joy of my life; it is for him, and from
him, that I am incited to seek after all that is lovely and of good
report." To which William Wordsworth, speaking of his sister
but answering the other as if one nightingale called to another in
the forests of the past, replies:

> The Blessing of my later years
> Was with me when a Boy:
> She gave me eyes, she gave me ears;
> And humble cares, and delicate fears;
> A heart, the fountain of sweet tears;
> And love, and thought, and joy.[12]

Such was, such perhaps still is, the relationship of many
brothers and sisters in private, as individuals. They respect each
other and help each other and have aims in common. Why then,
if such can be their private relationship, as biography and poetry
prove, should their public relationship, as law and history prove,
be so very different? And here, since you are a lawyer, with a
lawyer's memory, it is not necessary to remind you of certain
decrees of English law from its first records to the year 1919
by way of proving that the public, the society relationship of
brother and sister has been very different from the private. The
very word "society" sets tolling in memory the dismal bells of a
harsh music: shall not, shall not, shall not. You shall not learn;
you shall not earn; you shall not own; you shall not—such was
the society relationship of brother to sister for many centuries.
And though it is possible, and to the optimistic credible, that in
time a new society may ring a carillon of splendid harmony, and
your letter heralds it, that day is far distant. Inevitably we ask
ourselves, is there not something in the conglomeration of
people into societies that releases what is most selfish and vio-

lent, least rational and humane in the individuals themselves? Inevitably we look upon society, so kind to you, so harsh to us, as an ill-fitting form that distorts the truth; deforms the mind; fetters the will. Inevitably we look upon societies as conspiracies that sink the private brother, whom many of us have reason to respect, and inflate in his stead a monstrous male, loud of voice, hard of fist, childishly intent upon scoring the floor of the earth with chalk marks, within whose mystic boundaries human beings are penned, rigidly, separately, artificially; where, daubed red and gold, decorated like a savage with feathers he goes through mystic rites and enjoys the dubious pleasures of power and dominion while we, "his" women, are locked in the private house without share in the many societies of which his society is composed. For such reasons compact as they are of many memories and emotions—for who shall analyse the complexity of a mind that holds so deep a reservoir of time past within it?—it seems both wrong for us rationally and impossible for us emotionally to fill up your form and join your society. For by so doing we should merge our identity in yours; follow and repeat and score still deeper the old worn ruts in which society, like a gramophone whose needle has stuck, is grinding out with intolerable unanimity "Three hundred millions spent upon arms." We should not give effect to a view which our own experience of "society" should have helped us to envisage. Thus, Sir, while we respect you as a private person and prove it by giving you a guinea to spend as you choose, we believe that we can help you most effectively by refusing to join your society; by working for our common ends—justice and equality and liberty for all men and women—outside your society, not within.

But this, you will say, if it means anything, can only mean that you, the daughters of educated men, who have promised us your positive help, refuse to join our society in order that you may make another of your own. And what sort of society do you propose to found outside ours, but in co-operation with it, so that we may both work together for our common ends? That is a question which you have every right to ask, and which we must try to answer in order to justify our refusal to sign the form you send. Let us then draw rapidly in outline the kind of society which the daughters of educated men might found and join outside your society but in co-operation with its ends. In the first place, this new society, you will be relieved to learn, would have no honorary treasurer, for it would need no funds. It would have no office, no committee, no secretary; it would call no meetings; it would hold no conferences. If name it must have, it could be called the Outsiders' Society. That is not a resonant name, but it has the advantage that it squares with facts—the facts of history, of law, of biography; even, it may be, with the still hidden facts of our still unknown psychology. It would consist of educated men's daughters working in their own class—how indeed can they work in any other?[13]—and by their own methods for liberty, equality and peace. Their first duty, to which they would bind themselves not by oath, for oaths and ceremonies have no part in a society which must be anonymous and elastic before everything, would be not to fight with arms. This is easy for them to observe, for in fact, as the papers inform us, "the Army Council have no intention of opening recruiting for any women's corps."[14] The country ensures it. Next they would refuse in the event of war to make munitions or nurse the wounded. Since in the last war both these activities were mainly discharged by the daughters of working men, the pressure upon them here too would be slight, though probably disagreeable. On the other hand the next duty to which they would pledge themselves is one of considerable difficulty, and calls not only for courage and initiative, but for the special knowledge of the educated man's daughter. It is, briefly, not to incite their brothers to fight, or to dissuade them, but to maintain an attitude of complete indifference. But the attitude expressed by the word "indifference" is so complex and of such importance that it needs even here further definition. Indifference in the first place must be given a firm footing upon fact. As it is a fact that she cannot understand what instinct compels him, what glory, what interest, what manly satisfaction fighting provides for him—"without war there would be no outlet for the manly qualities which fighting develops"—as fighting thus is a sex characteristic which she cannot share, the counterpart some claim of the maternal instinct which he cannot share, so is it an instinct which she cannot judge. The outsider therefore must leave him free to deal with this instinct by himself, because liberty of opinion must be respected, especially when it is based upon an instinct which is as foreign to her as centuries of tradition and education can make it.[15] This is a fundamental and instinctive distinction upon which indifference may be based. But the outsider will make it her duty not merely to base her indifference upon instinct, but upon reason. When he says, as history proves that he has said, and may say again, "I am fighting to protect our country" and thus seeks to rouse her patriotic emotion, she will ask herself, "What does 'our country' mean to me an outsider?" To decide this she will analyse the meaning of patriotism in her own case. She will inform herself of the position of her sex and her class in the past. She will inform herself of the amount of land, wealth and property in the possession of her own sex and class in the present—how much of "England" in fact belongs to her. From the same sources she will inform herself of the legal protection which the law has given her in the past and now gives her. And if he adds that he is fighting to protect her body, she will reflect upon the degree of physical protection that she now enjoys when the words "Air Raid Precaution" are written on blank walls. And if he says that he is fighting to protect England from foreign rule, she will reflect that for her there are no "foreigners," since by law she becomes a foreigner if she marries a foreigner. And she will do her best to make this a fact, not by forced fraternity, but by human sympathy. All these facts will convince her reason (to put it in a nutshell) that her sex and class has very little to thank England for in the past; not much to thank England for in the present; while the security of her person in the future is highly dubious. But probably she will have imbibed, even from the governess, some romantic notion that Englishmen, those fathers and grandfathers whom she sees marching in the picture of history, are "superior" to the men of other countries. This she will consider it her duty to check by comparing French historians with English; German with French; the testimony of the ruled—the Indians or the Irish, say—with the claims made by their rulers. Still some "patriotic" emotion, some ingrained belief in the intellectual superiority of her own country over other countries may remain. Then she will compare English painting with French painting; English music with German music; English literature with Greek literature, for translations abound. When all these comparisons have been faithfully made by the use of reason, the outsider will find herself in possession of very good reasons for her indifference. She will find that she has no good reason to ask her brother to fight on her behalf to protect "our" country. "'Our country,'" she will say, "throughout the greater part of its history has treated me as a slave; it has denied me education or any share in its possessions. 'Our' country still ceases to be mine if I marry a foreigner. 'Our' country denies me the means of protecting myself, forces me to pay others a very large sum annually to protect me, and is so little able, even so, to protect me that Air Raid precautions are written on the wall. Therefore if you insist upon fighting to protect me, or 'our' country, let it be understood, soberly and rationally between us, that you are

fighting to gratify a sex instinct which I cannot share; to procure benefits which I have not shared and probably will not
share; but not to gratify my instincts, or to protect either myself
or my country. For," the outsider will say, "in fact, as a woman,
I have no country. As a woman I want no country. As a woman
my country is the whole world." And if, when reason has said
its say, still some obstinate emotion remains, some love of England dropped into a child's ears by the cawing of rooks in an
elm tree, by the splash of waves on a beach, or by English voices
murmuring nursery rhymes, this drop of pure, if irrational, emotion she will make serve her to give to England first what she
desires of peace and freedom for the whole world.

Such then will be the nature of her "indifference" and from
this indifference certain actions must follow. She will bind herself to take no share in patriotic demonstrations; to assent to no
form of national self-praise; to make no part of any claque or
audience that encourages war; to absent herself from military
displays, tournaments, tattoos, prize-givings and all such ceremonies as encourage the desire to impose "our" civilization or
"our" dominion upon other people. The psychology of private
life, moreover, warrants the belief that this use of indifference
by the daughters of educated men would help materially to prevent war. For psychology would seem to show that it is far
harder for human beings to take action when other people are
indifferent and allow them complete freedom of action, than
when their actions are made the centre of excited emotion. The
small boy struts and trumpets outside the window: implore him
to stop; he goes on; say nothing; he stops. That the daughters
of educated men then should give their brothers neither the
white feather of cowardice nor the red feather of courage, but
no feather at all; that they should shut the bright eyes that rain
influence, or let those eyes look elsewhere when war is discussed—that is the duty to which outsiders will train themselves

in peace before the threat of death inevitably makes reason powerless.

Such then are some of the methods by which the society, the anonymous and secret Society of Outsiders would help you, Sir, to prevent war and to ensure freedom. Whatever value you may attach to them you will agree that they are duties which your own sex would find it more difficult to carry out than ours; and duties moreover which are specially appropriate to the daughters of educated men. For they would need some acquaintance with the psychology of educated men, and the minds of educated men are more highly trained and their words subtler than those of working men.[16] There are other duties, of course—many have already been outlined in the letters to the other honorary treasurers. But at the risk of some repetition let us roughly and rapidly repeat them, so that they may form a basis for a society of outsiders to take its stand upon. First, they would bind themselves to earn their own livings. The importance of this as a method of ending war is obvious; sufficient stress has already been laid upon the superior cogency of an opinion based upon economic independence over an opinion based upon no income at all or upon a spiritual right to an income to make further proof unnecessary. It follows that an outsider must make it her business to press for a living wage in all the professions now open to her sex; further that she must create new professions in which she can earn the right to an independent opinion. Therefore she must bind herself to press for a money wage for the unpaid worker in her own class—the daughters and sisters of educated men who, as biographies have shown us, are now paid on the truck system, with food, lodging and a pittance of £40 a year. But above all she must press for a wage to be paid by the State legally to the mothers of educated men. The importance of this to our common fight is immeasurable; for it is the most effective way in which we can ensure that the large and very honourable class of married women shall have a mind and a will of their own, with which, if his mind and will are good in her eyes, to support her husband, if bad to resist him, in any case to cease to be "his woman" and to be her self. You will agree, Sir, without any aspersion upon the lady who bears your name, that to depend upon her for your income would effect a most subtle and undesirable change in your psychology. Apart from that, this measure is of such importance directly to yourselves, in your own fight for liberty and equality and peace, that if any condition were to be attached to the guinea it would be this: that you should provide a wage to be paid by the State to those whose profession is marriage and motherhood. Consider, even at the risk of a digression, what effect this would have upon the birth-rate, in the very class where the birth-rate is falling, in the very class where births are desirable—the educated class. Just as the increase in the pay of soldiers has resulted, the papers say, in additional recruits to the force of arms-bearers, so the same inducement would serve to recruit the child-bearing force, which we can hardly deny to be as necessary and as honourable, but which, because of its poverty, and its hardships, is now failing to attract recruits. That method might succeed where the one in use at present—abuse and ridicule—has failed. But the point which, at the risk of further digression, the outsiders would press upon you is one that vitally concerns your own lives as educated men and the honour and vigour of your professions. For if your wife were paid for her work, the work of bearing and bringing up children, a real wage, a money wage, so that it became an attractive profession instead of being as it is now an unpaid profession, an unpensioned profession, and therefore a precarious and dishonoured profession,[17] your own slavery would be lightened. No longer need you go to the office at nine-thirty and stay there till six. Work could be equally distributed. Patients could be sent to the patientless. Briefs to the briefless. Articles could be left unwritten. Culture would thus be stimulated. You could see the fruit trees flower in spring. You could share the prime of life with your children. And after that prime was over no longer need you be thrown from the machine on to the scrap heap without any life left or interests surviving to parade the environs of Bath or Cheltenham in the care of some unfortunate slave. No longer would you be the Saturday caller, the albatross on the neck of society, the sympathy addict, the deflated work slave calling for replenishment; or, as Herr Hitler puts it, the hero requiring recreation, or, as Signor Mussolini puts it, the wounded warrior requiring female dependants to bandage his wounds.[18] If the State paid your wife a living wage for her work which, sacred though it is, can scarcely be called more sacred than that of the clergyman, yet as his work is paid without derogation so may hers be — if this step which is even more essential to your freedom than to hers were taken the old mill in which the professional man now grinds out his round, often so wearily, with so little pleasure to himself or profit to his profession, would be broken; the opportunity of freedom would be yours; the most degrading of all servitudes, the intellectual servitude, would be ended; the half-man might become whole. But since three hundred millions or so have to be spent upon the arms-bearers, such expenditure is obviously, to use a convenient word supplied by the politicians, "impracticable" and it is time to return to more feasible projects.

The outsiders then would bind themselves not only to earn their own livings, but to earn them so expertly that their refusal to earn them would be a matter of concern to the work master. They would bind themselves to obtain full knowledge of professional practices, and to reveal any instance of tyranny or abuse in their professions. And they would bind themselves not to continue to make money in any profession, but to cease all competition and to practise their profession experimentally, in the interests of research and for love of the work itself, when they had earned enough to live upon. Also they would bind themselves to remain outside any profession hostile to freedom, such as the making or the improvement of the weapons of war. And they would bind themselves to refuse to take office or honour from any society which, while professing to respect liberty, restricts it, like the universities of Oxford and Cambridge. And they would consider it their duty to investigate the claims of all public societies to which, like the Church and the universities, they are forced to contribute as taxpayers as carefully and fearlessly as they would investigate the claims of private societies to which they contribute voluntarily. They would make it their business to scrutinize the endowments of the schools and universities and the objects upon which that money is spent. As with the educational, so with the religious profession. By reading the New Testament in the first place and next those divines and historians whose works are all easily accessible to the daughters of educated men, they would make it their business to have some knowledge of the Christian religion and its history. Further they would inform themselves of the practice of that religion by attending Church services, by analysing the spiritual and intellectual value of sermons; by criticizing the opinions of men whose profession is religion as freely as they would criticize the opinions of any other body of men. Thus they would be creative in their activities, not merely critical. By criticizing education they would help to create a civilized society which protects culture and intellectual liberty. By criticizing religion they would attempt to free the religious spirit from its present servitude and would help, if need be, to create a new religion based, it might well be, upon the New Testament, but, it might well be, very different from the religion now erected upon that basis. And in all this, and in much more than we have time to particularize, they would be helped, you will agree, by their position as outsiders, that freedom from unreal loyalties, that freedom from interested motives which are at present assured them by the State.

It would be easy to define in greater number and more exactly the duties of those who belong to the Society of Outsiders, but not profitable. Elasticity is essential; and some degree of secrecy, as will be shown later, is at present even more essential. But the description thus loosely and imperfectly given is enough to show you, Sir, that the Society of Outsiders has the same ends as your society—freedom, equality, peace; but that it seeks to achieve them by the means that a different sex, a different tradition, a different education, and the different values which result from those differences have placed within our reach. Broadly speaking, the main distinction between us who are outside society and you who are inside society must be that whereas you will make use of the means provided by your position—leagues, conferences, campaigns, great names, and all such public measures as your wealth and political influence place within your reach—we, remaining outside, will experiment not with public means in public but with private means in private. Those experiments will not be merely critical but creative. To take two obvious instances:—the outsiders will dispense with pageantry not from any puritanical dislike of beauty. On the contrary, it will be one of their aims to increase private beauty; the beauty of spring, summer, autumn; the beauty of flowers, silks, clothes; the beauty which brims not only every field and wood but every barrow in Oxford Street; the scattered beauty which needs only to be combined by artists in order to become visible to all. But they will dispense with the dictated, regimented, official pageantry, in which only one sex takes an active part—those ceremonies, for example, which depend upon the deaths of kings, or their coronations to inspire them. Again, they will dispense with personal distinctions—medals, ribbons, badges, hoods, gowns—not from any dislike of personal adornment, but because of the obvious effect of such distinctions to constrict, to stereotype and to destroy. Here, as so often, the example of the Fascist States is at hand to instruct us—for if we have no example of what we wish to be, we have, what is perhaps equally valuable, a daily and illuminating example of what we do not wish to be. With the example then, that they give us of the power of medals, symbols, orders and even, it would seem, of decorated ink-pots[19] to hypnotize the human mind it must be our aim not to submit ourselves to such hypnotism. We must extinguish the coarse glare of advertisement and publicity, not merely because the limelight is apt to be held in incompetent hands, but because of the psychological effect of such illumination upon those who receive it. Consider next time you drive along a country road the attitude of a rabbit caught in the glare of a head-lamp—its glazed eyes, its rigid paws. Is there not good reason to think without going outside our own country, that the "attitudes," the false and unreal positions taken by the human form in England as well as in Germany, are due to the limelight which paralyses the free action of the human faculties and inhibits the human power to change and create new wholes much as a strong head-lamp paralyses the little creatures who run out of the darkness into its beams? It is a guess; guessing is dangerous; yet we have some reason to guide us in the guess that ease and freedom, the power to change and the power to grow, can only be preserved by obscurity; and that if we wish to help the human mind to create, and to prevent it from scoring the same rut repeatedly, we must do what we can to shroud it in darkness.

But enough of guessing. To return to facts—what chance is there, you may ask, that such a Society of Outsiders without office, meetings, leaders or any hierarchy, without so much as a form to be filled up, or a secretary to be paid, can be brought into existence, let alone work to any purpose? Indeed it would

have been waste of time to write even so rough a definition of
the Outsiders' Society were it merely a bubble of words, a covert
form of sex or class glorification, serving, as so many such expressions do, to relieve the writer's emotion, lay the blame elsewhere, and then burst. Happily there is a model in being, a
model from which the above sketch has been taken, furtively it
is true, for the model, far from sitting still to be painted, dodges
and disappears. That model then, the evidence that such a body,
whether named or unnamed, exists and works is provided not
yet by history or biography, for the outsiders have only had a
positive existence for twenty years—that is since the professions were opened to the daughters of educated men. But evidence of their existence is provided by history and biography in
the raw—by the newspapers that is—sometimes openly in the
lines, sometimes covertly between them. There, anyone who
wishes to verify the existence of such a body, can find innumerable proofs. Many, it is obvious, are of dubious value. For example, the fact that an immense amount of work is done by the
daughters of educated men without pay or for very little pay
need not be taken as a proof that they are experimenting of their
own free will in the psychological value of poverty. Nor need
the fact that many daughters of educated men do not "eat properly"[20] serve as a proof that they are experimenting in the physical value of undernourishment. Nor need the fact that a very
small proportion of women compared with men accept honours be held to prove that they are experimenting in the virtues
of obscurity. Many such experiments are forced experiments
and therefore of no positive value. But others of a much more
positive kind are coming daily to the surface of the Press. Let us
examine three only, in order that we may prove our statement
that the Society of Outsiders is in being. The first is straightfor-
ward enough.

Speaking at a bazaar last week at the Plumstead Common Baptist Church the Mayoress (of Woolwich) said: "... I myself would not even do as much as darn a sock to help in a war." These remarks are resented by the majority of the Woolwich public, who hold that the Mayoress was, to say the least, rather tactless. Some 12,000 Woolwich electors are employed in Woolwich Arsenal on armament making.[21]

There is no need to comment upon the tactlessness of such a statement made publicly, in such circumstances; but the courage can scarcely fail to command our admiration, and the value of the experiment, from a practical point of view, should other mayoresses in other towns and other countries where the electors are employed in armament making follow suit, may well be immeasurable. At any rate, we shall agree that the Mayoress of Woolwich, Mrs. Kathleen Rance, has made a courageous and effective experiment in the prevention of war by not knitting socks. For a second proof that the outsiders are at work let us choose another example from the daily paper, one that is less obvious, but still you will agree an outsider's experiment, a very original experiment, and one that may be of great value to the cause of peace.

Speaking of the work of the great voluntary associations for the playing of certain games, Miss Clarke [Miss E. R. Clarke of the Board of Education] referred to the women's organizations for hockey, lacrosse, netball, and cricket, and pointed out that under the rules there could be no cup or award of any kind to a successful team. The gates for their matches might be a little smaller than for the men's games, but their players played the game for the love of it, and they seemed to be proving that cups and awards are not necessary to stimulate interest for each year the numbers of players steadily continued to increase.[22]

That, you will agree, is an extraordinarily interesting experiment, one that may well bring about a psychological change of great value in human nature, and be of real help in preventing war. It is further of interest because it is an experiment that outsiders, owing to their comparative freedom from certain inhibitions and persuasions, can carry out much more easily than those who are necessarily exposed to such influences inside. That statement is corroborated in a very interesting way by the following quotation:

> Official football circles here [Wellingborough Northants] regard with anxiety the growing popularity of girls' football. A secret meeting of the Northants Football Association's consultative committee was held here last night to discuss the playing of a girls' match on the Peterborough ground. Members of the Committee are reticent. . . . One member, however, said today: "The Northants Football Association is to forbid women's football. This popularity of girls' football comes when many men's clubs in the country are in a parlous state through lack of support. Another serious aspect is the possibility of grave injury to women players."[23]

There we have proof positive of those inhibitions and persuasions which make it harder for your sex to experiment freely in altering current values than for ours; and without spending time upon the delicacies of psychological analysis even a hasty glance at the reasons given by this Association for its decision will throw a valuable light upon the reasons which lead other and even more important associations to come to their decisions. But to return to the outsiders' experiments. For our third example let us choose what we may call an experiment in passivity.

A remarkable change in the attitude of young women to the Church was discussed by Canon F. R. Barry, vicar of St. Mary the Virgin (the University Church), at Oxford last night.... The task before the Church, he said, was nothing less than to make civilization moral, and this was a great co-operative task which demanded all that Christians could bring to it. It simply could not be carried through by men alone. For a century, or a couple of centuries, women had predominated in the congregations in roughly the ratio of 75 per cent to 25 per cent. The whole situation was now changing, and what the keen observer would notice in almost any church in England was the paucity of young women.... Among the student population the young women were, on the whole, farther away from the Church of England and the Christian faith than the young men.[24]

That again is an experiment of very great interest. It is, as we have said, a passive experiment. For while the first example was an outspoken refusal to knit socks in order to discourage war, and the second was an attempt to prove whether cups and awards are necessary to stimulate interest in games, the third is an attempt to discover what happens if the daughters of educated men absent themselves from church. Without being in itself more valuable than the others, it is of more practical interest because it is obviously the kind of experiment that great numbers of outsiders can practise with very little difficulty or danger. To absent yourself—that is easier than to speak aloud at a bazaar, or to draw up rules of an original kind for playing games.

Therefore it is worth watching very carefully to see what effect the experiment of absenting oneself has had—if any. The results are positive and they are encouraging. There can be no doubt that the Church is becoming concerned about the attitude to the Church of educated men's daughters at the universities. The report of the Archbishops' Commission on the Ministry of Women is there to prove it. This document, which costs only one shilling and should be in the hands of all educated men's daughters, points out that "one outstanding difference between men's colleges and women's colleges is the absence in the latter of a chaplain." It reflects that "It is natural that in this period of their lives they [the students] exercise to the full their critical faculties." It deplores the fact that "Very few women coming to the universities can now afford to offer continuous voluntary service either in social or in directly religious work." And it concludes that "There are many special spheres in which such services are particularly needed, and the time has clearly come when the functions and position of women within the Church require further determination."[25] Whether this concern is due to the empty churches at Oxford, or whether the voices of the "older schoolgirls" at Isleworth expressing "very grave dissatisfaction"[26] at the way in which organized religion was carried on have somehow penetrated to those august spheres where their sex is not supposed to speak, or whether our incorrigibly idealistic sex is at last beginning to take to heart Bishop Gore's warning, "Men do not value ministrations which are gratuitous,"[27] and to express the opinion that a salary of £150 a year—the highest that the Church allows her daughters as deaconesses—is not enough—whatever the reason, considerable uneasiness at the attitude of educated men's daughters is apparent; and this experiment in passivity, whatever our belief in the value of the Church of England as a spiritual agency, is highly encouraging to us as outsiders. For it seems to show that to be passive is to be active; those also serve who remain outside. By making their absence felt their presence becomes desirable. What light this throws upon the power of outsiders to abolish or modify other institutions of which they disapprove, whether public dinners, public speeches, Lord Mayors' banquets and other obsolete ceremonies are pervious to indifference and will yield to its pressure, are questions, frivolous questions, that may well amuse our leisure and stimulate our curiosity. But that is not now the object before us. We have tried to prove to you, Sir, by giving three different examples of three different kinds of experiment that the Society of Outsiders is in being and at work. When you consider that these examples have all come to the surface of the newspaper you will agree that they represent a far greater number of private and submerged experiments of which there is no public proof. Also you will agree that they substantiate the model of the society given above, and prove that it was no visionary sketch drawn at random but based upon a real body working by different means for the same ends that you have set before us in your own society. Keen observers, like Canon Barry, could, if they liked, discover many more proofs that experiments are being made not only in the empty churches of Oxford. Mr. Wells even might be led to believe if he put his ear to the ground that a movement is going forward, not altogether imperceptibly, among educated men's daughters against the Nazi and the Fascist. But it is essential that the movement should escape the notice even of keen observers and of famous novelists.

Secrecy is essential. We must still hide what we are doing and thinking even though what we are doing and thinking is for our common cause. The necessity for this, in certain circumstances, is not hard to discover. When salaries are low, as Whitaker proves that they are, and jobs are hard to get and keep, as everybody knows them to be, it is, "to say the least, rather tactless," as the newspaper puts it, to criticize your master. Still, in country districts, as you yourself may be aware, farm labourers will not vote Labour. Economically, the educated man's daughter is much on a level with the farm labourer. But it is scarcely necessary for us to waste time in searching out what reason it is that inspires both his and her secrecy. Fear is a powerful reason; those who are economically dependent have strong reasons for fear. We need explore no further. But here you may remind us of a certain guinea, and draw our attention to the proud boast that our gift, small though it was, had made it possible not merely to burn a certain corrupt word, but to speak freely without fear or flattery. The boast it seems had an element of brag in it. Some fear, some ancestral memory prophesying war, still remains, it seems. There are still subjects that educated people, when they are of different sexes, even though financially independent, veil, or hint at in guarded terms and then pass on. You may have observed it in real life; you may have detected it in biography. Even when they meet privately and talk, as we have boasted, about "politics and people, war and peace, barbarism and civilization," yet they evade and conceal. But it is so important to accustom ourselves to the duties of free speech, for without private there can be no public freedom, that we must try to uncover this fear and to face it. What then can be the nature of the fear that still makes concealment necessary between educated people and reduces our boasted freedom to a farce? . . . Again there are three dots; again they represent a gulf—of silence this time, of silence inspired by fear. And since we lack both the courage to explain it and the skill, let us lower the veil of St. Paul between us—in other words take shelter behind an interpreter. Happily we have one at hand whose credentials are above suspicion. It is none other than the pamphlet from which quotation has already been made, the Report of the Archbishops' Commission on the Ministry of Women—a document of the highest interest for many reasons. For not only does it throw light of a searching and scientific nature upon this fear, but it gives us an opportunity to consider that profession which, since it is the highest of all, may be taken as the type of all, the profession of religion, about which, purposely, very little has yet been said. And since it is the type of all it may throw light upon the other professions about which something has been said. You will pardon us therefore if we pause here to examine this report in some detail.

The Commission was appointed by the Archbishops of Canterbury and York "in order to examine any theological or other relevant principles which have governed or ought to govern the Church in the development of the Ministry of Women."[28] Now the profession of religion, for our purposes the Church of England, though it seems on the surface to resemble the others in certain respects—it enjoys, Whitaker says, a large income, owns much property, and has a hierarchy of officials drawing salaries and taking precedence one of the other—yet ranks above all the other professions. The Archbishop of Canterbury precedes the Lord High Chancellor; the Archbishop of York precedes the Prime Minister. And it is the highest of all the professions because it is the profession of religion. But what, we may ask, is "religion"? What the Christian religion is has been laid down once and for all by the founder of that religion in words that can be read by all in a translation of singular beauty; and whether or not we accept the interpretation that has been put on them, we cannot deny them to be words of the most profound meaning. It can thus safely be said that whereas few people know what medicine is, or what law is, everyone who owns a copy of the New Testament knows what religion meant in the mind of its founder. Therefore, when in the year 1935 the daughters of educated men said that they wished to have the profession of religion opened to them, the priests of that profession,

who correspond roughly to the doctors and barristers in the
other professions, were forced not merely to consult some
statute or charter which reserves the right to practise that profession professionally to the male sex; they were forced to consult the New Testament. They did so; and the result, as the
Commissioners point out, was that they found that "the Gospels
show us that our Lord regarded men and women alike as members of the same spiritual kingdom, as children of God's family,
and as possessors of the same spiritual capacities. . . ." In proof
of this they quote: "There is neither male nor female: for ye are
all one in Christ Jesus" (Gal. iii, 28). It would seem then that the
founder of Christianity believed that neither training nor sex was
needed for this profession. He chose his disciples from the
working class from which he sprang himself. The prime qualification was some rare gift which in those early days was bestowed
capriciously upon carpenters and fishermen, and upon women
also. As the Commission points out there can be no doubt that
in those early days there were prophetesses—women upon
whom the divine gift had descended. Also they were allowed to
preach. St. Paul, for example, lays it down that women, when
praying in public, should be veiled. "The implication is that if
veiled a woman might prophesy [i.e. preach] and lead in prayer."
How then can they be excluded from the priesthood since they
were thought fit by the founder of the religion and by one of his
apostles to preach? That was the question, and the Commission
solved it by appealing not to the mind of the founder, but to the
mind of the Church. That, of course, involved a distinction. For
the mind of the Church had to be interpreted by another mind,
and that mind was St. Paul's mind; and St. Paul, in interpreting
the other mind, changed his own mind. For after summoning
from the depths of the past certain venerable if obscure figures—
Lydia and Chloe, Euodia and Syntyche, Tryphaena and Tryphosa
and Persis, debating their status, and deciding what was the

difference between a prophetess and presbyteress, what the
standing of a deaconess in the pre-Nicene Church and what in
the post-Nicene Church, the Commissioners once more have recourse to St. Paul, and say: "In any case it is clear that the author
of the Pastoral Epistles, be he St. Paul or another, regarded
woman as being debarred on the ground of her sex from the position of an official 'teacher' in the Church, or from any office
involving the exercise of a governmental authority over a man
(1 Tim. ii, 12)." That, it may frankly be said, is not so satisfactory
as it might be; for we cannot altogether reconcile the ruling of
St. Paul, or another, with the ruling of Christ himself who "regarded men and women alike as members of the same spiritual
kingdom . . . and as possessors of the same spiritual capacities."
But it is futile to quibble over the meaning of words, when we
are so soon in the presence of facts. Whatever Christ meant,
or St. Paul meant, the fact was that in the fourth or fifth century
the profession of religion had become so highly organized that
"the deacon (unlike the deaconess) may, 'after serving unto well-
pleasing the ministry committed unto him,' aspire to be appointed eventually to higher offices in the Church; whereas for
the deaconess the Church prays simply that God 'would grant
unto her the Holy Spirit . . . that she may worthily accomplish
the work committed to her.'" In three or four centuries, it appears, the prophet or prophetess whose message was voluntary
and untaught became extinct; and their places were taken by the
three orders of bishops, priests and deacons, who are invariably
men, and invariably, as Whitaker points out, paid men, for when
the Church became a profession its professors were paid. Thus
the profession of religion seems to have been originally much
what the profession of literature is now.[29] It was originally open
to anyone who had received the gift of prophecy. No training
was needed; the professional requirements were simple in the ex-

treme—a voice and a market-place, a pen and paper. Emily
Brontë, for instance, who wrote

> No coward soul is mine,
> No trembler in the world's storm-troubled sphere;
> I see Heaven's glories shine,
> And faith shines equal, arming me from fear.
>
> O God within my breast,
> Almighty, ever-present Deity!
> Life—that in me has rest,
> As I—undying Life—have power in Thee!

though not worthy to be a priest in the Church of England, is
the spiritual descendant of some ancient prophetess, who
prophesied when prophecy was a voluntary and unpaid for occupation. But when the Church became a profession, required
special knowledge of its prophets and paid them for imparting
it, one sex remained inside; the other was excluded. "The deacons rose in dignity—partly no doubt from their close association with the bishops—and become subordinate ministers of
worship and of the sacraments; but the deaconess shared only
in the preliminary stages of this evolution." How elementary
that evolution has been is proved by the fact that in England in
1938 the salary of an archbishop is £15,000; the salary of a
bishop is £10,000 and the salary of a dean is £3,000. But the
salary of a deaconess is £150; and as for the "parish worker,"
who "is called upon to assist in almost every department of
parish life," whose "work is exacting and often solitary..." she
is paid from £120 to £150 a year, nor is there anything to surprise us in the statement that "prayer needs to be the very
centre of her activities." Thus we might even go further than the

Commissioners and say that the evolution of the deaconess is not merely "elementary," it is positively stunted; for though she is ordained, and "ordination . . . conveys an indelible character, and involves the obligation of lifelong service," she must remain outside the Church; and rank beneath the humblest curate. Such is the decision of the Church. For the Commission, having consulted the mind and tradition of the Church, reported finally: "While the Commission as a whole would not give their positive assent to the view that a woman is inherently incapable of receiving the grace of Order, and consequently to admission to any of the three Orders, we believe that the general mind of the Church is still in accord with the continuous tradition of a male priesthood."

By thus showing that the highest of all the professions has many points of similarity with the other professions our interpreter, you will admit, has thrown further light upon the soul or essence of those professions. We must now ask him to help us, if he will, to analyse the nature of that fear which still, as we have admitted, makes it impossible for us to speak freely as free people should. Here again he is of service. Though identical in many respects, one very profound difference between the religious profession and the other professions has been noted above: the Church being a spiritual profession has to give spiritual and not merely historical reasons for its actions; it has to consult the mind, not the law.[29] Therefore when the daughters of educated men wished to be admitted to the profession of the Church it seemed advisable to the Commissioners to give psychological and not merely historical reasons for their refusal to admit them. They therefore called in Professor Grensted, D.D., the Nolloth Professor of the Philosophy of the Christian Religion in the University of Oxford, and asked him "to summarize the relevant psychological and physiological material," and to indicate "the grounds for the opinions and recommendations put forward by the Commission." Now psychology is not theology; and the psychology of the sexes, as the Professor insisted, and "its bearing upon human conduct, is still a matter for specialists ... and ... its interpretation remains controversial and in many respects obscure." But he gave his evidence for what it was worth, and it is evidence that throws so much light upon the origin of the fear which we have admitted and deplored that we can do no better than follow his words exactly.

> "It was represented," he said, "in evidence before the Commission that man has a natural precedence of woman. This view, in the sense intended, cannot be supported psychologically. Psychologists fully recognize the fact of male dominance, but this must not be confused with male superiority, still less with any type of precedence which could have a bearing upon questions as to the admissibility of one sex rather than the other to Holy Orders."

The psychologist, therefore, can only throw light upon certain facts. And this was the first fact that he investigated.

> It is clearly a fact of the very greatest practical importance that strong feeling is aroused by any suggestion that women should be admitted to the status and functions of the threefold Order of the Ministry. The evidence before the Commission went to show that this feeling is predominantly hostile to such proposals. . . . This strength of feeling, conjoined with a wide variety of rational explanations, is clear evidence of the presence of powerful and widespread subconscious motive. In the absence of detailed analytical material, of which there seems to be no

record in this particular connection, it nevertheless remains clear that infantile fixation plays a predominant part in determining the strong emotion with which this whole subject is commonly approached.

The exact nature of this fixation must necessarily differ with different individuals, and suggestions which can be made as to its origin can only be general in character. But whatever be the exact value and interpretation of the material upon which theories of the "Oedipus complex" and the "castration complex" have been founded, it is clear that the general acceptance of male dominance, and still more of feminine inferiority, resting upon subconscious ideas of woman as "man manque," has its background in infantile conceptions of this type. These commonly, and even usually, survive in the adult, despite their irrationality, and betray their presence, below the level of conscious thought, by the strength of the emotions to which they give rise. It is strongly in support of this view that the admission of women to Holy Orders, and especially to the ministry of the sanctuary, is so commonly regarded as something shameful. This sense of shame cannot be regarded in any other light than as a nonrational sex-taboo.

Here we can skip; we can take the Professor's word for it that he has sought, and found, "ample evidence of these unconscious forces," both in Pagan religions and in the Old Testament, and so follow him to his conclusion:

At the same time it must not be forgotten that the Christian conception of the priesthood rests not upon these subconscious emotional factors, but upon the institution of Christ. It thus not only fulfils but supersedes the priesthoods of paganism and the Old Testament. So far as psychology is concerned there is no theoretical reason why this Christian priesthood should not be exercised by women as well as by men and in exactly the same sense. The difficulties which the psychologist foresees are emotional and practical only.[30]

With that conclusion we may leave him.

The Commissioners, you will agree, have performed the delicate and difficult task that we asked them to undertake. They have acted as interpreters between us. They have given us an admirable example of a profession in its purest state; and shown us how a profession bases itself upon mind and tradition. They have further explained why it is that educated people when they are of different sexes do not speak openly upon certain subjects. They have shown why the outsiders, even when there is no question of financial dependence, may still be afraid to speak freely or to experiment openly. And, finally, in words of scientific precision, they have revealed to us the nature of that fear. For as Professor Grensted gave his evidence, we, the daughters of educated men, seemed to be watching a surgeon at work— an impartial and scientific operator, who, as he dissected the human mind by human means laid bare for all to see what cause, what root lies at the bottom of our fear. It is an egg. Its scientific name is "infantile fixation." We, being unscientific, have named it wrongly. An egg we called it; a germ. We smelt it in the atmosphere; we detected its presence in Whitehall, in the universities, in the Church. Now undoubtedly the Professor has defined it and described it so accurately that no daughter of an educated man, however uneducated she may be, can miscall it or misinterpret it in future. Listen to the description. "Strong feeling is aroused by any suggestion that women be admitted"—it matters not to which priesthood; the priesthood of

medicine or the priesthood of science or the priesthood of the
Church. Strong feeling, she can corroborate the Professor, is
undoubtedly shown should she ask to be admitted. "This
strength of feeling is clear evidence of the presence of powerful
and subconscious motive." She will take the Professor's word
for that, and even supply him with some motives that have escaped him. Let us draw attention to two only. There is the
money motive for excluding her, to put it plainly. Are not
salaries motives now, whatever they may have been in the time
of Christ? The archbishop has £15,000, the deaconess £150; and
the Church, so the Commissioners say, is poor. To pay women
more would be to pay men less. Secondly, is there not a motive,
a psychological motive, for excluding her, hidden beneath what
the Commissioners call a "practical consideration"? "At present
a married priest," they tell us, "is able to fulfil the requirements
of the ordination service 'to forsake and set aside all worldly
cares and studies' largely because his wife can undertake the
care of the household and the family, . . ."[31] To be able to set
aside all worldly cares and studies and lay them upon another
person is a motive, to some of great attractive force; for some
undoubtedly wish to withdraw and study, as theology with its
refinements, and scholarship with its subtleties, prove; to others,
it is true, the motive is a bad motive, a vicious motive, the cause
of that separation between the Church and the people; between
literature and the people; between the husband and the wife
which has had its part in putting the whole of our Commonwealth out of gear. But whatever the powerful and subconscious
motives may be that lie behind the exclusion of women from
the priesthoods, and plainly we cannot count them, let alone dig
to the roots of them here, the educated man's daughter can testify from her own experience that they "commonly, and even
usually, survive in the adult and betray their presence, below the
level of conscious thought, by the strength of the emotions to

which they give rise." And you will agree that to oppose strong emotion needs courage; and that when courage fails, silence and evasion are likely to manifest themselves.

But now that the interpreters have performed their task, it is time for us to raise the veil of St. Paul and to attempt, face to face, a rough and clumsy analysis of that fear and of the anger which causes that fear; for they may have some bearing upon the question you put us, how we can help you to prevent war. Let us suppose, then, that in the course of that bi-sexual private conversation about politics and people, war and peace, barbarism and civilization, some question has cropped up, about admitting, shall we say, the daughters of educated men to the Church or the Stock Exchange or the diplomatic service. The question is adumbrated merely; but we on our side of the table become aware at once of some "strong emotion" on your side "arising from some motive below the level of conscious thought" by the ringing of an alarm bell within us; a confused but tumultuous clamour: You shall not, shall not, shall not. . . . The physical symptoms are unmistakable. Nerves erect themselves; fingers automatically tighten upon spoon or cigarette; a glance at the private psychometer shows that the emotional temperature has risen from ten to twenty degrees above normal. Intellectually, there is a strong desire either to be silent; or to change the conversation; to drag in, for example, some old family servant, called Crosby, perhaps, whose dog Rover has died . . . and so evade the issue and lower the temperature.

But what analysis can we attempt of the emotions on the other side of the table—your side? Often, to be candid, while we are talking about Crosby, we are asking questions—hence a certain flatness in the dialogue—about you. What are the powerful and subconscious motives that are raising the hackles on your side of the table? Is the old savage who has killed a bison asking the other old savage to admire his prowess? Is the tired professional man demanding sympathy and resenting competition? Is the patriarch calling for the siren? Is dominance craving for submission? And, most persistent and difficult of all the questions that our silence covers, what possible satisfaction can dominance give to the dominator?[32] Now, since Professor Grensted has said that the psychology of the sexes is "still a matter for specialists," while "its interpretation remains controversial and in many respects obscure," it would be politic perhaps to leave these questions to be answered by specialists. But since, on the other hand, if common men and women are to be free they must learn to speak freely, we cannot leave the psychology of the sexes to the charge of specialists. There are two good reasons why we must try to analyse both our fear and your anger; first, because such fear and anger prevent real freedom in the private house; second, because such fear and anger may prevent real freedom in the public world: they may have a positive share in causing war. Let us then grope our way amateurishly enough among these very ancient and obscure emotions which we have known ever since the time of Antigone and Ismene and Creon at least; which St. Paul himself seems to have felt; but which the Professors have only lately brought to the surface and named "infantile fixation," "Oedipus complex," and the rest. We must try, however feebly, to analyse those emotions since you have asked us to help you in any way we can to protect liberty and to prevent war.

Let us then examine this "infantile fixation," for such it seems is the proper name, in order that we may connect it with the question you have put to us. Once more, since we are generalists not specialists, we must rely upon such evidence as we can collect from history, biography, and from the daily paper— the only evidence that is available to the daughters of educated men. We will take our first example of infantile fixation from biography, and once more we will have recourse to Victorian biography because it is only in the Victorian age that biography becomes rich and representative. Now there are so many cases of infantile fixation as defined by Professor Grensted in Victorian biography that we scarcely know which to choose. The case of Mr. Barrett of Wimpole Street is, perhaps, the most famous and the best authenticated. Indeed, it is so famous that the facts scarcely require repetition. We all know the story of the father who would allow neither sons nor daughters to marry; we all know in greatest detail how his daughter Elizabeth was forced to conceal her lover from her father; how she fled with her lover from the house in Wimpole Street; and how her father never forgave her for that act of disobedience. We shall agree that Mr. Barrett's emotions were strong in the extreme; and their strength makes it obvious that they had their origin in some dark place below the level of conscious thought. That is a typical, a classical case of infantile fixation which we can all bear in mind. But there are others less famous which a little investigation will bring to the surface and show to be of the same nature. There is the case of the Rev. Patrick Brontë. The Rev. Arthur Nicholls was in love with his daughter, Charlotte; "What his words were," she wrote, when Mr. Nicholls proposed to her, "you can imagine; his manner you can hardly realize nor can I forget it. . . . I asked if he had spoken to Papa. He said he dared not." Why did he dare not? He was strong and young and passionately in love; the father was old. The reason is immediately apparent. "He [the Rev. Patrick Brontë] always disapproved of marriages, and constantly talked against them. But he more than disapproved this time; he could not bear the idea of this attachment of Mr. Nicholls to his daughter. Fearing the consequences . . . she made haste to give her father a promise that, on the morrow, Mr. Nicholls should have a distinct refusal."[33] Mr. Nicholls left

Haworth; Charlotte remained with her father. Her married life — it was to be a short one — was shortened still further by her father's wish.

For a third example of infantile fixation let us choose one that is less simple, but for that reason more illuminating. There is the case of Mr. Jex-Blake. Here we have the case of a father who is not confronted with his daughter's marriage but with his daughter's wish to earn her living. That wish also would seem to have aroused in the father a very strong emotion and an emotion which also seems to have its origin in the levels below conscious thought. Again with your leave we will call it a case of infantile fixation. The daughter, Sophia, was offered a small sum for teaching mathematics; and she asked her father's permission to take it. That permission was instantly and heatedly refused. "Dearest, I have only this moment heard that you contemplate being *paid* for the tutorship. It would be quite beneath you, darling, and I *cannot consent* to it. [The italics are the father's.] Take the post as one of honour and usefulness, and I shall be glad. . . . But to be *paid* for the work would be to alter the thing *completely*, and would lower you sadly in the eyes of almost everybody." That is a very interesting statement. Sophia, indeed, was led to argue the matter. Why was it beneath her, she asked, why should it lower her? Taking money for work did not lower Tom in anybody's eyes. That, Mr. Jex-Blake explained, was quite a different matter; Tom was a man; Tom "feels bound as a *man* . . . to support his wife and family"; Tom had therefore taken "the *plain path* of duty." Still Sophia was not satisfied. She argued — not only was she poor and wanted the money; but also she felt strongly "the honest, and I believe perfectly justifiable pride of earning." Thus pressed Mr. Jex-Blake at last gave, under a semi-transparent cover, the real reason why he objected to her taking money. He offered to give her the money himself if she would refuse to take it from the College. It was plain, therefore, that he did not object to her taking money; what he objected to was her taking money from another man. The curious nature of his proposal did not escape Sophia's scrutiny. "In that case," she said, "I must say to the Dean, not, 'I am willing to work without payment,' but, 'My Father prefers that I should receive payment from *him*, not from the College,' and I think the Dean would think us both ridiculous, or at least foolish." Whatever interpretation the Dean might have put upon Mr. Jex-Blake's behavior, we can have no doubt what emotion was at the root of it. He wished to keep his daughter in his own power. If she took money from him she remained in his power; if she took it from another man not only was she becoming independent of Mr. Jex-Blake, she was becoming dependent upon another man. That he wished her to depend upon him, and felt obscurely that this desirable dependence could only be secured by financial dependence is proved indirectly by another of his veiled statements. "If you married tomorrow to my liking—and I don't believe you would ever marry otherwise—I should give you a good fortune."[34] If she became a wage-earner, she could dispense with the fortune and marry whom she liked. The case of Mr. Jex-Blake is very easily diagnosed, but it is a very important case because it is a normal case, a typical case. Mr. Jex-Blake was no monster of Wimpole Street; he was an ordinary father; he was doing what thousands of other Victorian fathers whose cases remain unpublished were doing daily. It is a case, therefore, that explains much that lies at the root of Victorian psychology—that psychology of the sexes which is still, Professor Grensted tells us, so obscure. The case of Mr. Jex-Blake shows that the daughter must not on any account be allowed to make money because if she makes money she will be independent of her father and free to marry any man she chooses. Therefore the daughter's desire to earn her living rouses two different forms of jealousy. Each is strong separately; together they are very strong. It is further significant that in order to justify this very strong emotion which has its origin below the levels of conscious thought Mr. Jex-Blake had recourse to one of the commonest of all evasions; the argument which is not an argument but an appeal to the emotions. He appealed to the very deep, ancient and complex emotion which we may, as amateurs, call the womanhood emotion. To take money was beneath her he said; if she took money she would lower herself in the eyes of almost everybody. Tom being a man would not be lowered; it was her sex that made the difference. He appealed to her womanhood.

Whenever a man makes that appeal to a woman he rouses in her, it is safe to say, a conflict of emotions of a very deep and primitive kind which it is extremely difficult for her to analyse or to reconcile. It may serve to transmit the feeling if we compare it with the confused conflict of manhood emotions that is roused in you, Sir, should a woman hand you a white feather.[35] It is interesting to see how Sophia, in the year 1859, tried to deal with this emotion. Her first instinct was to attack the most obvious form of womanhood, that which lay uppermost in her consciousness and seemed to be responsible for her father's attitude — her ladyhood. Like other educated men's daughters Sophia Jex-Blake was what is called "a lady." It was the lady who could not earn money; therefore the lady must be killed. "Do you honestly, father, think," she asked, "any lady lowered by the mere act of receiving money? Did you think the less of Mrs. Teed because you paid her?" Then, as if aware that Mrs. Teed, being a governess, was not on a par with herself who came of an upper-middle-class family, "whose lineage will be found in *Burke's Landed Gentry*," she quickly called in to help her to kill the lady "Mary Jane Evans . . . one of the proudest families of our relations," and then Miss Wodehouse, "whose family is better and older than mine" — they both thought her right in wishing to earn money. And not only did Miss Wodehouse think her right in wishing to earn money; Miss Wodehouse "showed she agreed with my opinions by her actions. She sees no meanness in earning, but in those that think it mean. When accepting Maurice's school, she said to him, most nobly, I think, 'If you think it better that I should work as a paid mistress, I will take any salary you please; if not, I am willing to do the work freely and for nothing.'" The lady, sometimes, was a noble lady; and that lady it was hard to kill; but killed she must be, as Sophia realized, if Sophia were to enter that Paradise where "lots of girls walk about London when and where they please," that "Elysium upon earth," which is (or was) Queen's College, Harley Street, where the daughters of educated men enjoy the happiness not of ladies "but of Queens—Work and independence!"[36] Thus Sophia's first instinct was to kill the lady;[37] but when the lady was killed the woman still remained. We can see her, concealing and excusing the disease of infantile fixation, more clearly in the other two cases. It was the woman, the human being whose sex made it her sacred duty to sacrifice herself to the father, whom Charlotte Brontë and Elizabeth Barrett had to kill. If it was difficult to kill the lady, it was even more difficult to kill the woman. Charlotte found it at first almost impossible. She refused her lover. ". . . thus thoughtfully for her father, and unselfishly for herself [she] put aside all consideration of how she should reply, excepting as he wished." She loved Arthur Nicholls; but she refused him. ". . . she held herself simply passive, as far as words and actions went, while she suffered acute pain from the strong expressions which her father used in speaking of Mr. Nicholls." She waited; she suffered; until "the great conqueror Time," as Mrs. Gaskell puts it, "achieved his victory over strong prejudice and human resolve." At last her father consented. The great conqueror, however, had met his match in Mr. Barrett; Elizabeth Barrett waited; Elizabeth suffered; at last Elizabeth fled.

The extreme force of the emotions to which the infantile fixation gives rise is proved by these three cases. It is remarkable, we may agree. It was a force that could quell not only Charlotte Brontë but Arthur Nicholls; not only Elizabeth Barrett but Robert Browning. It was a force thus that could do battle with the strongest of human passions — the love of men and women; and could compel the most brilliant and the boldest of Victorian sons and daughters to quail before it; to cheat the father, to deceive the father, and then to fly from the father. But to what did it owe this amazing force? Partly, as these cases make clear, to the fact that the infantile fixation was protected by society. Nature, law and property were all ready to excuse and conceal it. It was easy for Mr. Barrett, Mr. Jex-Blake and the Rev. Patrick Brontë to hide the real nature of their emotions from themselves. If they wished that their daughter should stay at home, society agreed that they were right. If the daughter protested, then nature came to their help. A daughter who left her father was an unnatural daughter; her womanhood was suspect. Should she persist further, then law came to his help. A daughter who left her father had no means of supporting herself. The lawful professions were shut to her. Finally, if she earned money in the one profession that was open to her, the oldest profession of all, she unsexed herself. There can be no question — the infantile fixation is powerful, even when a mother is infected. But when the father is infected it has a threefold power; he has nature to protect him; law to protect him; and property to protect him. Thus protected it was perfectly possible for the Rev. Patrick Brontë to cause "acute pain" to his daughter Charlotte for several months, and to steal several months of her short married happiness without incurring any censure from the society in which he practised the profession of a priest of the Church of England; though had he tortured a dog, or stolen a watch, that same society would have unfrocked him and cast him forth. Society it seems was a father, and afflicted with the infantile fixation too.

Since society protected and indeed excused the victims of the infantile fixation in the nineteenth century, it is not surprising that the disease, though unnamed, was rampant. Whatever biography we open we find almost always the familiar symptoms—the father is opposed to his daughter's marriage; the father is opposed to his daughter's earning her living. Her wish either to marry, or to earn her living, rouses strong emotion in him; and he gives the same excuses for that strong emotion; the lady will debase her ladyhood; the daughter will outrage her womanhood. But now and again, very rarely, we find a father who was completely immune from the disease. The results are then extremely interesting. There is the case of Mr. Leigh Smith.[38] This gentleman was contemporary with Mr. Jex-Blake, and came of the same social caste. He, too, had property in Sussex; he, too, had horses and carriages; and he, too, had children. But there the resemblance ends. Mr. Leigh Smith was devoted to his children; he objected to schools; he kept his children at home. It would be interesting to discuss Mr. Leigh Smith's educational methods; how he had masters to teach them; how, in a large carriage built like an omnibus, he took them with him on long journeys yearly all over England. But like so many experimentalists, Mr. Leigh Smith remains obscure; and we must content ourselves with the fact that he "held the unusual opinion that daughters should have an equal provision with sons." So completely immune was he from the infantile fixation that "he did not adopt the ordinary plan of paying his daughter's bills and giving them an occasional present, but when Barbara came of age in 1848 he gave her an allowance of £300 a year." The results of that immunity from the infantile fixation were remarkable. For "treating her money as a power to do good, one of the first uses to which Barbara put it was educational." She started a school; a school that was open not only to different sexes and different classes, but to different creeds; Roman Catholics, Jews and "pupils from families of advanced free thought" were received in it. "It was a most unusual school," an outsiders' school. But that was not all that she attempted upon three hundred a year. One thing led to another. A friend, with her help, started a co-operative evening class for ladies "for drawing from an undraped model." In 1858 only one life class in London was open to ladies. And then a petition was got up to the Royal Academy; its schools were actually, though as so often happens only nominally, opened to women in 1861;[39] next Barbara went into the question of the laws concerning women; so that actually in 1871 married women were allowed to own their property; and finally she helped Miss Davies to found Girton. When we reflect what one father who was immune from infantile fixation could do by allowing one daughter £300 a year we need not wonder that most fathers firmly refused to allow their daughters more than £40 a year with bed and board thrown in.

The infantile fixation in the fathers then was, it is clear, a strong force, and all the stronger because it was a concealed force. But the fathers were met, as the nineteenth century drew on, by a force which had become so strong in its turn that it is much to be hoped that the psychologists will find some name for it. The old names as we have seen are futile and false. "Feminism," we have had to destroy. "The emancipation of women" is equally inexpressive and corrupt. To say that the daughters were inspired prematurely by the principles of anti-Fascism is merely to repeat the fashionable and hideous jargon of the moment. To call them champions of intellectual liberty and culture is to cloud the air with the dust of lecture halls and the damp dowdiness of public meetings. Moreover, none of these tags and labels express the real emotions that inspired the daughters' opposition to the infantile fixation of the fathers, because, as biography shows, that force had behind it many different emotions, and many that were contradictory. Tears were behind it, of course—tears, bitter tears: the tears of those whose desire for knowledge was frustrated. One daughter longed to learn chemistry; the books at home only taught her alchemy. She "cried bitterly at not being taught things." Also the desire for an open and rational love was behind it. Again there were tears—angry tears. "She flung herself on the bed in tears. . . . 'Oh,' she said, 'Harry is on the roof.' 'Who's Harry?' said I; 'which roof? Why?' 'Oh, don't be silly,' she said; 'he had to go.'"[40] But again the desire not to love, to lead a rational existence without love, was behind it. "I make the confession humbly. . . . I know nothing myself of love,"[41] wrote one of them. An odd confession from one of the class whose only profession for so many centuries had been marriage; but significant. Others wanted to travel; to explore Africa; to dig in Greece and Palestine. Some wanted to learn music, not to tinkle domestic airs, but to compose—operas, symphonies, quartets. Others wanted to paint, not ivy-clad cottages, but naked bodies. They all wanted—but what one word can sum up the variety of the things that they wanted, and had wanted, consciously or subconsciously, for so long? Josephine Butler's label—Justice, Equality, Liberty—is a fine one; but it is only a label, and in our age of innumerable labels, of multi-coloured labels, we have become suspicious of labels; they kill and constrict. Nor does the old word "freedom" serve, for it was not freedom in the sense of license that they wanted; they wanted, like Antigone, not to break the laws, but to find the law.[42] Ignorant as we are of human motives and ill supplied with words, let us then admit that no one word expresses the force which in the nineteenth century opposed itself to the force of the fathers. All we can safely say about that force was that it was a force of tremendous power. It forced open the doors of the private house. It opened Bond Street and Piccadilly; it opened cricket grounds and football grounds; it shrivelled flounces and stays; it made the oldest profession in the world (but Whitaker supplies no figures) unprofitable. In fifty years, in short, that force made the life lived by Lady Lovelace and Gertrude Bell unlivable, and almost incredible. The fathers, who had triumphed over the strongest emotions of strong men, had to yield.

If that full stop were the end of the story, the final slam of the door, we could turn at once to your letter, Sir, and to the form which you have asked us to fill up. But it was not the end; it was the beginning. Indeed though we have used the past, we shall soon find ourselves using the present tense. The fathers in private, it is true, yielded; but the fathers in public, massed together in societies, in professions, were even more subject to the fatal disease than the fathers in private. The disease had acquired a motive, had connected itself with a right, or a conception, which made it still more virulent outside the house than within. The desire to support wife and children—what motive could be more powerful, or deeply rooted? For it was connected with manhood itself—a man who could not support his family failed in his own conception of manliness. And was not that conception as deep in him as the conception of womanhood in his daughter? It was those motives, those rights and conceptions that were now challenged. To protect them, and from women, gave, and gives, rise it can scarcely be doubted to an emotion perhaps below the level of conscious thought but certainly of the utmost violence. The infantile fixation develops, directly the priest's right to practise his profession is challenged, to an aggravated and exacerbated emotion to which the name sex taboo is scientifically applied. Take two instances; one private, the other public. A scholar has "to mark his disapproval of the admission of women to his university by refusing to enter his beloved college or city."[43] A hospital has to decline an offer to endow a scholarship because it is made by a woman on behalf of women.[44] Can we doubt that both actions are inspired by that sense of shame which, as Professor Grensted says "cannot be regarded in any other light than as a non-rational sex taboo"? But since the emotion itself had increased in strength it became necessary to invoke the help of stronger allies to excuse and conceal it. Nature was called in; Nature it was claimed who is not only omniscient but unchanging, had made the brain of woman of the wrong shape or size. "Anyone," writes Bertrand Russell, "who desires amusement may be advised to look up the tergiversations of eminent craniologists in their attempts to prove from brain measurements that women are stupider than men."[45] Science, it would seem is not sexless; she is a man, a father, and infected too. Science, thus infected, produced measurements to order: the brain was too small to be examined. Many years were spent waiting before the sacred gates of the universities and hospitals for permission to have the brains that the professors said that Nature had made incapable of passing examinations examined. When at last permission was granted the examinations were passed. A long and dreary list of those barren, if necessary, triumphs lies presumably along with other broken records[46] in college archives, and harassed head mistresses still consult them, it is said, when desiring official proof of impeccable mediocrity. Still Nature held out. The brain that could pass examinations was not the creative brain; the brain that can bear responsibility and earn the higher salaries. It was a practical brain, a pettifogging brain, a brain fitted for routine work under the command of a superior. And since the professions were shut, it was undeniable — the daughters had not ruled Empires, commanded fleets, or led armies to victory; only a few trivial books testified to their professional ability, for literature was the only profession that was open to them. And, moreover, whatever the brain might do when the professions were opened to it, the body remained. Nature, the priests said, in her infinite wisdom, had laid down the unalterable law that man is the creator. He enjoys; she only passively endures. Pain was more beneficial than pleasure to the body that endures. "The views of medical men on pregnancy, childbirth, and lactation were until fairly recently," Bertrand Russell writes, "impregnated with sadism. It required, for example, more evidence to persuade them that anaesthetics may be used in childbirth than it would have required to persuade them of the opposite." So science argued, so the professors agreed. And when at last the daughters interposed, But are not brain and body affected by training? Does not the wild rabbit differ from the rabbit in the hutch? And must we not, and do we not change this unalterable nature? By setting a match to a fire frost is defied; Nature's decree of death is postponed. And the breakfast egg, they persisted, is it all the work of the cock? Without yolk, without white, how far would your breakfasts, oh, priests and professors, be fertile? Then the priests and professors in solemn unison intoned: But childbirth itself, that burden you cannot deny, is laid upon woman alone. Nor could they deny it, nor wish to renounce it. Still they declared, consulting the statistics in books, the time occupied by woman in childbirth is under modern conditions—remember we are in the twentieth century now—only a fraction.[47] Did that fraction incapacitate us from working in Whitehall, in fields and factories, when our country was in danger? To which the fathers replied: The war is over; we are in England now.

And if, Sir, pausing in England now, we turn on the wireless of the daily press we shall hear what answer the fathers who are infected with infantile fixation now are making to those questions now. "Homes are the real places of the women. . . . Let them go back to their homes. . . . The Government should give work to men. . . . A strong protest is to be made by the Ministry of Labour. . . . Women must not rule over men. . . .

There are two worlds, one for women, the other for men.... Let them learn to cook our dinners.... Women have failed.... They have failed.... They have failed...."

Even here, even now, the clamour, the uproar that infantile fixation is making is such that we can hardly hear ourselves speak; it takes the words out of our mouths; it makes us say what we have not said. As we listen to the voices we seem to hear an infant crying in the night, the black night that now covers Europe, and with no language but a cry, Ay, ay, ay, ay.... But it is not a new cry, it is a very old cry. Let us shut off the wireless and listen to the past. We are in Greece now; Christ has not been born yet, nor St. Paul either. But listen:

"Whomsoever the city may appoint, that man must be obeyed, in little things and great, in just things and unjust... disobedience is the worst of evils.... We must support the cause of order, and in no wise suffer a woman to worst us.... They must be women, and not range at large. Servants, take them within." That is the voice of Creon, the dictator. To whom Antigone, who was to have been his daughter, answered, "Not such are the laws set among men by the justice who dwells with the gods below." But she had neither capital nor force behind her. And Creon said: "I will take her where the path is loneliest, and hide her, living, in a rocky vault." And he shut her not in Holloway or in a concentration camp, but in a tomb. And Creon we read brought ruin on his house, and scattered the land with the bodies of the dead. It seems, Sir, as we listen to the voices of the past, as if we were looking at the photograph again, at the picture of dead bodies and ruined houses that the Spanish Government sends us almost weekly. Things repeat themselves it seems. Pictures and voices are the same today as they were 2,000 years ago.

Such then is the conclusion to which our enquiry into the nature of fear has brought us—the fear which forbids freedom in the private house. That fear, small, insignificant and private as it is, is connected with the other fear, the public fear, which is neither small nor insignificant, the fear which has led you to ask us to help you to prevent war. Otherwise we should not be looking at the picture again. But it is not the same picture that caused us at the beginning of this letter to feel the same emotions—you called them "horror and disgust"; we called them horror and disgust. For as this letter has gone on, adding fact to fact, another picture has imposed itself upon the foreground. It is the figure of a man; some say, others deny, that he is Man himself,[48] the quintessence of virility, the perfect type of which all the others are imperfect adumbrations. He is a man certainly. His eyes are glazed; his eyes glare. His body, which is braced in an unnatural position, is tightly cased in a uniform. Upon the breast of that uniform are sewn several medals and other mystic symbols. His hand is upon a sword. He is called in German and Italian Führer or Duce; in our own language Tyrant or Dictator. And behind him lie ruined houses and dead bodies— men, women and children. But we have not laid that picture before you in order to excite once more the sterile emotion of hate. On the contrary it is in order to release other emotions such as the human figure, even thus crudely in a coloured photograph, arouses in us who are human beings. For it suggests a connection and for us a very important connection. It suggests that the public and the private worlds are inseparably connected; that the tyrannies and servilities of the one are the tyrannies and servilities of the other. But the human figure even in a photograph suggests other and more complex emotions. It suggests that we cannot dissociate ourselves from that figure but are ourselves that figure. It suggests that we are not passive spectators doomed to unresisting obedience but by our thoughts and actions can ourselves change that figure. A common interest unites us; it is one world, one life. How essential it is that we should realise that unity the dead bodies, the ruined houses prove. For such will be our ruin if you, in the immensity of your public abstractions forget the private figure, or if we in the intensity of our private emotions forget the public world. Both houses will be ruined, the public and the private, the material and the spiritual, for they are inseparably connected. But with your letter before us we have reason to hope. For by asking our help you recognise that connection; and by reading your words we are reminded of other connections that lie far deeper than the facts on the surface. Even here, even now your letter tempts us to shut our ears to these little facts, these trivial details, to listen not to the bark of the guns and the bray of the gramophones but to the voices of the poets, answering each other, assuring us of a unity that rubs out divisions as if they were chalk marks only; to discuss with you the capacity of the human spirit to overflow boundaries and make unity out of multiplicity. But that would be to dream—to dream the recurring dream that has haunted the human mind since the beginning of time; the dream of peace, the dream of freedom. But, with the sound of the guns in your ears you have not asked us to dream. You have not asked us what peace is; you have asked us how to prevent war. Let us then leave it to the poets to tell us what the dream is; and fix our eyes upon the photograph again: the fact.

Whatever the verdict of others may be upon the man in uniform—and opinions differ—there is your letter to prove that to you the picture is the picture of evil. And though we look upon that picture from different angles our conclusion is the same as yours—it is evil. We are both determined to do what we can to destroy the evil which that picture represents, you by your methods, we by ours. And since we are different, our help must be different. What ours can be we have tried to show— how imperfectly, how superficially there is no need to say.[49] But as a result the answer to your question must be that we can best help you to prevent war not by repeating your words and following your methods but by finding new words and creating new methods. We can best help you to prevent war not by joining your society but by remaining outside your society but in co-operation with its aim. That aim is the same for us both. It is to assert "the rights of all—all men and women—to the respect in their persons of the great principles of Justice and Equality and Liberty." To elaborate further is unnecessary, for we have every confidence that you interpret those words as we do. And excuses are unnecessary, for we can trust you to make allowances for those deficiencies which we foretold and which this letter has abundantly displayed.

To return then to the form that you have sent and ask us to fill up: for the reasons given we will leave it unsigned. But in order to prove as substantially as possible that our aims are the same as yours, here is the guinea, a free gift, given freely, without any other conditions than you choose to impose upon yourself. It is the third of three guineas; but the three guineas, you will observe, though given to three different treasurers are all given to the same cause, for the causes are the same and inseparable.

Now, since you are pressed for time, let me make an end; apologising three times over to the three of you, first for the length of this letter, second for the smallness of the contribution, and thirdly for writing at all. The blame for that however rests upon you, for this letter would never have been written had you not asked for an answer to your own.

ONE

1. *The Life of Mary Kingsley,* by Stephen Gwynn, p. 15. It is difficult to get exact figures of the sums spent on the education of educated men's daughters. About £20 or £30 presumably covered the entire cost of Mary Kingsley's education (*b.* 1862; *d.* 1900). A sum of £100 may be taken as about the average in the nineteenth century and even later. The women thus educated often felt the lack of education very keenly. "I always feel the defects of my education most painfully when I go out," wrote Anne J. Clough, the first Principal of Newnham. (*Life of Anne J. Clough,* by B. A. Clough, p. 60.) Elizabeth Haldane, who came, like Miss Clough, of a highly literate family, but was educated in much the same way, says that when she grew up, "My first conviction was that I was not educated, and I thought of how this could be put right. I should have loved going to college, but college in those days was unusual for girls, and the idea was not encouraged. It was also expensive. For an only daughter to leave a widowed mother was indeed considered to be out of the question, and no one made the plan seem feasible. There was in those days a new movement for carrying on correspondence classes. . . ." (*From One Century to Another,* by Elizabeth Haldane, p. 73.) The efforts of such uneducated women to conceal their ignorance were often valiant, but not always successful. "They talked agreeably on current topics, carefully avoiding controversial subjects. What impressed me was their ignorance and

indifference concerning anything outside their own circle ... no less a personage than the mother of the Speaker of the House of Commons believed that California belonged to us, part of our Empire!" (*Distant Fields,* by H. A. Vachell, p. 109.) That ignorance was often simulated in the nineteenth century owing to the current belief that educated men enjoyed it is shown by the energy with which Thomas Gisborne, in his instructive work *On the Duties of Women* (p. 278), rebuked those who recommend women "studiously to refrain from discovering to their partners in marriage the full extent of their abilities and attainments." "This is not discretion but art. It is dissimulation, it is deliberate imposition.... It could scarcely be practised long without detection."

But the educated man's daughter in the nineteenth century was even more ignorant of life than of books. One reason for that ignorance is suggested by the following quotation: "It was supposed that most men were not 'virtuous,' that is, that nearly all would be capable of accosting and annoying—or worse—any unaccompanied young woman whom they met." ("Society and the Season," by Mary, Countess of Lovelace, in *Fifty Years,* 1882–1932, p. 37.) She was therefore confined to a very narrow circle; and her "ignorance and indifference" to anything outside it was excusable. The connection between that ignorance and the nineteenth century conception of manhood, which—witness the Victorian hero—made "virtue" and virility incompatible is obvious. In a well-known passage, Thackeray complains of the limitations which virtue and virility between them imposed upon his art.

2. Our ideology is still so inveterately anthropocentric that it has been necessary to coin this clumsy term—educated man's daughter—to describe the class whose fathers have been educated at public schools and universities. Obviously, if the term "bourgeois" fits her brother, it is grossly incorrect to use it of one who differs so profoundly in the two prime characteristics of the bourgeoisie—capital and environment.

3. The number of animals killed in England for sport during the past century must be beyond computation. 1,212 head of game is given as the average for a day's shooting at Chatsworth in 1909. (*Men, Women and Things,* by the Duke of Portland, p. 251.) Little mention is made in sporting memoirs of women guns; and their appearance in the hunting field was the cause of much caustic comment. "Skittles," the famous nineteenth-century horsewoman, was a lady of easy morals. It is highly probable that there was held to be some connection between sport and unchastity in women in the nineteenth century.

4. *Francis and Riversdale Grenfell,* by John Buchan, pp. 189, 205.

5. *Antony (Viscount Knebworth),* by the Earl of Lytton, p. 355.

6. *The Poems of Wilfred Owen,* edited by Edmund Blunden, pp. 25, 41.

7. Lord Hewart, proposing the toast of "England" at the banquet of the Society of St. George at Cardiff.

8 and 9. *The Daily Telegraph,* February 5th, 1937.

10. There is of course one essential that the educated woman can supply: children. And one method by which she can help to prevent war is to refuse to bear children. Thus Mrs. Helena Normanton is of opinion that "The only thing that women in any country can do to prevent war is to stop the supply of 'cannon fodder.'" (Report of the Annual Council for Equal Citizenship, *Daily Telegraph,* March 5th, 1937.) Letters in the newspapers frequently support this view. "I can tell Mr. Harry Campbell why women refuse to have children in these times. When men have learnt how to run the lands they govern so that wars shall hit only those who make the quarrels, instead of mowing down those who do not, then women may again feel like having large families. Why should women bring children into such a world as this one is today?" (Edith Maturin-Porch, in the *Daily Telegraph,* September 6th, 1937.) The fact that the birth rate in the educated class is falling would seem to show that educated women are taking Mrs. Normanton's

advice. It was offered them in very similar circumstances over two thousand years ago by Lysistrata.

11. There are of course innumerable kinds of influence besides those specified in the text. It varies from the simple kind described in the following passage: "Three years later . . . we find her writing to him as Cabinet Minister to solicit his interest on behalf of a favourite parson for a Crown living . . ." (*Henry Chaplin, a Memoir,* by Lady Londonderry, p. 57) to the very subtle kind exerted by Lady Macbeth upon her husband. Somewhere between the two lies the influence described by D. H. Lawrence: "It is hopeless for me to try to do anything without I have a woman at the back of me . . . I daren't sit in the world without I have a woman behind me. . . . But a woman that I love sort of keeps me in direct communication with the unknown, in which otherwise I am a bit lost" (*Letters of D. H. Lawrence,* pp. 93–4), with which we may compare, though the collocation is strange, the famous and very similar definition given by the ex-King Edward VIII upon his abdication. Present political conditions abroad seem to favour a return to the use of interested influence. For example: "A story serves to illustrate the present degree of women's influence in Vienna. During the past autumn a measure was planned to further diminish women's professional opportunities. Protests, pleas, letters, all were of no avail. Finally, in desperation, a group of well-known ladies of the city . . . got together and planned. For the next fortnight, for a certain number of hours per day, several of these ladies got on to the telephone to the Ministers they knew personally, ostensibly to ask them to dinner at their homes. With all the charm of which the Viennese are capable, they kept the Ministers talking, asking about this and that, and finally mentioning the matter that distressed them so much. When the Ministers had been rung up by several ladies, all of whom they did not wish to offend, and kept from urgent State affairs by this manoeuvre, they decided on compromise — and so the measure was postponed." (*Women Must Choose,*

by Hilary Newitt, p. 129.) Similar use of influence was often deliberately made during the battle for the franchise. But women's influence is said to be impaired by the possession of a vote. Thus Marshal von Bieberstein was of opinion that "Women led men always ... but he did not wish them to vote." (*From One Century to Another,* by Elizabeth Haldane, p. 258.)

12. English women were much criticized for using force in the battle for the franchise. When in 1910 Mr. Birrell had his hat "reduced to pulp" and his shins kicked by suffragettes, Sir Almeric Fitzroy commented, "an attack of this character upon a defenceless old man by an organized band of 'janissaries' will, it is hoped, convince many people of the insane and anarchical spirit actuating the movement." (*Memoirs of Sir Almeric Fitzroy,* Vol. II, p. 425.) These remarks did not apply apparently to the force in the European War. The vote indeed was given to English women largely because of the help they gave to Englishmen in using force in that war. "On the 14th August [1916], Mr. Asquith himself gave up his opposition [to the franchise]. 'It is true,' he said, '(that women) cannot fight in the sense of going out with rifles and so forth, but ... they have aided in the most effective way in the prosecution of the war.'" ("*The Cause,*" by Ray Strachey, p. 354.) This raises the difficult question whether those who did not aid in the prosecution of the war, but did what they could to hinder the prosecution of the war, ought to use the vote to which they are entitled chiefly because others "aided in the prosecution of the war"? That they are stepdaughters, not full daughters, of England is shown by the fact that they change nationality on marriage. A woman, whether or not she helped to beat the Germans, becomes a German if she marries a German. Her political views must then be entirely reversed, and her filial piety transferred.

13. *Sir Ernest Wild, K.C.,* by Robert J. Blackburn, pp. 174–5.

14. That the right to vote has not proved negligible is shown by the facts published from time to time by the National Union of

Societies for Equal Citizenship. "This publication (*What the Vote Has Done*) was originally a single-page leaflet; it has now (1927) grown to a six-page pamphlet, and has to be constantly enlarged." (*Josephine Butler*, by M. G. Fawcett and E. M. Turner, note, p. 101.)

15. There are no figures available with which to check facts that must have a very important bearing upon the biology and psychology of the sexes. A beginning might be made in this essential but strangely neglected preliminary by chalking on a large-scale map of England property owned by men, red; by women, blue. Then the number of sheep and cattle consumed by each sex must be compared; the hogsheads of wine and beer; the barrels of tobacco; after which we must examine carefully their physical exercises; domestic employments; facilities for sexual intercourse, etc. Historians are of course mainly concerned with war and politics; but sometimes throw light upon human nature. Thus Macaulay, dealing with the English country gentleman in the seventeenth century, says: "His wife and daughter were in tastes and acquirements below a housekeeper or still room maid of the present day. They stitched and spun, brewed gooseberry wine, cured marigolds, and made the crust for the venison pasty."

Again, "The ladies of the house, whose business it had commonly been to cook the repast, retired as soon as the dishes had been devoured, and left the gentlemen to their ale and tobacco." (Macaulay, *History of England*, Chapter Three.) But the gentlemen were still drinking and the ladies were still withdrawing a great deal later. "In my mother's young days before her marriage, the old hard-drinking habits of the Regency and of the eighteenth century still persisted. At Woburn Abbey it was the custom for the trusted old family butler to make his nightly report to my grandmother in the drawing-room. 'The gentlemen have had a good deal tonight; it might be as well for the young ladies to retire,' or, 'The gentlemen have had very little tonight,' was announced according to circumstances by this faithful family retainer. Should the young girls be packed off upstairs, they liked standing on an upper gallery of the staircase to watch the shouting, riotous crowd issuing from the dining-room." (*The Days Before Yesterday,* by Lord F. Hamilton, p. 322.) It must be left to the scientist of the future to tell us what effect drink and property have had upon chromosomes.

16. The fact that both sexes have a very marked though dissimilar love of dress seems to have escaped the notice of the dominant sex owing largely it must be supposed to the hypnotic power of dominance. Thus the late Mr. Justice MacCardie, in summing up the case of Mrs. Frankau, remarked: "Women cannot be expected to renounce an essential feature of femininity or to abandon one of nature's solaces for a constant and insuperable physical handicap. . . . Dress, after all, is one of the chief methods of women's self-expression. . . . In matters of dress women often remain children to the end. The psychology of the matter must not be overlooked. But whilst bearing the above matters in mind the law has rightly laid it down that the rule of prudence and proportion must be observed." The Judge who thus dictated was wearing a scarlet robe, an ermine cape, and a vast wig of artificial curls. Whether he was enjoying "one of nature's solaces for a constant and insuperable physical handicap," whether again he was himself observing "the rule of prudence and proportion" must be doubtful. But "the psychology of the matter must not be overlooked"; and the fact that the singularity of his own appearance together with that of Admirals, Generals, Heralds, Life Guards, Peers, Beefeaters, etc., was completely invisible to him so that he was able to lecture the lady without any consciousness of sharing her weakness, raises two questions: how often must an act be performed before it becomes traditional, and therefore venerable; and what degree of social prestige causes blindness to the remarkable nature of one's own clothes? Singularity of dress, when not associated with office, seldom escapes ridicule.

17. In the New Year's Honours List for 1937, 147 men accepted honours as against seven women. For obvious reasons this cannot

be taken as a measure of their comparative desire for such advertisement. But that it should be easier, psychologically, for a woman
to reject honours than for a man seems to be indisputable. For the
fact that intellect (roughly speaking) is man's chief professional
asset, and that stars and ribbons are his chief means of advertising
intellect, suggests that stars and ribbons are identical with powder
and paint, a woman's chief method of advertising her chief professional asset: beauty. It would therefore be as unreasonable to ask
him to refuse a Knighthood as to ask her to refuse a dress. The
sum paid for a Knighthood in 1901 would seem to provide a very
tolerable dress allowance: "21st April (Sunday)—To see Meynell,
who was as usual full of gossip. It appears that the King's debts have
been paid off privately by his friends, one of whom is said to have
lent £100,000, and satisfies himself with £25,000 in repayment plus
a Knighthood." (*My Diaries,* Wilfrid Scawen Blunt, Part II, p. 8.)

18. What the precise figures are it is difficult for an outsider to
know. But that the incomes are substantial can be conjectured
from a delightful review some years ago by Mr. J. M. Keynes in *The
Nation* of a history of Clare College, Cambridge. The book "it is
rumoured cost six thousand pounds to produce." Rumour has it
also that a band of students returning at dawn from some festivity
about that time saw a cloud in the sky; which as they gazed assumed the shape of a woman; who, being supplicated for a sign, let
fall in a shower of radiant hail the one word "Rats." This was interpreted to signify what from another page of the same number
of *The Nation* would seem to be the truth; that the students of one
of the women's colleges suffered greatly from "cold gloomy
ground floor bedrooms overrun with mice." The apparition, it was
supposed, took this means of suggesting that if the gentlemen of
Clare wished to do her honour a cheque for £6,000 payable to the
Principal of —— would celebrate her better than a book even
though "clothed in the finest dress of paper and black buck-
ram. . . ." There is nothing mythical, however, about the fact

recorded in the same number of *The Nation* that "Somerville received with pathetic gratitude the £7,000 which went to it last year from the Jubilee gift and a private bequest."

19. A great historian has thus described the origin and character of the universities, in one of which he was educated: "The schools of Oxford and Cambridge were founded in a dark age of false and barbarous science; and they are still tainted by the vices of their origin. . . . The legal incorporation of these societies by the charters of popes and kings had given them a monopoly of public instruction; and the spirit of monopolists is narrow, lazy, and oppressive: their work is more costly and less productive than that of independent artists; and the new improvements so eagerly grasped by the competition of freedom, are admitted with slow and sullen reluctance in those proud corporations, above the fear of a rival, and below the confession of an error. We may scarcely hope that any reformation will be a voluntary act; and so deeply are they rooted in law and prejudice, that even the omnipotence of parliament would shrink from an inquiry into the state and abuses of the two universities." (Edward Gibbon, *Memoirs of My Life and Writings*.) "The omnipotence of Parliament" did however institute an inquiry in the middle of the nineteenth century "into the state of the University [of Oxford], its discipline, studies, and revenues. But there was so much passive resistance from the Colleges that the last item had to go by the board. It was ascertained however that out of 542 Fellowships in all the Colleges of Oxford only twenty-two were really open to competition without restrictive conditions of patronage, place or kin. . . . The Commissioners . . . found that Gibbon's indictment had been reasonable. . . ." (*Herbert Warren of Magdalen*, by Laurie Magnus, pp. 47–49.) Nevertheless the prestige of a university education remained high; and Fellowships were considered highly desirable. When Pusey became a Fellow of Oriel, "The bells of the parish church at Pusey expressed the satisfaction of his father and family." Again, when Newman was elected a

Fellow, "all the bells of the three towers [were] set pealing—at Newman's expense." (*Oxford Apostles,* by Geoffrey Faber, pp. 131, 69.) Yet both Pusey and Newman were men of a distinctly spiritual nature.

20. *The Crystal Cabinet,* by Mary Butts, p. 138. The sentence in full runs: "For just as I was told that desire for learning in woman was against the will of God, so were many innocent freedoms, innocent delights, denied in the same Name"—a remark which makes it desirable that we should have a biography from the pen of an educated man's daughter of the Deity in whose Name such atrocities have been committed. The influence of religion upon women's education, one way or another, can scarcely be overestimated. "If, for example," says Thomas Gisborne, "the uses of music are explained, let not its effect in heightening devotion be overlooked. If drawing is the subject of remark, let the student be taught habitually to contemplate in the works of creation the power, the wisdom and the goodness of their Author." (*The Duties of the Female Sex,* by Thomas Gisborne, p. 85.) The fact that Mr. Gisborne and his like—a numerous band—base their educational theories upon the teaching of St. Paul would seem to hint that the female sex was to be "taught habitually to contemplate in the works of creation, the power and wisdom and the goodness," not so much of the Deity, but of Mr. Gisborne. And from that we are led to conclude that a biography of the Deity would resolve itself into a Dictionary of Clerical Biography.

21. *Mary Astell,* by Florence M. Smith. "Unfortunately, the opposition to so new an idea (a college for women) was greater than the interest in it, and came not only from the satirists of the day, who, like the wits of all ages, found the progressive woman a source of laughter and made Mary Astell the subject of stock jokes in comedies of the *Femmes Savantes* types, but from churchmen, who saw in the plan an attempt to bring back popery. The strongest opponent of the idea was a celebrated bishop, who, as

Ballard asserts, prevented a prominent lady from subscribing £10,000 to the plan. Elizabeth Elstob gave to Ballard the name of this celebrated bishop in reply to an inquiry from him. 'According to Elizabeth Elstob . . . it was Bishop Burnet that prevented that good design by dissuading that lady from encouraging it.'" (*Op. cit.,* pp. 21–2.) "That lady" may have been Princess Anne, or Lady Elizabeth Hastings; but there seems reason to think that it was the Princess. That the Church swallowed the money is an assumption, but one perhaps justified by the history of the Church.

22. *Ode for Music,* performed in the Senate House at Cambridge, July 1st, 1769.

23. "I assure you I am not an enemy of women. I am very favourable to their employment as *labourers* or in other *menial* capacity. I have, however, doubts as to the likelihood of their succeeding in business as capitalists. I am sure the nerves of most women would break down under the anxiety, and that most of them are utterly destitute of the disciplined reticence necessary to every sort of co-operation. Two thousand years hence you may have changed it all, but the present women will only flirt with men, and quarrel with one another." Extract from a letter from Walter Bagehot to Emily Davies, who had asked his help in founding Girton. But compare Mr. Baldwin at Downing St. (March 31st, 1936.)

24. *Recollections and Reflections,* by Sir J. J. Thomson, pp. 86–7–8, 296–7.

25. "Cambridge University still refuses to admit women to the full rights of membership; it grants them only titular degrees and they have therefore no share in the government of the University." (*Memorandum on the Position of English Women in Relation to that of English Men,* by Philippa Strachey, p. 26. (1935.)) Nevertheless, the Government makes a "liberal grant" from public money to Cambridge University.

26. "The total number of students at recognized institutions for the higher education of women who are receiving instruction in

the University or working in the University laboratories or museums shall not at any time exceed five hundred." (*The Student's
Handbook to Cambridge,* 1934–5, p. 616.) Whitaker informs us that
the number of male students who were in residence at Cambridge
in October 1935 was 5,328. Nor would there appear to be any
limitation.

27. The men's scholarship list at Cambridge printed in *The Times*
of December 20th, 1937, measures roughly thirty-one inches; the
women's scholarship list at Cambridge measures roughly five
inches. There are, however, seventeen colleges for men and the list
here measured includes only eleven. The thirty-one inches must
therefore be increased. There are only two colleges for women;
both are here measured.

28. Until the death of Lady Stanley of Alderley, there was no
chapel at Girton. "When it was proposed to build a chapel, she objected, on the ground that all the available funds should be spent
on education. 'So long as I live, there shall be no chapel at Girton,'
I heard her say. The present chapel was built immediately after her
death." (*The Amberley Papers,* Patricia and Bertrand Russell, Vol. I,
p. 17.) Would that her ghost had possessed the same influence as
her body! But ghosts, it is said, have no cheque books.

29. "I have also a feeling that girls' schools have, on the whole,
been content to take the general lines of their education from the
older-established institutions for my own, the weaker sex. My own
feeling is that the problem ought to be attacked by some original
genius on quite different lines. . . ." (*Things Ancient and Modern,* by
C. A. Alington, pp. 216–17.) It scarcely needs genius or originality
to see that "the lines," in the first place, must be cheaper. But it
would be interesting to know what meaning we are to attach to the
word "weaker" in the context. For since Dr. Alington is a former
head master of Eton he must be aware that his sex has not only acquired, but retained the vast revenues of that ancient foundation—
a proof, one would have thought, not of sexual weakness but of

sexual strength. That Eton is not "weak," at least from the material point of view, is shown by the following quotation from Dr. Alington: "Following out the suggestion of one of the Prime Minister's Committees on Education, the Provost and Fellows in my time decided that all scholarships at Eton should be of a fixed value, capable of being liberally augmented in case of need. So liberal has been this augmentation that there are several boys in College whose parents pay nothing towards either their board or education." One of the benefactors was the late Lord Rosebery. "He was a generous benefactor to the school," Dr. Alington informs us, "and endowed a history scholarship, in connection with which a characteristic episode occurred. He asked me whether the endowment was adequate, and I suggested that a further £200 would provide for the payment to the examiner. He sent a cheque for £2,000: his attention was called to the discrepancy, and I have in my scrap book the reply in which he said that he thought a good round sum would be better than a fraction." (*Op. cit.,* pp. 163, 186.) The entire sum spent at Cheltenham College for Girls in 1854 upon salaries and visiting teachers was £1,300; "and the accounts in December showed a deficit of £400." (*Dorothea Beale of Cheltenham,* by Elizabeth Raikes, p. 91.)

30. The words "vain and vicious" require qualification. No one would maintain that all lecturers and all lectures are "vain and vicious"; many subjects can only be taught with diagrams and personal demonstration. The words in the text refer only to the sons and daughters of educated men who lecture their brothers and sisters upon English literature; and for the reasons that it is an obsolete practice dating from the Middle Ages when books were scarce; that it owes its survival to pecuniary motives; or to curiosity; that the publication in book form is sufficient proof of the evil effect of an audience upon the lecturer intellectually; and that psychologically eminence upon a platform encourages vanity and the desire to impose authority. Further, the reduction of English literature to

an examination subject must be viewed with suspicion by all who have firsthand knowledge of the difficulty of the art, and therefore of the very superficial value of an examiner's approval or disapproval; and with profound regret by all who wish to keep one art at least out of the hands of middlemen and free, as long as may be, from all association with competition and money making. Again, the violence with which one school of literature is now opposed to another, the rapidity with which one school of taste succeeds another, may not unreasonably be traced to the power which a mature mind lecturing immature minds has to infect them with strong, if passing, opinions, and to tinge those opinions with personal bias. Nor can it be maintained that the standard of critical or of creative writing has been raised. A lamentable proof of the mental docility to which the young are reduced by lecturers is that the demand for lectures upon English literature steadily increases (as every writer can bear witness) and from the very class which should have learnt to read at home — the educated. If, as is sometimes urged in excuse, what is desired by college literary societies is not knowledge of literature but acquaintance with writers, there are cocktails, and there is sherry; both better unmixed with Proust. None of this applies of course to those whose homes are deficient in books. If the working class finds it easier to assimilate English literature by word of mouth they have a perfect right to ask the educated class to help them thus. But for the sons and daughters of that class after the age of eighteen to continue to sip English literature through a straw, is a habit that seems to deserve the terms vain and vicious; which terms can justly be applied with greater force to those who pander to them.

31. It is difficult to procure exact figures of the sums allowed the daughters of educated men before marriage. Sophia Jex-Blake had an allowance of from £30 to £40 annually; her father was an upper-middle-class man. Lady M. Lascelles, whose father was an Earl, had, it seems, an allowance of about £100 in 1860; Mr. Bar-

rett, a rich merchant, allowed his daughter Elizabeth "from forty to forty-five pounds . . . every three months, the income tax being first deducted." But this seems to have been the interest upon £8,000, "or more or less . . . it is difficult to ask about it," which she had "in the funds," "the money being in two different per cents," and apparently, though belonging to Elizabeth, under Mr. Barrett's control. But these were unmarried women. Married women were not allowed to own property until the passing of the Married Woman's Property Act in 1870. Lady St. Helier records that since her marriage settlements had been drawn up in conformity with the old law, "What money I had was settled on my husband, and no part of it was reserved for my private use . . . I did not even possess a cheque book, nor was I able to get any money except by asking my husband. He was kind and generous, but he acquiesced in the position then existing that a woman's property belonged to her husband . . . he paid all my bills, he kept my bank book, and gave me a small allowance for my personal expenses." (*Memories of Fifty Years,* by Lady St. Helier, p. 341.) But she does not say what the exact sum was. The sums allowed to the sons of educated men were considerably larger. An allowance of £200 was considered to be only just sufficient for an undergraduate at Balliol, "which still had traditions of frugality," about 1880. On that allowance "they could not hunt and they could not gamble. . . . But with care, and with a home to fall back on in the vacations, they could make this do." (*Anthony Hope and His Books,* by Sir C. Mallet, p. 38.) The sum that is now needed is considerably more. Gino Watkins "never spent more than the £400 yearly allowance with which he paid all his college and vacation bills." (*Gino Watkins,* by J. M. Scott, p. 59.) This was at Cambridge, a few years ago.

32. How incessantly women were ridiculed throughout the nineteenth century for attempting to enter their solitary profession, novel readers know, for those efforts provide half the stock-in-trade of fiction. But biography shows how natural it was, even in

the present century, for the most enlightened of men to conceive of all women as spinsters, all desiring marriage. Thus: "'Oh dear, what is to happen to them?' he [G. L. Dickinson] once murmured sadly as a stream of aspiring but uninspiring spinsters flowed round the front court of King's; 'I don't know and they don't know.' And then in still lower tones as if his bookshelves might overhear him, 'Oh dear! What they want is a husband!'" (*Goldsworthy Lowes Dickinson,* by E. M. Forster, p. 106.) "What they wanted" might have been the Bar, the Stock Exchange or rooms in Gibbs's Buildings, had the choice been open to them. But it was not; and therefore Mr. Dickinson's remark was a very natural one.

33. "Now and then, at least in the larger houses, there would be a set party, selected and invited long beforehand, and over these always one idol dominated—the pheasant. Shooting had to be used as a lure. At such times the father of the family was apt to assert himself. If his house was to be filled to bursting, his wines drunk in quantities, and his best shooting provided, then for that shooting he would have the best guns possible. What despair for the mother of daughters to be told that the one guest whom of all others she secretly desired to invite was a bad shot and totally inadmissible!" ("Society and the Season," by Mary, Countess of Lovelace, in *Fifty Years,* 1882–1932, p. 29.)

34. Some idea of what men hoped that their wives might say and do, at least in the nineteenth century, may be gathered from the following hints in a letter "addressed to a young lady for whom he had a great regard a short time before her marriage" by John Bowdler. "Above all, avoid everything which has the *least tendency* to indelicacy or indecorum. Few women have *any idea* how much men are disgusted at the slightest approach to these in any female, and especially in one to whom they are attached. By attending the nursery, or the sick bed, women are too apt to acquire a habit of conversing on such subjects in language which men of delicacy are shocked at." (*Life of John Bowdler,* p. 123.) But though delicacy was

essential, it could, after marriage, be disguised. "In the 'seventies of last century, Miss Jex-Blake and her associates were vigorously fighting the battle for admission of women to the medical profession, and the doctors were still more vigorously resisting their entry, alleging that it must be improper and demoralizing for a woman to have to study and deal with delicate and intimate medical questions. At that time, Ernest Hart, the Editor of the *British Medical Journal,* told me that the majority of the contributions sent to him for publication in the *Journal* dealing with delicate and intimate medical questions were in the handwriting of the doctors' wives, to whom they had obviously been dictated. There were no typewriters or stenographers available in those days." (*The Doctor's Second Thoughts,* by Sir J. Crichton-Browne, pp. 73, 74.)

The duplicity of delicacy was observed long before this, however. Thus Mandeville in *The Fable of the Bees* (1714) says: ". . . I would have it first consider'd that the Modesty of Women is the result of Custom and Education, by which all unfashionable Denudations and filthy Expressions are render'd frightful and abominable to them, and that notwithstanding this, the most Virtuous Young Woman alive will often, in spite of her Teeth, have Thoughts and confus'd Ideas of Things arise in her Imagination, which she would not reveal to some People for a Thousand Worlds." The real nature of delicacy and the real nature of chastity (let alone the real nature of marriage) are still therefore highly conjectural.

1. To quote the exact words of one such appeal: "This letter is to ask you to set aside for us garments for which you have no further use. . . . Stockings, of every sort, no matter how worn, are also most acceptable. . . . The Committee find that by offering these clothes at bargain prices . . . they are performing a really useful service to women whose professions require that they should have presentable day and evening dresses which they can ill afford to buy." (Extract from a letter received from the London and National Society for Women's Service. (1938.))

2. *The Testament of Joad,* by C. E. M. Joad, pp. 210–11. Since the number of societies run directly or indirectly by Englishwomen in the cause of peace is too long to quote (see *The Story of the Disarmament Declaration,* p. 15, for a list of the peace activities of professional, business and working-class women) it is unnecessary to take Mr. Joad's criticism seriously, however illuminating psychologically.

3. *Experiment in Autobiography,* by H. G. Wells, p. 486. The men's "movement to resist the practical obliteration of their freedom by Nazis or Fascists" may have been more perceptible. But that it has been more successful is doubtful. "Nazis now control the whole of Austria" (Daily paper, March 12th, 1938).

4. "Women, I think, ought not to sit down to table with men; their presence ruins conversation, tending to make it trivial and genteel, or at best merely clever." (*Under the Fifth Rib,* by C. E. M.

Joad, p. 58.) This is an admirably outspoken opinion, and if all who share Mr. Joad's sentiments were to express them as openly, the hostess's dilemma—whom to ask, whom not to ask—would be lightened and her labour saved. If those who prefer the society of their own sex at table would signify the fact, the men, say, by wearing a red, the women by wearing a white rosette, while those who prefer the sexes mixed wore parti-coloured buttonholes of red and white blended, not only would much inconvenience and misunderstanding be prevented, but it is possible that the honesty of the buttonhole would kill a certain form of social hypocrisy now all too prevalent. Meanwhile Mr. Joad's candour deserves the highest praise, and his wishes the most implicit observance.

5. According to Mrs. H. M. Swanwick, the W.S.P.U. had "an income from gifts, in the year 1912, of £42,000." (*I Have Been Young*, by H. M. Swanwick, p. 189.) The total spent in 1912 by the Women's Freedom League was £26,772 12s. 9d. (*"The Cause,"* by Ray Strachey, p. 311.) Thus the joint income of the two societies was £68,772 12s. 9d. But the two societies were, of course, opposed.

6. "But, exceptions apart, the general run of women's earnings is low, and £250 a year is quite an achievement, even for a highly qualified woman with years of experience." (*Careers and Openings for Women,* by Ray Strachey, p. 70.) Nevertheless "The numbers of women doing professional work have increased very fast in the last twenty years, and were about 400,000 in 1931, in addition to those doing secretarial work or employed in the Civil Service." (*Op. cit.,* p. 44.)

7. The income of the Labour party in 1936 was £50,153. (*Daily Telegraph,* September 1937.)

8. *The British Civil [Servant]. The Public Service,* by William A. Robson, p. 16.

Professor Ernest Barker suggests that there should be an alternative Civil Service Examination for "men and women of an older

growth" who have spent some years in social work and social service. "Women candidates in particular might benefit. It is only a
very small proportion of women students who succeed in the present open competition: indeed very few compete. On the alternative system here suggested it is possible, and indeed probable, that
a much larger proportion of women would be candidates. Women
have a genius and a capacity for social work and service. The alternative form of competition would give them a chance of showing
that genius and that capacity. It might give them a new incentive
to compete for entry into the administrative service of the state, in
which their gifts and their presence are needed." (*The British Civil
Servant.* "The Home Civil Service," by Professor Ernest Barker, p.
41.) But while the home service remains as exacting as it is at present, it is difficult to see how any incentive can make women free
to give "their gifts and their presence" to the service of the state,
unless the state will undertake the care of elderly parents; or make
it a penal offence for elderly people of either sex to require the services of daughters at home.

9. Mr. Baldwin, speaking at Downing Street, at a meeting on behalf of Newnham College Building Fund, March 31st, 1936.

10. The effect of a woman in the pulpit is thus defined in *Women
and the Ministry, Some Considerations on the Report of the Archbishops'
Commission on the Ministry of Women* (1936), p. 24. "But we maintain
that the ministration of women . . . will tend to produce a lowering
of the spiritual tone of Christian worship, such as is not produced
by the ministrations of men before congregations largely or exclusively female. It is a tribute to the quality of Christian womanhood
that it is possible to make this statement; but it would appear to be
a simple matter of fact that in the thoughts and desires of that sex
the natural is more easily made subordinate to the supernatural, the
carnal to the spiritual than is the case with men; and that the ministrations of a male priesthood do not normally arouse that side of
female human nature which should be quiescent during the times

of the adoration of almighty God. We believe, on the other hand, that it would be impossible for the male members of the average Anglican congregation to be present at a service at which a woman ministered without becoming unduly conscious of her sex."

In the opinion of the Commissioners, therefore, Christian women are more spiritually minded than Christian men—a remarkable, but no doubt adequate, reason for excluding them from the priesthood.

11. *Daily Telegraph,* January 20th, 1936.

12. *Daily Telegraph,* 1936.

13. *Daily Telegraph,* January 22nd, 1936.

14. "There are, so far as I know, no universal rules on this subject [i.e., sexual relations between civil servants]; but civil servants and municipal officers of both sexes are certainly expected to observe the conventional proprieties and to avoid conduct which might find its way into the newspapers and there be described as 'scandalous.' Until recently sexual relations between men and women officers of the Post Office were punishable with immediate dismissal of both parties. . . . The problem of avoiding newspaper publicity is a fairly easy one to solve so far as court proceedings are concerned: but official restriction extends further so as to prevent women civil servants (who usually have to resign on marriage) from cohabiting openly with men if they desire to do so. The matter, therefore, takes on a different complexion." (*The British Civil Servant. The Public Service,* by William A. Robson, pp. 14, 15.)

15. Most men's clubs confine women to a special room, or annexe, and exclude them from other apartments, whether on the principle observed at St. Sofia that they are impure, or whether on the principle observed at Pompeii that they are too pure, is matter for speculation.

16. The power of the Press to burke discussion of any undesirable subject was, and still is, very formidable. It was one of the "extraordinary obstacles" against which Josephine Butler had to fight

in her campaign against the Contagious Diseases Act. "Early in 1870 the London Press began to adopt that policy of silence with regard to the question, which lasted for many years, and called forth from the Ladies' Association the famous 'Remonstrance against the Conspiracy of Silence,' signed by Harriet Martineau and Josephine E. Butler, which concluded with the following words: 'Surely, while such a conspiracy of silence is possible and practised among leading journalists, we English greatly exaggerate our privileges as a free people when we profess to encourage a free press, and to possess the right to hear both sides in a momentous question of morality and legislation.'" (*Personal Reminiscences of a Great Crusade,* by Josephine E. Butler, p. 49.) Again, during the battle for the vote the Press used the boycott with great effect. And so recently as July 1937 Miss Philippa Strachey in a letter headed "A Conspiracy of Silence," printed (to its honour) by the *Spectator,* almost repeats Mrs. Butler's words: "Many hundreds and thousands of men and women have been participating in an endeavour to induce the Government to abandon the provision in the new Contributory Pensions Bill for the black-coated workers which for the first time introduces a differential income limit for men and women entrants. . . . In the course of the last month the Bill has been before the House of Lords, where this particular provision has met with strong and determined opposition from all sides of the Chamber. . . . These are events one would have supposed to be of sufficient interest to be recorded in the daily Press. But they have been passed over in complete silence by the newspapers from *The Times* to the *Daily Herald.* . . . The differential treatment of women under this Bill has aroused a feeling of resentment among them such as has not been witnessed since the granting of the franchise. . . . How is one to account for this being completely concealed by the Press?"

17. Flesh wounds were of course inflicted during the battle of Westminster. Indeed the fight for the vote seems to have been

more severe than is now recognized. Thus Flora Drummond says: "Whether we won the vote by our agitation, as I believe, or whether we got it for other reasons, as some people say, I think many of the younger generation will find it hard to believe the fury and brutality aroused by our claim for votes for women less than thirty years ago." (Flora Drummond in the *Listener,* August 25th, 1937.) The younger generation is presumably so used to the fury and brutality that claims for liberty arouse that they have no emotion available for this particular instance. Moreover, that particular fight has not yet taken its place among the fights which have made England the home, and Englishmen the champions, of liberty. The fight for the vote is still generally referred to in terms of sour deprecation: "... and the women ... had not begun that campaign of burning, whipping, and picture-slashing which was finally to prove to both Front Benches their eligibility for the Franchise." (*Reflections and Memories,* by Sir John Squire, p. 10.) The younger generation therefore can be excused if they believe that there was nothing heroic about a campaign in which only a few windows were smashed, shins broken, and Sargent's portrait of Henry James damaged, but not irreparably, with a knife. Burning, whipping and picture-slashing only it would seem become heroic when carried out on a large scale by men with machine-guns.

18. *The Life of Sophia Jex-Blake,* by Margaret Todd, M.D., p. 72.

19. "Much has lately been said and written of the achievements and accomplishments of Sir Stanley Baldwin during his Premierships and too much would be impossible. Might I be permitted to call attention to what Lady Baldwin has done? When I first joined the committee of this hospital in 1929, analgesics (pain deadeners) for normal maternity cases in the wards were almost unknown, now their use is ordinary routine and they are availed of in practically 100 per cent of cases, and what is true of this hospital is true virtually for all similar hospitals. This remarkable change in so short a time is due to the inspiration and the tireless efforts and

encouragement of Mrs. Stanley Baldwin, as she then was. . . ." (Letter to *The Times* from C. S. Wentworth Stanley, Chairman House Committee, The City of London Maternity Hospital, 1937.) Since chloroform was first administered to Queen Victoria on the birth of Prince Leopold in April 1853, "normal maternity cases in the wards" have had to wait for seventy-six years and the advocacy of a Prime Minister's wife to obtain this relief.

20. According to *Debrett* the Knights and Dames of the Most Excellent Order of the British Empire wear a badge consisting of "a cross patonce, enamelled pearl, fimbriated or surmounted by a gold medallion with a representation of Britannia seated within a circle gules inscribed with the motto 'For God and the Empire.'" This is one of the few orders open to women, but their subordination is properly marked by the fact that the ribbon in their case is only two inches and one-quarter in breadth; whereas the ribbon of the Knights is three inches and three-quarters in breadth. The stars also differ in size. The motto, however, is the same for both sexes, and must be held to imply that those who thus ticket themselves see some connection between the Deity and the Empire, and hold themselves prepared to defend them. What happens if Britannia seated within a circle gules is opposed (as is conceivable) to the other authority whose seat is not specified on the medallion, *Debrett* does not say, and the Knights and Dames must themselves decide.

21. *Life of Sir Ernest Wild, K.C.,* by R. J. Rackham, p. 91.

22. Lord Baldwin, speech reported in *The Times,* April 20th, 1936.

23. *Life of Charles Gore,* by G. L. Prestige, D.D., pp. 240–1.

24. *Life of Sir William Broadbent, K.C.V.O., F.R.S.,* edited by his daughter, M. E. Broadbent, p. 242.

25. *The Lost Historian, a Memoir of Sir Sidney Low,* by Desmond Chapman-Huston, p. 198.

26. *Thoughts and Adventures,* by the Rt. Hon. Winston Churchill, p. 57.

27. Speech at Belfast by Lord Londonderry, reported in *The Times,* July 11th, 1936.

28. *Thoughts and Adventures,* by the Rt. Hon. Winston Churchill, p. 279.

29. *Daily Herald,* February 13th, 1935.

30. Goethe's *Faust,* translated by Melian Stawell and G. L. Dickinson.

31. *The Life of Charles Tomlinson,* by his niece, Mary Tomlinson, p. 30.

32. *Miss Weeton, Journal of a Governess, 1807–1811,* edited by Edward Hall, pp. 14, xvii.

33. *A Memoir of Anne Jemima Clough,* by B. A. Clough, p. 32.

34. *Personal Reminiscences of a Great Crusade,* by Josephine Butler, p. 189.

35. "You and I know that it matters little if we have to be the out-of-sight piers driven deep into the marsh, on which the visible ones are carried, that support the bridge. We do not mind if, hereafter, people forget that there are any low down at all; if some have to be used up in trying experiments, before the best way of building the bridge is discovered. We are quite willing to be among these. The bridge is what we care for, and not our place in it; and we believe that, to the end, it may be kept in remembrance that this is alone to be our object." (Letter from Octavia Hill to Mrs. N. Senior, September 20th, 1874. *The Life of Octavia Hill,* by C. Edmund Maurice, pp. 307–8.)

Octavia Hill (1838–1912) initiated the movement for "securing better homes for the poor and open spaces for the public. . . . The 'Octavia Hill System' has been adopted over the whole planned extension of [Amsterdam]. In January 1928 no less than 28,648 dwellings had been built." (*Octavia Hill,* from letters edited by Emily S. Maurice, pp. 10–11.)

36. The maid played so important a part in English upper-class life from the earliest times until the year 1914, when the Hon.

Monica Grenfell went to nurse wounded soldiers accompanied by a maid (*Bright Armour,* by Monica Salmond, p. 20), that some recognition of her services seems to be called for. Her duties were peculiar. Thus she had to escort her mistress down Piccadilly "where a few club men might have looked at her out of a window," but was unnecessary in Whitechapel, "where malefactors were possibly lurking round every corner." But her office was undoubtedly arduous. Wilson's part in Elizabeth Barrett's private life is well known to readers of the famous letters. Later in the century (about 1889–92) Gertrude Bell "went with Lizzie, her maid, to picture exhibitions; she was fetched by Lizzie from dinner parties; she went with Lizzie to see the Settlement in Whitechapel where Mary Talbot was working. . . ." (*[The Earlier] Letters of Gertrude Bell,* edited by Lady Richmond.) We have only to consider the hours she waited in cloak rooms, the acres she toiled in picture galleries, the miles she trudged along West End pavements to conclude that if Lizzie's day is now almost over, it was in its day a long one. Let us hope that the thought that she was putting into practice the commands laid down by St. Paul in his Letters to Titus and the Corinthians was a support; and the knowledge that she was doing her utmost to deliver her mistress's body intact to her master a solace. Even so in the weakness of the flesh and in the darkness of the beetle-haunted basement she must sometimes have bitterly reproached St. Paul on the one hand for his chastity, and the gentlemen of Piccadilly on the other for their lust. It is much to be regretted that no lives of maids, from which a more fully documented account could be constructed, are to be found in the *Dictionary of National Biography.*

37. *The Earlier Letters of Gertrude Bell,* collected and edited by Elsa Richmond, pp. 217–18.

38. The question of chastity, both of mind and body, is of the greatest interest and complexity. The Victorian, Edwardian and much of the Fifth Georgian conception of chastity was based, to go no further back, upon the words of St. Paul. To understand

their meaning we should have to understand his psychology and environment—no light task in view of his frequent obscurity and the lack of biographical material. From internal evidence it seems clear that he was a poet and a prophet, but lacked logical power, and was without that psychological training which forces even the least poetic or prophetic nowadays to subject their personal emotions to scrutiny. Thus his famous pronouncement on the matter of veils, upon which the theory of women's chastity seems to be based, is susceptible to criticism from several angles. In the Letter to the Corinthians his argument that a woman must be veiled when she prays or prophesies is based upon the assumption that to be unveiled "is one and the same thing as if she were shaven." That assumption granted, we must ask next, What shame is there in being shaven? Instead of replying, St. Paul proceeds to assert, "For a man indeed ought not to have his head veiled, forasmuch as he is the image and glory of God": from which it appears that it is not being shaven in itself that is wrong; but to be a woman and to be shaven. It is wrong, it appears, for the woman because "the woman is the glory of the man." If St. Paul had said openly that he liked the look of women's long hair many of us would have agreed with him, and thought the better of him for saying so. But other reasons appeared to him preferable, as appears from his next remark: "For the man is not of the woman; but the woman of the man; for neither was the man created for the woman; but the woman for the man: for this cause ought the woman to have a sign of authority on her head, because of the angels." What view the angels took of long hair we have no means of knowing; and St. Paul himself seems to have been doubtful of their support or he would not think it necessary to drag in the familiar accomplice nature. "Doth not even nature itself teach you, that, if a man have long hair, it is a dishonour to him? But if a woman have long hair, it is a glory to her: for her hair is given her for a covering. But if any man seemeth to be contentious, we have no such custom, neither the churches of God." The argument from nature may seem to us susceptible of amendment; nature, when allied with financial advantage, is seldom of divine origin; but if the basis of the argument is shifty, the conclusion is firm. "Let the women keep silence in the churches: for it is not permitted unto them to speak; but let them be in subjection, as also saith the law." Having thus invoked the familiar but always suspect trinity of accomplices, Angels, nature and law, to support his personal opinion, St. Paul reaches the conclusion which has been looming unmistakably ahead of us: "And if they would learn anything, let them ask their own husbands at home: for it is shameful for a woman to speak in the church." The nature of that "shame," which is closely connected with chastity has, as the letter proceeds, been considerably alloyed. For it is obviously compounded of certain sexual and personal prejudices. St. Paul, it is obvious, was not only a bachelor (for his relations with Lydia see Renan, *Saint Paul,* p. 149: "Est-il cependant absolument impossible que Paul ait contracté avec cette sœur une union plus intime? On ne saurait l'affirmer"); and, like many bachelors, suspicious of the other sex; but a poet and like many poets preferred to prophesy himself rather than to listen to the prophecies of others. Also he was of the virile or dominant type, so familiar at present in Germany, for whose gratification a subject race or sex is essential. Chastity then as defined by St. Paul is seen to be a complex conception, based upon the love of long hair; the love of subjection; the love of an audience; the love of laying down the law, and, subconsciously, upon a very strong and natural desire that the woman's mind and body shall be reserved for the use of one man and one only. Such a conception when supported by the Angels, nature, law, custom and the Church, and enforced by a sex with a strong personal interest to enforce it, and the economic means, was of undoubted power. The grip of its white if skeleton fingers can be found upon whatever page of history we open from St. Paul to Gertrude Bell. Chastity was invoked to prevent her from studying medicine; from painting from the nude; from reading Shakespeare; from playing in orchestras; from walking down Bond Street alone. In 1848 it was "an unpardonable solecism" for the daughters of a gardener to drive down Regent Street in a hansom cab (*Paxton and the Bachelor Duke,* by Violet Markham, p. 288); that solecism became a crime, of what magnitude theologians must decide, if the flaps were left open. In the beginning of the present century the daughter of an ironmaster (for let us not flout distinctions said today to be of prime importance), Sir Hugh Bell, had "reached the age of 27 and married without ever having walked alone down Piccadilly. . . . Gertrude, of course, would never have dreamt of doing that. . . ." The West End was the contaminated area. "It was one's own class that was taboo; . . ." (*The Earlier Letters of Gertrude Bell,* collected and edited by Elsa Richmond, pp. 217–18.) But the complexities and inconsistencies of chastity were such that the same girl who had to be veiled, i.e., accompanied by a male or a maid, in Piccadilly, could visit Whitechapel, or Seven Dials, then haunts of vice and disease, alone and with her parents' approval. This anomaly did not altogether escape comment. Thus Charles Kingsley as a boy exclaimed: ". . . and the girls have their heads crammed full of schools, and district visiting, and baby linen, and penny clubs. Confound!!! and going about among the most abominable scenes of filth and wretchedness, and indecency to visit the poor and read the Bible to them. My own mother says that the places they go into are fit for no girl to see, and that they should not know such things exist."(*Charles Kingsley,* by Margaret Farrand Thorp, p. 12.) Mrs. Kingsley, however, was exceptional. Most of the daughters of educated men saw such "abominable scenes," and knew that such things existed. That they concealed their knowledge is probable; what effect that concealment had psychologically it is impossible here to inquire. But that chastity, whether real or imposed, was an immense power, whether good or bad, it is impossible to doubt. Even today it is probable that a woman has to fight a psychological battle of some severity with the ghost of St. Paul, before she can have intercourse with a man other than her husband. Not only was the social stigma strongly exerted on behalf of chastity, but the Bastardy Act did its utmost to impose chastity by financial pressure. Until women had the vote in 1918, "the Bastardy Act of 1872 fixed the sum of 5s. a week as the maximum which a father, whatever his wealth, could be made to pay towards the maintenance of his child." (*Josephine Butler,* by M. G. Fawcett and E. M. Turner, note, p. 101.) Now that St. Paul and many of his apostles have been unveiled themselves by modern science chastity has undergone considerable revision. Yet there is said to be a reaction in favour of some degree of chastity for both sexes. This is partly due to economic causes; the protection of chastity by maids is an expensive item in the bourgeois budget. The psychological argument in favour of chastity is well expressed by Mr. Upton Sinclair: "Nowadays we hear a great deal about mental troubles caused by sex repression; it is the mood of the moment. We do not hear anything about the complexes which may be caused by sex indulgence. But my observation has been that those who permit themselves to follow every sexual impulse are quite as miserable as those who repress every sexual impulse. I remember a classmate in College; I said to him: 'Did it ever occur to you to stop and look at your own mind? Everything that comes to you is turned into sex.' He looked surprised, and I saw that it was a new idea to him; he thought it over, and said: 'I guess you are right.'" (*Candid Reminiscences,* by Upton Sinclair, p. 63.) Further illustration is supplied by the following anecdote: "In the splendid library of Columbia University were treasures of beauty, costly volumes of engravings and in my usual greedy fashion I went at these, intending to learn all there was to know about Renaissance art in a week or two. But I found myself overwhelmed by this mass of nakedness; my senses reeled, and I had to quit." (*Op. cit.,* pp. 62–3.)

39. The translation here used is by Sir Richard Jebb (*Sophocles, the Plays and Fragments*, with critical notes, commentary and translation in English prose.) It is impossible to judge any book from a translation, yet even when thus read the *Antigone* is clearly one of the great masterpieces of dramatic literature. Nevertheless, it could undoubtedly be made, if necessary, into anti-Fascist propaganda. Antigone herself could be transformed either into Mrs. Pankhurst, who broke a window and was imprisoned in Holloway; or into Frau Pommer, the wife of a Prussian mines official at Essen, who said: "'The thorn of hatred has been driven deep enough into the people by the religious conflicts, and it is high time that the men of today disappeared.' . . . She has been arrested and is to be tried on a charge of insulting and slandering the State and the Nazi movement." (*The Times*, August 12th, 1935.) Antigone's crime was of much the same nature and was punished in much the same way. Her words, "See what I suffer, and from whom, because I feared to cast away the fear of heaven! . . . And what law of heaven have I transgressed? Why, hapless one, should I look to the gods any more—what ally should I invoke—when by piety I have earned the name of impious?" could be spoken either by Mrs. Pankhurst, or by Frau Pommer; and are certainly topical. Creon, again, who "thrust the children of the sunlight to the shades, and ruthlessly lodged a living soul in the grave"; who held that "disobedience is the worst of evils," and that "whomsoever the city may appoint, that man must be obeyed, in little things and great, in just things and unjust" is typical of certain politicians in the past, and of Herr Hitler and Signor Mussolini in the present. But though it is easy to squeeze these characters into up-to-date dress, it is impossible to keep them there. They suggest too much; when the curtain falls we sympathize, it may be noted, even with Creon himself. This result, to the propagandist undesirable, would seem to be due to the fact that Sophocles (even in a translation) uses freely all the faculties

that can be possessed by a writer; and suggests, therefore, that if we use art to propagate political opinions, we must force the artist to clip and cabin his gift to do us a cheap and passing service. Literature will suffer the same mutilation that the mule has suffered; and there will be no more horses.

40. The five words of Antigone are: *Οὔτοι συνέχθει ἄλλα συμωιλεῖν ἔωυν.* 'Tis not my nature to join in hating, but in loving (*Antigone,* line 523 (Jebb).) To which Creon replied: "Pass, then, to the world of the dead, and, if thou must needs love, love them. While I live, no woman shall rule me."

41. Even at a time of great political stress like the present it is remarkable how much criticism is still bestowed upon women. The announcement, "A shrewd, witty and provocative study of modern woman," appears on an average three times yearly in publishers' lists. The author, often a doctor of letters, is invariably of the male sex; and "to mere man," as the blurb puts it (see *Times Lit. Sup.,* March 12th, 1938), "this book will be an eye-opener." Presumably the need for a scapegoat is largely responsible, and the role is traditionally a woman's. (See Genesis.) It is a curious fact that although the "practical obliteration" of her freedom is assured if certain characteristics generally if erroneously associated with aggravated masculinity remain unchecked, the educated woman not only accepts criticism, but, if publishers' lists are to be taken as evidence, makes no attempt to return it. This may be attributed to poverty which, as the poet says, makes cowards of us all. On the other hand, a statement in the *Times* (Sept. 1st, 1937) that "in the last few years women have developed a great taste for oysters" suggests that an increase of spending power may in time develop the critical faculty as well as the sensual.

THREE

1. It is to be hoped that some methodical person has made a collection of the various manifestoes and questionnaires issued broadcast during the years 1936–7. Private people of no political training were invited to sign appeals asking their own and foreign governments to change their policy; artists were asked to fill up forms stating the proper relations of the artist to the State, to religion, to morality; pledges were required that the writer should use English grammatically and avoid vulgar expressions; and dreamers were invited to analyse their dreams. By way of inducement it was generally proposed to publish the results in the daily or weekly press. What effect this inquisition has had upon governments it is for the politician to say. Upon literature, since the output of books is unstaunched, and grammar would seem to be neither better nor worse, the effect is problematical. But the inquisition is of great psychological and social interest. Presumably it originated in the state of mind suggested by Dean Inge (The Rickman Godlee Lecture, reported in *The Times,* November 23rd, 1937), "whether in our own interests we were moving in the right direction. If we went on as we were doing now, would the man of the future be superior to us or not? . . . Thoughtful people were beginning to realize that before congratulating ourselves on moving fast we ought to have some idea where we were moving to": a general self-dissatisfaction and desire "to live differently." It also points, indirectly, to the

death of the Siren, that much ridiculed and often upper-class lady who by keeping open house for the aristocracy, plutocracy, intelligentsia, ignorantsia, etc., tried to provide all classes with a talking-ground or scratching-post where they could rub up minds, manners and morals more privately, and perhaps as usefully. The part that the Siren played in promoting culture and intellectual liberty in the eighteenth century is held by historians to be of some importance. Even in our own day she had her uses. Witness W. B. Yeats—"How often I have wished that he [Synge] might live long enough to enjoy that communion with idle, charming cultivated women which Balzac in one of his dedications calls 'the chief consolation of genius'!" (*Dramatis Personae*, W. B. Yeats, p. 127.) Lady St. Helier who, as Lady Jeune, preserved the eighteenth-century tradition, informs us, however, that "Plovers' eggs at 2s. 6d. apiece, forced strawberries, early asparagus, *petits poussins* . . . are now considered almost a necessity by anyone aspiring to give a good dinner" (1909); and her remark that the reception day was "very fatiguing . . . how exhausted I felt when half-past seven came, and how gladly at eight o'clock I sat down to a peaceful *tête-à-tête* dinner with my husband!" (*Memories of Fifty Years*, by Lady St. Helier, pp. 3, 5, 182) may explain why such houses are shut, why such hostesses are dead, and why therefore the intelligentsia, the ignorantsia, the aristocracy, the bureaucracy, the bourgeoisie, etc., are driven (unless somebody will revive that society on an economic basis) to do their talking in public. But in view of the multitude of manifestoes and questionnaires now in circulation it would be foolish to suggest another into the minds and motives of the Inquisitors.

2. "He did begin however on May 13th (1844) to lecture weekly at Queen's College which Maurice and other professors at King's had established a year before, primarily for the examination and training of governesses. Kingsley was ready to share in this unpopular task because he believed in the higher education of women." (*Charles Kingsley*, by Margaret Farrand Thorp, p. 65.)

3. The French, as the above quotation shows, are as active as the English in issuing manifestoes. That the French, who refuse to allow the women of France to vote, and still inflict upon them laws whose almost medieval severity can be studied in *The Position of Women in Contemporary France,* by Frances Clark, should appeal to English women to help them to protect liberty and culture must cause surprise.

4. Strict accuracy, here slightly in conflict with rhythm and euphony, requires the word "port." A photograph in the daily Press of "Dons in a Senior Common Room after dinner" (1937) shows "a railed trolley in which the port decanter travels across a gap between diners at the fireplace, and thus continues its round without passing against the sun." Another picture shows the "sconce" cup in use. "This old Oxford custom ordains that mention of certain subjects in Hall shall be punished by the offender drinking three pints of beer at one draught. . . ." Such examples are by themselves enough to prove how impossible it is for a woman's pen to describe life at a man's college without committing some unpardonable solecism. But the gentlemen whose customs are often, it is to be feared, travestied, will extend their indulgence when they reflect that the female novelist, however reverent in intention, works under grave physical drawbacks. Should she wish, for example, to describe a Feast at Trinity, Cambridge, she has to "listen through the peephole in the room of Mrs. Butler (the Master's wife) to the speeches taking place at the Feast which was held in Trinity College." Miss Haldane's observation was made in 1907, when she reflected that "The whole surroundings seemed mediaeval." (*From One Century to Another,* by E. Haldane, p. 235.)

5. According to Whitaker there is a Royal Society of Literature and also the British Academy, both presumably, since they have offices and officers, official bodies, but what their powers are it is impossible to say, since if Whitaker had not vouched for their existence it would scarcely have been suspected.

6. Women were apparently excluded from the British Museum Reading-Room in the eighteenth century. Thus: "*Miss Chudleigh* solicits permission to be received into the reading-room. The only female student who as yet has honoured us was *Mrs. Macaulay;* and your Lordship may recollect what an untoward event offended her delicacy." (Daniel Wray to Lord Harwicke, October 22nd, 1768. Nichols, *Literary Anecdotes of the Eighteenth Century,* Vol. I, p. 137.) The editor adds in a footnote: "This alludes to the indelicacy of a gentleman there, in *Mrs. Macaulay's* presence; of which the particulars will not bear to be repeated."

7. *The Autobiography and Letters of Mrs. M. O. W. Oliphant,* arranged and edited by Mrs. Harry Coghill. Mrs. Oliphant (1825–97) "lived in perpetual embarrassment owing to her undertaking education and maintenance of her widowed brother's children in addition to her own two sons . . ." (*Dictionary of National Biography.*)

8. Macaulay's *History of England,* Vol. III, p. 278 (standard edition).

9. Mr. Littlewood, until recently dramatic critic of the *Morning Post,* described the condition of Journalism at Present at a dinner given in his honour, December 6th, 1937. Mr. Littlewood said "that he had in season and out of season fought for more space for the theatre in the columns of the London daily papers. It was Fleet Street where, between eleven and half-past twelve, not to mention before and after, thousands of beautiful words and thoughts were systematically massacred. It had been his lot for at least two out of his four decades to return to that shambles every night with the sure and certain prospect of being told that the paper was already full with important news, and that there was no room for any sanguinary stuff about the theatre. It had been his luck to wake up the next morning to find himself answerable for the mangled remains of what was once a good notice. . . . It was not the fault of the men in the office. Some of them put the blue pencil through with tears in their eyes. The real culprit was that huge public who knew noth-

ing about the theatre and could not be expected to care." (*The Times,* December 6th, 1937.)

Mr. Douglas Jerrold describes the treatment of politics in the Press. "In those few brief years [between 1928–33] truth had fled from Fleet Street. You could never tell all the truth all the time. You never will be able to do so. But you used at least to be able to tell the truth about other countries. By 1933, you did it at your peril. In 1928 there was no direct political pressure from advertisers. Today it is not only direct but effective."

Literary criticism would seem to be in much the same case and for the same reason: "There are no critics in whom the public have any more confidence. They trust, if at all, to the different Book Societies, and the selections of individual newspapers, and on the whole they are wise. . . . The Book Society are frankly book sellers, and the great national newspapers cannot afford to puzzle their readers. They must all choose books which have, at the prevailing level of public taste, a potentially large sale." (*Georgian Adventure,* by Douglas Jerrold, pp. 282, 283, 298.)

10. While it is obvious that under the conditions of journalism at present the criticism of literature must be unsatisfactory, it is also obvious that no change can be made, without changing the economic structure of society and the psychological structure of the artist. Economically, it is necessary that the reviewer should herald the publication of a new book with his town-crier's shout, "O yez, O yez, O yez, such and such a book has been published; its subject is this, that or the other." Psychologically, vanity and the desire for "recognition" are still so strong among artists that to starve them of advertisement and to deny them frequent if contrasted shocks of praise and blame would be as rash as the introduction of rabbits into Australia: the balance of nature would be upset and the consequences might well be disastrous. The suggestion in the text is not to abolish public criticism; but to supplement it by a new

service based on the example of the medical profession. A panel of critics recruited from reviewers (many of whom are potential critics of genuine taste and learning) would practise like doctors and in strictest privacy. Publicity removed, it follows that most of the distractions and corruptions which inevitably make contemporary criticism worthless to the writer would be abolished; all inducement to praise or blame for personal reasons would be destroyed; neither sales nor vanity would be affected; the author could attend to criticism without considering the effect upon public or friends; the critic could criticize without considering the editor's blue pencil or the public taste. Since criticism is much desired by the living, as the constant demand for it proves, and since fresh books are as essential for the critic's mind as fresh meat for his body, each would gain; literature even might benefit. The advantages of the present system of public criticism are mainly economic; the evil effects psychologically are shown by the two famous *Quarterly* reviews of Keats and Tennyson. Keats was deeply wounded; and "the effect . . . upon Tennyson himself was penetrating and prolonged. His first act was at once to withdraw from the press *The Lover's Tale.* . . . We find him thinking of leaving England altogether, of living abroad." (*Tennyson,* by Harold Nicolson, p. 118.) The effect of Mr. Churton Collins upon Sir Edmund Gosse was much the same: "His self-confidence was undermined, his personality reduced . . . was not everyone watching his struggles regarding him as doomed? . . . His own account of his sensations was that he went about feeling that he had been flayed alive." (*The Life and Letters of Sir Edmund Gosse,* by Evan Charteris, p. 196.)

11. "A-ring-the-bell-and-run-away-man." This word has been coined in order to define those who make use of words with the desire to hurt but at the same time to escape detection. In a transitional age when many qualities are changing their value, new words to express new values are much to be desired. Vanity, for ex-

ample, which would seem to lead to severe complications of cruelty and tyranny, judging from evidence supplied abroad, is still masked by a name with trivial associations. A supplement to the *Oxford English Dictionary* is indicated.

12. *Memoir of Anne J. Clough,* by B. A. Clough, pp. 38, 67.

"The Sparrow's Nest," by William Wordsworth.

13. In the nineteenth century much valuable work was done for the working class by educated men's daughters in the only way that was then open to them. But now that some of them at least have received an expensive education, it is arguable that they can work much more effectively by remaining in their own class and using the methods of that class to improve a class which stands much in need of improvement. If on the other hand the educated (as so often happens) renounce the very qualities which education should have bought—reason, tolerance, knowledge—and play at belonging to the working class and adopting its cause, they merely expose that cause to the ridicule of the educated class, and do nothing to improve their own. But the number of books written by the educated about the working class would seem to show that the glamour of the working class and the emotional relief afforded by adopting its cause, are today as irresistible to the middle class as the glamour of the aristocracy was twenty years ago (*see A La Recherche du Temps Perdu*). Meanwhile it would be interesting to know what the true-born working man or woman thinks of the playboys and playgirls of the educated class who adopt the working-class cause without sacrificing middle-class capital, or sharing working-class experience. "The average housewife," according to Mrs. Murphy, Home Service Director of the British Commercial Gas Association, "washed an acre of dirty dishes, a mile of glass and three miles of clothes and scrubbed five miles of floor yearly." (*Daily Telegraph,* September 29th, 1937.) For a more detailed account of working-class life, see *Life as We Have Known It,* by Co-operative working

women, edited by Margaret Llewelyn Davies. The *Life of Joseph Wright* also gives a remarkable account of working-class life at first hand and not through pro-proletarian spectacles.

14. "It was stated yesterday at the War Office that the Army Council have no intention of opening recruiting for any women's corps." (*The Times,* October 22nd, 1937.) This marks a prime distinction between the sexes. Pacifism is enforced upon women. Men are still allowed liberty of choice.

15. The following quotation shows, however, that if sanctioned the fighting instinct easily develops. "The eyes deeply sunk into the sockets, the features acute, the amazon keeps herself very straight on the stirrups at the head of her squadron. . . . Five English parliamentaries look at this woman with the respectful and a bit restless admiration one feels for a 'fauve' of an unknown species. . . .

— Come nearer Amalia—orders the commandant. She pushes her horse towards us and salutes her chief with the sword.

—Sergeant Amalia Bonilla—continues the chief of the squadron—how old are you?—Thirty-six.—Where were you born?—In Granada.—Why have you joined the army?—My two daughters were militiawomen. The younger has been killed in the Alto de Leon. I thought I had to supersede her and avenge her.— And how many enemies have you killed to avenge her?—You know it, commandant, five. The sixth is not sure.—No, but you have taken his horse. The amazon Amalia rides in fact a magnificent dapple-grey horse, with glossy hair, which flatters like a parade horse. . . . This woman who has killed five men—but who feels not sure about the sixth—was for the envoys of the House of Commons an excellent introducer to the Spanish War." (*The Martyrdom of Madrid,* Inedited Witnesses, by Louis Delaprée, pp. 34, 5, 6. Madrid, 1937.)

16. By way of proof, an attempt may be made to elucidate the reasons given by various Cabinet Ministers in various Parliaments from about 1870 to 1918 for opposing the Suffrage Bill. An able

effort has been made by Mrs. Oliver Strachey (see chapter "The Deceitfulness of Politics" in her *"The Cause"*).

17. "We have had women's civil and political status before the League only since 1935." From reports sent in as to the position of the woman as wife, mother and home maker, "the sorry fact was discovered that her economic position in many countries (including Great Britain) was unstable. She is entitled neither to salary nor wages and has definite duties to perform. In England, though she may have devoted her whole life to husband and children, her husband, no matter how wealthy, can leave her destitute at his death and she has no legal redress. We must alter this—by legislation. . . ." (Linda P. Littlejohn, reported in the *Listener*, November 10th, 1937.)

18. This particular definition of woman's task comes not from an Italian but from a German source. There are so many versions and all are so much alike that it seems unnecessary to verify each separately. But it is curious to find how easy it is to cap them from English sources. Mr. Gerhardi for example writes: "Never yet have I committed the error of looking on women writers as serious fellow artists. I enjoy them rather as spiritual helpers who, endowed with a sensitive capacity for appreciation, may help the few of us afflicted with genius to bear our cross with good grace. Their true role, therefore, is rather to hold out the sponge to us, cool our brow, while we bleed. If their sympathetic understanding may indeed be put to a more romantic use, how we cherish them for it!" (*Memoirs of a Polyglot*, by William Gerhardi, pp. 320, 321.) This conception of woman's role tallies almost exactly with that quoted above.

19. To speak accurately, "a large silver plaque in the form of the Reich eagle . . . was created by President Hindenburg for scientists and other distinguished civilians. . . . It may not be worn. It is usually placed on the writing-desk of the recipient." (Daily paper, April 21st, 1936.)

20. "It is a common thing to see the business girl contenting herself with a bun or a sandwich for her midday meal; and though there are theories that this is from choice . . . the truth is that they often cannot afford to eat properly." (*Careers and Openings for Women,* by Ray Strachey, p. 74.) Compare also Miss E. Turner: ". . . many offices had been wondering why they were unable to get through their work as smoothly as formerly. It had been found that junior typists were fagged out in the afternoons because they could afford only an apple and a sandwich for lunch. Employers should meet the increased cost of living by increased salaries." (*The Times,* March 28th, 1938.)

21. The Mayoress of Woolwich (Mrs. Kathleen Rance) speaking at a bazaar, reported in *Evening Standard,* December 20th, 1937.

22. Miss E. R. Clarke, reported in *The Times,* September 24th, 1937.

23. Reported in *Daily Herald,* August 15th, 1936.

24. Canon F. R. Barry, speaking at conference arranged by Anglican Group at Oxford, reported in *The Times,* January 10th, 1933.

25. *The Ministry of Women. Report of the Archbishops' Commission.* VII. Secondary Schools and Universities, p. 65.

26. "Miss D. Carruthers, Head Mistress of the Green School, Isleworth, said there was a 'very grave dissatisfaction' among older schoolgirls at the way in which organized religion was carried on. 'The Churches seem somehow to be failing to supply the spiritual needs of young people,' she said. 'It is a fault that seems common to all churches.'" (*Sunday Times,* November 21st, 1937.)

27. *Life of Charles Gore,* by G. L. Prestige, D.D., p. 353.

28. *The Ministry of Women. Report of the Archbishops' Commission, passim.*

29. Whether or not the gift of prophecy and the gift of poetry were originally the same, a distinction has been made between those gifts and professions for many centuries. But the fact that the Song of Songs, the work of a poet, is included among the sacred

books, and that propagandist poems and novels, the works of prophets, are included among the secular, points to some confusion. Lovers of English literature can scarcely be too thankful that Shakespeare lived too late to be canonized by the Church. Had the plays been ranked among the sacred books they must have received the same treatment as the Old and the New Testaments; we should have had them doled out on Sundays from the mouths of priests in snatches; now a soliloquy from *Hamlet;* now a corrupt passage from the pen of some drowsy reporter; now a bawdy song; now half a page from *Antony and Cleopatra,* as the Old and New Testaments have been sliced up and interspersed with hymns in the Church of England service; and Shakespeare would have been as unreadable as the Bible. Yet those who have not been forced from childhood to hear it thus dismembered weekly assert that the Bible is a work of the greatest interest, much beauty, and deep meaning.

30. *The Ministry of Women,* Appendix I. "Certain Psychological and Physiological Considerations," by Professor Grensted, D.D., pp. 79–87.

31. "At present a married priest is able to fulfil the requirements of the ordination service, 'to forsake and set aside all worldly cares and studies,' largely because his wife can undertake the care of the household and the family. . . ." (*The Ministry of Women,* p. 32.)

The Commissioners are here stating and approving a principle which is frequently stated and approved by the dictators. Herr Hitler and Signor Mussolini have both often in very similar words expressed the opinion that "There are two worlds in the life of the nation, the world of men and the world of women"; and proceeded to much the same definition of the duties. The effect which this division has had upon the woman; the petty and personal nature of her interests; her absorption in the practical; her apparent incapacity for the poetical and adventurous—all this has been made the staple of so many novels, the target for so much satire, has confirmed so many theorists in the theory that by the law of nature the woman is less spiritual than the man, that nothing more need be said to prove that she has carried out, willingly or unwillingly, her share of the contract. But very little attention has yet been paid to the intellectual and spiritual effect of this division of duties upon those who are enabled by it "to forsake all worldly cares and studies." Yet there can be no doubt that we owe to this segregation the immense elaboration of modern instruments and methods of war; the astonishing complexities of theology; the vast deposit of notes at the bottom of Greek, Latin and even English texts; the innumerable carvings, chasings and unnecessary ornamentations of our common furniture and crockery; the myriad distinctions of *Debrett* and *Burke;* and all those meaningless but highly ingenious turnings and twistings into which the intellect ties itself when rid of "the cares of the household and the family." The emphasis which both priests and dictators place upon the necessity for two worlds is enough to prove that it is essential to their domination.

32. Evidence of the complex nature of satisfaction of dominance is provided by the following quotation: "My husband insists that I call him 'Sir,'" said a woman at the Bristol Police Court yesterday, when she applied for a maintenance order. "To keep the peace I have complied with his request," she added. "I also have to clean his boots, fetch his razor when he shaves, and speak up promptly when he asks me questions." In the same issue of the same paper Sir E. F. Fletcher is reported to have "urged the House of Commons to stand up to dictators." (*Daily Herald,* August 1st, 1936.) This would seem to show that the common consciousness which includes husband, wife and House of Commons is feeling at one and the same moment the desire to dominate, the need to comply in order to keep the peace, and the necessity of dominating the desire for dominance—a psychological conflict which serves to explain much that appears inconsistent and turbulent in contemporary opinion. The pleasure of dominance is of course further complicated by the fact that it is still, in the educated class,

closely allied with the pleasures of wealth, social and professional prestige. Its distinction from the comparatively simple pleasures—e.g., the pleasure of a country walk—is proved by the fear of ridicule which great psychologists, like Sophocles, detect in the dominator; who is also peculiarly susceptible according to the same authority either to ridicule or defiance on the part of the female sex. An essential element in this pleasure therefore would seem to be derived not from the feeling itself but from the reflection of other people's feelings, and it would follow that it can be influenced by a change in those feelings. Laughter as an antidote to dominance is perhaps indicated.

33. *The Life of Charlotte Brontë,* by Mrs. Gaskell.

34. *The Life of Sophia Jex-Blake,* by Margaret Todd, pp. 67–9, 70–1, 72.

35. External observation would suggest that a man still feels it a peculiar insult to be taunted with cowardice by a woman in much the same way that a woman feels it a peculiar insult to be taunted with unchastity by a man. The following quotation supports this view. Mr. Bernard Shaw writes: "I am not forgetting the gratification that war gives to the instinct of pugnacity and admiration of courage that are so strong in women. . . . In England on the outbreak of war civilized young women rush about handing white feathers to all young men who are not in uniform. This," he continues, "like other survivals from savagery is quite natural," and he points out that "in old days a woman's life and that of her children depended on the courage and killing capacity of her mate." Since vast numbers of young men did their work all through the war in offices without any such adornment, and the number of "civilized young women" who stuck feathers in coats must have been infinitesimal compared with those who did nothing of the kind, Mr. Shaw's exaggeration is sufficient proof of the immense psychological impression that fifty or sixty feathers (no actual statistics are available) can still make. This would seem to show that the male

still preserves an abnormal susceptibility to such taunts; therefore that courage and pugnacity are still among the prime attributes of manliness; therefore that he still wishes to be admired for possessing them; therefore that any derision of such qualities would have a proportionate effect. That "the manhood emotion" is also connected with economic independence seems probable. "We have never known a man who was not, openly or secretly, proud of being able to support women; whether they were his sisters or his mistresses. We have never known a woman who did not regard the change from economic independence on an employer to economic dependence on a man, as an honourable promotion. What is the good of men and women lying to each other about these things? It is not we that have made them"—(*A. H. Orage,* by Philip Mairet, vii)—an interesting statement, attributed by G. K. Chesterton to A. H. Orage.

36. Until the beginning of the 'eighties, according to Miss Haldane, the sister of R. B. Haldane, no lady could work. "I should, of course, have liked to study for a profession, but that was an impossible idea unless one were in the sad position of 'having to work for one's bread' and that would have been a terrible state of affairs. Even a brother wrote of the melancholy fact after he had been to see Mrs. Langtry act. 'She was a lady and acted like a lady, but what a sad thing it was that she should have to do so!'" (*From One Century to Another,* by Elizabeth Haldane, pp. 73–4.) Harriet Martineau earlier in the century was delighted when her family lost its money, for thus she lost her "gentility" and was allowed to work.

37. *Life of Sophia Jex-Blake,* by Margaret Todd, pp. 69, 70.

38. For an account of Mr. Leigh Smith, see *The Life of Emily Davies,* by Barbara Stephen. Barbara Leigh Smith became Madame Bodichon.

39. How nominal that opening was is shown by the following account of the actual conditions under which women worked in the R.A. Schools about 1900. "Why the female of the species

should never be given the same advantages as the male it is difficult to understand. At the R.A. Schools we women had to compete
against men for all the prizes and medals that were given each year,
and we were only allowed half the amount of tuition and less than
half their opportunities for study. . . . No nude model was allowed
to be posed in the women's painting room at the R.A. Schools. . . .
The male students not only worked from nude models, both male
and female, during the day, but they were given an evening class as
well, at which they could make studies from the figure, the visiting
R.A. instructing." This seemed to the women students "very unfair
indeed"; Miss Collyer had the courage and the social standing necessary to beard first Mr. Frank Dicksee, who argued that since girls
marry, money spent on their teaching is money wasted; next Lord
Leighton; and at length the thin edge of the wedge, that is the undraped figure, was allowed. But "the advantages of the night class
we never did succeed in obtaining. . . ." The women students therefore clubbed together and hired a photographer's studio in Baker
Street. "The money that we, as the committee, had to find, reduced
our meals to near starvation diet." (*Life of an Artist,* by Margaret
Collyer, pp. 79–81, 82.) The same rule was in force at the Notting-
ham Art School in the twentieth century. "Women were not allowed to draw from the nude. If the men worked from the living
figure I had to go into the Antique Room . . . the hatred of those
plaster figures stays with me till this day. I never got any benefit out
of their study." (*Oil Paint and Grease Paint,* by Dame Laura Knight,
p. 47.) But the profession of art is not the only profession that is
thus nominally open. The profession of medicine is "open," but
". . . nearly all the Schools attached to London Hospitals are barred
to women students, whose training in London is mainly carried on
at the London School of Medicine." (*Memorandum on the Position of
English Women in Relation to that of English Men,* by Philippa Strachey
(1935), p. 26.) "Some of the girl 'medicals' at Cambridge University
have formed themselves into a group to ventilate the grievance."

(*Evening News,* March 25th, 1937.) In 1922 women students were admitted to the Royal Veterinary College, Camden Town. ". . . since then the profession has attracted so many women that the number has recently been restricted to 50." (*Daily Telegraph,* October 1st, 1937.)

40 and 41. *The Life of Mary Kingsley,* by Stephen Gwynn, pp. 18, 26. In a fragment of a letter Mary Kingsley writes: "I am useful occasionally, but that is all—very useful a few months ago when on calling on a friend she asked me to go up to her bedroom and see her new hat—a suggestion that staggered me, I knowing her opinion of mine in such matters." "The letter," says Mr. Gwynn, "did not complete this adventure of an unauthorised *fiancé,* but I am sure she got him off the roof and enjoyed the experience riotously."

42. According to Antigone there are two kinds of law, the written and the unwritten, and Mrs. Drummond maintains that it may sometimes be necessary to improve the written law by breaking it. But the many and varied activities of the educated man's daughter in the nineteenth century were clearly not simply or even mainly directed towards breaking the laws. They were, on the contrary, endeavours of an experimental kind to discover what are the unwritten laws; that is the private laws that should regulate certain instincts, passions, mental and physical desires. That such laws exist, and are observed by civilized people, is fairly generally allowed; but it is beginning to be agreed that they were not laid down by "God," who is now very generally held to be a conception, of patriarchal origin, valid only for certain races, at certain stages and times; nor by nature, who is now known to vary greatly in her commands and to be largely under control; but have to be discovered afresh by successive generations, largely by their own efforts of reason and imagination. Since, however, reason and imagination are to some extent the product of our bodies, and there are two kinds of body, male and female, and since these two bodies have been proved within the past few years to differ fundamentally, it is

clear that the laws that they perceive and respect must be differently interpreted. Thus Professor Julian Huxley says: ". . . from the moment of fertilization onwards, man and woman differ in every cell of their body in regard to the number of their chromosomes — those bodies which, for all the world's unfamiliarity, have been shown by the last decade's work to be the bearers of heredity, the determiners of our characters and qualities." In spite of the fact, therefore, that "the superstructure of intellectual and practical life is potentially the same in both sexes," and that "The recent Board of Education Report of the Committee on the Differentiation of the Curriculum for Boys and Girls in Secondary Schools (London, 1923) has established that the intellectual differences between the sexes are very much slighter than popular belief allows" (*Essays in Popular Science,* by Julian Huxley, pp. 62–3), it is clear that the sexes now differ and will always differ. If it were possible not only for each sex to ascertain what laws hold good in its own case, and to respect each other's laws; but also to share the results of those discoveries, it might be possible for each sex to develop fully and improve in quality without surrendering its special characteristics. The old conception that one sex must "dominate" another would then become not only obsolete, but so odious that if it were necessary for practical purposes that a dominant power should decide certain matters, the repulsive task of coercion and dominion would be relegated to an inferior and secret society, much as the flogging and execution of criminals is now carried out by masked beings in profound obscurity. But this is to anticipate.

43. From *The Times* obituary notice of H. W. Greene, fellow of Magdalen College, Oxford, familiarly called "Grugger," February 6th, 1933.

44. "In 1747 the quarterly court (of the Middlesex Hospital) decided to set apart some of the beds for lying-in cases under rules which precluded any woman from acting as midwife. The exclusion of women has remained the traditional attitude. In 1861 Miss

Garrett, afterwards Dr. Garrett Anderson, obtained permission to attend classes . . . and was permitted to visit the wards with the resident officers, but the students protested and the medical officers gave way. The Board declined an offer from her to endow a scholarship for women students." *The Times,* May 17th, 1935.

45. "There is, in the modern world, a great body of well-attested knowledge . . . but as soon as any strong passion intervenes to warp the expert's judgment he becomes unreliable, whatever scientific equipment he may possess." (*The Scientific Outlook,* by Bertrand Russell, p. 17.)

46. One of the record-breakers, however, gave a reason for record-breaking which must compel respect: "Then, too, there was my belief that now and then women should do for themselves what men have already done — and occasionally what men have not done — thereby establishing themselves as persons, and perhaps encouraging other women towards greater independence of thought and action. . . . When they fail, their failure must be a challenge to others." (*The Last Flight,* by Amelia Earhart, pp. 21, 65.)

47. "In point of fact this process [childbirth] actually disables women only for a very small fraction in most of their lives — even a woman who has six children is only necessarily laid up for twelve months out of her whole lifetime." (*Careers and Openings for Women,* by Ray Strachey, pp. 47–8.) At present, however, she is necessarily occupied for much longer. The bold suggestion has been made that the occupation is not necessarily maternal, but should be shared by both parents. And actually an English Member of Parliament has resigned in order to be with his children.

48. The nature of manhood and the nature of womanhood are frequently defined both by Italian and German dictators. Both repeatedly insist that it is the nature of man and indeed the essence of manhood to fight. Hitler, for example, draws a distinction between "a nation of pacifists and a nation of men." Both repeatedly insist that it is the nature of womanhood to heal the wounds of the

fighter. Nevertheless a very strong movement is on foot towards emancipating man from the old "natural and eternal law" that man is essentially a fighter; witness the growth of pacifism among the male sex today. Compare further Lord Knebworth's statement "that if permanent peace were ever achieved, and armies and navies ceased to exist, there would be no outlet for the manly qualities which fighting developed," with the following statement by another young man of the same social caste a few months ago: ". . . it is not true to say that every boy at heart longs for war. It is only other people who teach it us by giving us swords and guns, soldiers and uniforms to play with." (*Conquest of the Past,* by Prince Hubertus Loewenstein, p. 215.) It is possible that the Fascist States by revealing to the younger generation at least the need for emancipation from the old conception of virility are doing for the male sex what the Crimean and the European wars did for their sisters. Professor Huxley, however, warns us that "any considerable alteration of the hereditary constitution is an affair of millennia, not of decades." On the other hand, as science also assures us that our life on earth is "an affair of millennia, not of decades," some alteration in the hereditary constitution may be worth attempting.

49. Coleridge however expresses the views and aims of the outsiders with some accuracy in the following passage: "Man must be *free* or to what purpose was he made a Spirit of Reason, and not a Machine of Instinct? Man must *obey;* or wherefore has he a conscience? The powers, which create this difficulty, contain its solution likewise; for *their* service is perfect freedom. And whatever law or system of law compels any other service, disennobles our nature, leagues itself with the animal against the godlike, kills in us the very principle of joyous well-doing, and fights against humanity. . . . If therefore society is to be under a *rightful* constitution of government, and one that can impose on rational Beings a true and moral obligation to obey it, it must be framed on such principles that every individual follows his own Reason, while he obeys the

laws of the constitution, and performs the will of the state while he follows the dictates of his own Reason. This is expressly asserted by Rousseau, who states the problem of a perfect constitution of government in the following words: Trouver une forme d'Association—par laquelle chacun s'unisant a tous, n'obeisse pourtant qu'à lui même, et reste aussi libre qu'auparavant, i.e.: To find a form of society according to which each one uniting with the whole shall yet obey himself only and remain as free as before." (*The Friend,* by S. T. Coleridge, Vol. I, pp. 333, 334, 335, edition 1818.) To which may be added a quotation from Walt Whitman:

"Of Equality—as if it harm'd me, giving others the same chances and rights as myself—as if it were not indispensable to my own rights that others possess the same."

And finally the words of a half-forgotten novelist, George Sand, are worth considering:

"Toutes les existences sont solidaires les unes des autres, et tout être humain qui présenterait la sienne isolément, sans la rattacher à celle de ses semblables, n'offrirait qu'une énigme à débrouiller.... Cette individualité n'a par elle seule ni signification ni importance aucune. Elle ne prend un sens quelconque qu'en devenant une parcelle de la vie générale, en se fondant avec l'individualité de chacun de mes semblables, et c'est par là qu'elle devient de l'histoire." (*Histoire de ma Vie,* par George Sand, pp. 240–1.)

NOTES TO *Three Guineas*

These notes have been compiled to aid the American reader, though others unfamiliar with the references in this highly allusive text may also find them useful. Woolf's own notes, I believe, should be read as an integral part of the text. While some few of her notes simply give information, most are mini-essays on the topics of the text. Read together, they make a commentary on the form of the footnote itself, a critique of its scholarly function, and, as a series of extratextual appendages, a curious addendum to a set of answers to correspondents. Who are the footnotes meant for? Are they meant to enlighten those who have written to the narrator for contributions? Or are they little asides and interruptions composed for the delight of the reader? Perhaps they are the "nugget[s] of pure truth" she earlier refused to give the readers of *A Room of One's Own*, feeling that now was a time for explanations, for including all the left-over bits of feminist polemic she had hoped not to need to use.

References not included in either the introduction's list of works cited or the suggestions for further reading are given in full in these notes.

Three Guineas [title]   For people of Virginia Woolf's class in Britain in the 1930s, the guinea was an obsolete but still used monetary denomination written as a bank check, as in a doctor's fee, say, or for the purchase of expensive luxury goods. A check (British *cheque*) in guineas indicated the class of the writer and the expense of the purchase. Vanessa Bell's jacket design for the book's publication in 1938 represents the three checks (or cheques) with an old-fashioned quill pen and inkwell (see the introduction, note 7). Nowadays, and for American readers in particular, the word *guinea* is apt to suggest an ethnic slur against Italian Americans, and biographer Hermione Lee, in her introduction to the 1986 Hogarth Press edition of *Three Guineas,* confesses her mystification at its meaning. In all cases the reference is to black Africa. It is equally clear that for Woolf the reference is to race and the history of slavery on which Britain's wealth (including that of herself and women of her class) was built. Her title calls attention to slave-based capitalism while reinforcing the connections between fascism and the patriarchal structure of British society in the buildup to World War II. As the paper check is written in a guaranteed monetary exchange based on gold bullion, Woolf's inquiry is into the cultural foundations of the institutions of war and private property. Slave-owning is what she sees as the basis of the problem.

More important, the guinea is symbolic of the imperialist power that the English aristocracy had traditionally wielded. The guinea itself came into existence in 1663, the same year in which King Charles II bought stock in the Royal Adventurers into Africa, the contemporary incarnation of several slave-trading companies that had been known successively as the Guinea Company. The Royal Mint used gold that had been taken out of Angola, Guinea, and Benin to create the guinea coin, which features the engraving of an elephant. (A Google image search will turn up many examples.) By the time Woolf composed *Three Guineas,* the coin itself had become obsolete, although the wealthy continued to donate guineas to charity, or use them to buy paintings and other luxuries, as they had done for centuries, in the form of checks or the monetary equivalent of the guinea, a pound and a shilling. Subtle allusions throughout *Three Guineas* suggest that the condition of women in British society is analogous to the condition of slaves. The title is a clear reference to the racial issues that had earlier confounded her in *A Room of One's Own* (1929).

prodding your pigs . . . in Norfolk [6]   Possibly a sly reference to the prominent economist and family friend John Maynard Keynes as a country gentleman. He was deeply offended by *Three Guineas,* especially the photographs. Later (14) she describes her "horror and disgust" at Spanish Civil War photographs of "what might be a man's body, or a woman's; it is so mutilated that it might, on the other hand, be the body of a pig. . . ."

the great public schools [6]   The term *public* here refers to the prestigious private institutions that had traditionally educated the sons of the British upper classes, many of whom then attended Oxford or Cambridge University. Woolf mentions two of these, Eton College (founded 1440) and Harrow School (founded 1572) (7). Eton and Harrow are still single-sex schools today.

Mary Kingsley [6]   Major British Victorian explorer and travel writer (1862–1900). *Travels in West Africa* established her reputation. Mary Kingsley is one of the heroines of this book because, like Woolf herself, she was an autodidact who became a great success on her own efforts. But Woolf was also aware that such heroic women whose lives she cites here were often not to be claimed as sister pacifists and feminists, and Kingsley is remembered as an intrepid imperialist. Although Woolf makes a point of referring to Mary Kingsley in *Three Guineas* in order to contrast her work as an "uneducated" woman to that of her well-educated brother, Woolf alludes to the refrain of Charles Kingsley's poem "The Three Fishers" ("Men must work, and women must weep") through "Women Must Weep," the title of the truncated version of *Three Guineas* that appeared in the May and June 1938 editions of the *Atlantic Monthly* in the United States. In using this title, Woolf avoided having to explain to the American reading public the history and political relevance of "guineas" by instead enlisting her readers in the cause of seeing the oppression of women in 1938 as an obsolete Victorian sentimentalism. See also the first entry in Woolf's "Notes and References: One"; note 38 in "Notes and References: Two"; and notes 2, 40, and 41 in "Notes and References: Three." In the discourse of the women's suffrage movement surrounding the struggle for the vote, these lines from Kingsley's popular expression of the concept of separate spheres for men and women were often debated.

Arthur's Education Fund [7]   From the William Makepeace Thackeray novel *Pendennis* (1848–50), chapter 18.

the Pastons [7]   English landowners whose diaries recorded domestic life in the time of Chaucer. See Woolf's "The Pastons and Chaucer" in *The Common Reader* and in *The Essays,* volume 4.

K.C. [7]   King's Counsel, an honorary position of precedence in all courts of law for a barrister (called Q.C., Queen's Counsel, when the monarch is a woman).

allowance of £50 a year [8]   The sum Virginia and her sister, Vanessa, had as girls. It had to cover all their clothes, books, drawing materials, travel expenses, and, in Woolf's case, Greek and French lessons. In 1933 she gave her niece, Angelica, £100 a year for her expenses.

courts and quadrangles [8]   The college open spaces are called quadrangles at Oxford and courts at Cambridge. It was from one of these that the narrator of *A Room of One's Own* was expelled from the grass, on which only members of a college are allowed to walk.

educated men's daughters [8]   A term used to describe precisely the social position of women like herself, implying fathers' refusal to educate their daughters. Woolf repeats the phrase more than a hundred times in the text. Can such repetition create sympathy for middle- and upper-class Englishwomen as victims in today's readers?

that understanding of human beings . . . called psychology [9] Woolf's knowledge of psychology was based on her readings of Sigmund Freud, whose works were published in England by the Hogarth Press (see the discussion of infantile fixation in the third section of *Three Guineas*). Woolf's desire to separate psychology from science may indicate her distrust of a field that, beginning in the nineteenth century, had been used to "prove" the inferiority of women and ethnic minorities. Despite the irony here, she was learning a great deal from reading Freud during this period in her attempt to understand why men make war, in the present essay, and to assist her in recalling her childhood in order to write her memoirs. See Elizabeth Abel for a discussion of the influence of Freud on Woolf, and Willa Muir (introduction, note 6) on Woolf's early ideas about the difference between men and women.

year 1919 [9] In this year was passed the Sex Disqualification (Removal) Act, which opened to women nearly all public offices and professions. Viscountess Nancy Astor became the first female member of Parliament in 1919.

To that let us add this from an airman's life [10] Woolf is quoting from the Earl of Lytton's memoir of his son, Edward Antony James Bulwer-Lytton, Viscount Knebworth (see note 5 in "Notes and References: One"). Antony, as Viscount Knebworth was called, was a member of the Auxiliary Air Force and in 1933 died in a plane crash at age thirty.

the life of a poet who was killed in the European war: Wilfred Owen [11] *European* is the term by which the British commonly refer to the

First World War. Wilfred Owen (1893–1918) was a young soldier and war poet who died a week before the end of it. He is best known for "Dulce et Decorum Est," which details the physical agony of soldiers at war and ends by refuting the popular notion that a patriotic death is both proper and gratifying. "Dulce et Decorum Est" alludes to line thirteen of Ode 2 in Book 3 by the Roman poet Horace (65–8 B.C.). The English equivalent of the phrase "dulce et decorum est, pro patria mori" is "sweet and proper it is to die for one's country."

Here then on the table before us are photographs. [14]   Woolf was writing *Three Guineas* toward the end of 1936/beginning of 1937, approximately five to six months after the start of the Spanish Civil War. The elected government was attacked by Franco's forces, and international brigades were formed from all over the world to fight against fascism. The socialist and communist newspapers and pamphlets that arrived at the Woolf household on a regular basis contained photographs of the war damage wrought upon civilians. While bombing civilians and their cities has become commonplace now, the bombings of Madrid and the town of Guernica (represented in Picasso's famous painting) in this war were horrifying because they broke the earlier accepted rules of war in which civilians, especially women and children, were to be spared. England had in fact used bombs on civilians before this date, but the people bombed were interfering in the colonialist project in Afghanistan and North Africa. Woolf repeatedly refers to these photographs of "dead children" and "ruined houses" as a refrain in the text. The barbarity of such acts is called up again and again, the repetition sending the reader to search for those photographs in the text. But she does not satisfy the desire of the reader she has roused to share her rage. Instead she supplies five photographs of unidentified British professional men in their costumes of power—archbishops, academics, judges, military men. As with the title, the reader is meant to connect them with the Spanish Civil War, war in general, and fascism in particular. "Let us consider what other method of persuasion is left to us. Only, it would seem, to point to the photographs—the photographs of dead bodies and ruined houses. Can we bring out the connection between them and prostituted culture and intellectual slavery and make it so clear that the one implies the other . . ." (113), she writes later in the book. The connection between the two sets of photographs, those mentioned in the text and those actually published in the text, has been lost for many decades. This is the first American text to restore Woolf's devastating illustrations of her thesis. It is not known how the photographs were dropped from the English and American editions of *Three Guineas* for so many decades, or why. What is clear is that now readers will be able to read the photographs and the text together and "bring out the connection between them."

The famous Duchess of Devonshire, Lady Palmerston . . . all undoubtedly possessed of great political influence [17]   The reader is invited to look up these references as a lesson in the project employed by Woolf of using an interactive expectation regarding the allusions in the text to educate us to her own level regarding the history of women. If the reader refuses the role intended for her, see the note in the Shakespeare Head Press edition of *Three Guineas* edited by Naomi Black (Oxford: Blackwell, 2001) for extensive commentary. Woolf's point is that women were only allowed to exercise political power from behind the scenes, often gaining powerful political influence in salons.

the names of the great political leaders—Pitt, Fox . . . [17]   William Pitt the Younger (1759–1806), Robert Peel (1788–1850), Henry John Temple, Viscount Palmerston (1784–1865), Benjamin Disraeli (1804–1881), and William Gladstone (1809–1898) all served terms as Britain's prime minister. Charles James Fox (1749–1806) was appointed lord of the admiralty and, subsequently, lord of the treasury during the prime ministry of Lord Frederick North.

Sheridan at Devonshire House . . . the names of Jane Austen . . . do not occur [18]   Richard Brinsley Sheridan (1751–1816) was a playwright as well as a member of Parliament who held appointments as secretary of the treasury and treasurer of the navy. Likewise, Thomas Babington Macaulay (1800–1859) was both a writer and politician. Matthew Arnold (1822–1888) was a poet, and Thomas Carlyle (1795–1881) was an essayist and historian. Devonshire House was the London residence of the fifth Duke of Cavendish and his wife, the former Lady Georgiana Spencer. Holland House was the home of Henry Richard Vassall Fox, third Lord Holland, who served once as Lord of the Privy Seal and twice as chancellor of the duchy of Lancaster while in Parliament. Many distinguished individuals came to Holland House. Lansdowne House was the home of Henry Petty-Fitzmaurice, the fourth Marquess of Lansdowne, who employed Matthew Arnold as his personal secretary. Bath House was the London residence of William Bingham Baring, the second Baron Ashburton. Carlyle was friends with the Baroness Harriet Ashburton. Jane Austen (1775–1817), Charlotte Brontë (1816–1855), and George Eliot (1819–1880) were novelists. Woolf alludes to these writers to emphasize the extent to which women were excluded from participation in politics. She contrasts Sheridan, Macaulay, Arnold, and Carlyle with Austen, Brontë, and Eliot (whose real name was Mary Ann Evans) to show how accomplished male writers formed part of the Establishment while their female counterparts did not.

the late Sir Ernest Wild [18]   Wild (1869–1934) was a lawyer and member of Parliament.

Piccadilly Circus [19]   A major intersection in the West End of London linking the fashionable shops of Regent Street to the Shaftesbury Avenue theaters and often used by Woolf and her contemporaries to signify the haunt of prostitutes.

the Siren [21]   In the *Odyssey,* Homer's epic poem, the singing of the Sirens entices sailors to attempt landing on the Sirens' island, causing them to shipwreck and drown.

through the shadow of the veil that St. Paul still lays upon our eyes [22–23]   Woolf alludes to Saint Paul's first letter to the Corinthians (chapter 11): "*5:* But every woman that prayeth or prophesieth with her head uncovered dishonoureth her head: for that is even all one as if she were shaven. *6:* For if the woman be not covered, let her also be shorn: but if it be a shame for a woman to be shorn or shaven, let her be covered. *7:* For a man indeed ought not to cover his head, forasmuch as he is the image and glory of God: but the woman is the glory of the man. *8:* For the man is not of the woman; but the woman of the man. *9:* Neither was the man created for the woman; but the woman for the man" (King James version).

Within quite a small space are crowded together St. Paul's . . . and the Houses of Parliament [23]   St. Paul's Cathedral traditionally has been associated with events and individuals of national importance. For example, the Duke of Wellington's funeral took place at St. Paul's in 1852. The Lord Mayor of London lives at Mansion House during his tenure. Most of Britain's monarchs were crowned at Westminster, which is also the burial site of many prominent British citizens. In any case, Woolf is pointing out the geographic proximity of England's political, ecclesiastical, and economic institutions in order to emphasize the connections between them as a monolithic force.

Your clothes in the first place make us gape with astonishment [23]   In "The Plumage Bill" (*The Woman's Leader,* July 23, 1920; *Essays* 3:

241–45), Woolf responded to commentary published in the *Nation* on July 10 concerning legislation that would have made it illegal to import the feathers of foreign birds. In the *Nation*, "Wayfarer" charged that women's obsession with style and appearance is to blame for the birds' suffering and death. Woolf replied that both the (male) hunters who capture the birds for their own financial benefit and the MPs who allowed the bill to fail are responsible for the cruelty.

Lord Chancellor [26]   Leader of the House of Lords.

we can refuse all such distinctions [27]   Woolf herself refused all honors and honorary degrees, including to be made a Companion of Honour, one of England's highest honors (*Diary* 4: 314).

Mary Astell [34]   Writer and philosopher (1668–1731). It was in *A Serious Proposal to the Ladies for the Advancement of Their True and Greatest Interest,* published in 1694, that Astell elaborated on her idea to establish a women's college (see note 21 in "Notes and References: One.")

Princess Anne [34]   Anne (1665–1714) was the daughter of King James II and the younger sister of Queen Mary (1662–1694). She acceded to the throne of England in 1702 after the death of her brother-in-law, William III (1650–1702).

Bishop Burnet [34]   Author (ca. 1635–1715) of *History of the Reformation of the Church of England* and *History of My Own Times.* He was appointed bishop of Salisbury in 1689.

Church of England [34]   The Anglican Church. After King Henry VIII (1491–1547) left the Roman Catholic Church in order to marry Anne Boleyn, he founded the Church of England and established himself as its nominal leader. This divide resulted in a schism between Catholics and Anglicans. Although Henry's eldest daughter by Catherine of Aragon, Mary I (reigned 1553–58), attempted to reinstate Roman Catholicism as England's official religion by having her opposition murdered (which earned her the epithet "Bloody Mary"), the reign of Elizabeth I (1558–1603), Henry's daughter by Anne Boleyn, was a prosperous period for England that reestablished the Anglican Church as the official Church of England.

Church of Rome [34]   The Roman Catholic Church.

colleges for the sisters of educated men both at Oxford and at Cambridge [35] As of 1938, the women's colleges at Oxford were Lady Margaret Hall, Somerville, St. Hugh's, and St. Hilda's. The women's colleges at Cambridge were Girton and Newnham. Girton was founded in 1869; Newnham and the Oxford colleges were all founded between 1871 and 1893.

There is Gray's Ode *to prove it* [36]   Thomas Gray (1716–1771), English poet best known for "Elegy Written in a Country Churchyard." The ode to which Woolf refers is "Ode for Music" (see note 22 in "Notes and References: One").

and Anon. must receive whatever thanks Anon. will consent to receive [37] Anonymous. Woolf refers to the lack of acknowledgment given to donors of modest sums compared with the credit that is usually accorded to those who donate lavish amounts. In *A Room of One's Own,* Woolf "[ventures] to guess that Anon, who wrote so many poems without signing them, was often a woman."

Master of Trinity, Sir J. J. Thomson, O.M., F.R.S. [37]   Trinity College is one of the colleges of Cambridge University. As Master of Trinity between 1918 and 1940, Joseph John Thomson oversaw the college's affairs. "O.M." is the abbreviation for "Old Master," signaling Thomson's status as a Trinity alumnus. "F.R.S." stands for "Fellow of the Royal Society," an organization of prominent scientists founded in 1660. Thomson won the 1906 Nobel Prize in Physics.

Bryant & May's matches [42]   Alludes to the Match Girls' Strike, a classic incident in the history of women and labor in England. On June 23, 1888, an article appeared in the *Link* detailing the abominable working conditions of the employees at Bryant & May. The article, written by the social reformer Annie Besant (1847–1933), was based on interviews she solicited with some of the match girls. After the management of Bryant & May tried to force the girls to refute what Besant had said and one of the workers was fired for her alleged role in facilitating the interviews, close to two hundred match girls went on strike by fleeing to the offices of the *Link*. Shortly after, approximately fourteen hundred other match girls joined the initial two hundred. The strike occurred on July 5, 1888. By July 16, pressured by negative reports in the press, Bryant & May reached a settlement with representatives of the London Trades Council and the Match Girls Strike Committee that ensured better working conditions for the match girls.

Dean of Durham [45]   The dean is the cathedral's highest-ranking cleric after the bishop.

English tripos [46]   Final exams at Cambridge University. "Tripos," from the Greek prefix for "three," refers to the three-year curriculum leading up to the bachelor's degree.

an allowance of from £40 to £100 a year [47]   In the second part of *Three Guineas,* the writer states that the current average salary of the professional Englishwoman was £250 a year. In *A Room of One's Own,* Woolf asserts that women must have £500 a year if they are to "have the habit of freedom and the courage to write exactly what [they] think."

M.P.s [47]   Members of Parliament.

"our splendid Empire" [49]   That is to say, England. During the nineteenth century, England was the most dominant nation in

the world, an imperialist power that spanned five continents. By the 1930s, England's authority had begun to wane, as some of its various colonies gained independence.

that amazing outburst in August 1914 [49]   Outbreak of the First World War. Although the war technically began when Austria-Hungary went to war with Serbia on July 28, 1914, most of the countries involved entered the struggle during the first few days of August. England proclaimed itself at war with Germany after the latter sent troops into Belgium, a neutral country, on the fourth of August. Eight days later, England announced that it was also at war with Austria-Hungary. Virginia Woolf was also a pacifist during this war, but then there was a strong peace movement in England, as well as many friends in her Bloomsbury circle who opposed the war and refused military service. Her pacifist convictions were formed under the influence of her Quaker aunt, Caroline Emelia Stephen, as well as by the work of the great classics scholar Jane Ellen Harrison ("the great J- H-" of *A Room of One's Own*).

letter from another honorary treasurer [51]   The National Society for Women's Service. Woolf's speech to the London branch of this organization, "Professions for Women," is a brilliant discussion of the complicated realities of women in the professions between the wars. Various drafts of the speech are reprinted in *The Pargiters*.

C. E. M. Joad [52]   A philosopher and journalist (1891–1953) who in 1934 had published two articles in the *New Statesman and Nation* on the decline of the Bloomsbury Group as a cultural force. Woolf quotes here from his 1937 *Testament of Joad* (see also her note 4 to part 2).

W.S.P.U. [53]   The Women's Social and Political Union, a militant suffrage organization led by Emmeline Pankhurst, and later by her daughter Christabel.

H. G. Wells [54]   Herbert George Wells (1866–1946), novelist and
popularizer of science and history, four of whose works were
published by the Hogarth Press. In her diary, Woolf records that
reading Wells's views on women had set her mind running on
"A Knock at the Door," one of her early titles for *Three Guineas*
(*Diary* 4: 75).

'the woman's movement' has proved itself a failure [54]   According to
Wells and Joad. So the guinea she is sending to the NSWS "is to
be devoted not to paying your rent but burning your building."
This startlingly violent remark, along with the burning of the
word *feminism* because it has presumably outlived its usefulness,
puts us forcefully back in the thirties, when Hitler and Mussolini
were banning and burning books and issuing commands for
women to go "retire once more to the kitchen."

Society for the Abolition of Slavery [55]   The Society for the Abolition
of the Slave Trade was first formed in 1787 by Granville Sharp
and Thomas Clarkson. A new Anti-Slavery Society was formed
in 1823, among whose members were Clarkson and William
Wilberforce. Woolf's grandfather, Sir James Stephen, got the
Anti-Slavery bill through Parliament; it was framed by his father,
James Stephen.

How much peace will £42,000 a year buy [56]   Woolf attributes this figure to the Women's Social and Political Union (WSPU), but it
was actually collected by the National Union of Women's Suffrage Societies, representing a larger proportion of women and
so is even less impressive than it seems.

Cleopatra's needle [56]   London landmark obelisk, imperialist booty
from Egypt and phallic in shape. Two digs in one phrase.

Whitaker's Almanack [56]   Joseph Whitaker (1820–1895) published a
yearly almanac, a common reference book used throughout the

chapter as a foil for "facts" and utterly discredited by the time she is through with it. A copy was buried under the obelisk in 1878.

Dominions Office [56]   A branch of the British government that in 1938 was concerned with the affairs of Australia, Canada, New Zealand, South Africa, and other territories.

Friendly Societies [56]   Similar to credit unions, these societies were formalized by an act of Parliament in 1875.

open to both men and women equally [57]   Note the careful listing of civil service jobs women may hold, how low the salaries are, and how few Englishwomen work in the professions. See Michèle Barrett's introduction to her edition (*A Room of One's Own* and *Three Guineas* [Harmondsworth: Penguin, 1993]) to see how little the situation has improved.

Whitehall [58]   Used as a metonym for government because it names the area where the Houses of Parliament stand.

Mr. Baldwin [59]   Stanley Baldwin was prime minister from 1923 to 1929 and again from 1935 to 1937. He appears in the photograph of a graduation ceremony at Cambridge University ("A University Procession").

Brooks', White's, the Travellers', the Reform, the Athenaeum [68]   Exclusive private clubs in London for men only.

Here we go round . . . [72]   See the introduction, page xlvi.

Close at hand is a bridge [73]   See Christine Froula, "St. Virginia's Epistle," for a discussion of this famous passage.

Charing Cross [74]   A district in central London where there is a major railway station.

stirred the pot, while they rocked the cradle [77]   See Q. D. Leavis's review in *Scrutiny,* which accuses Virginia Woolf *ad feminam* of not knowing which end of the cradle to stir because she had no children.

Cenotaph [77]   Tomb of the Unknown Soldier in London, designed by Sir Edwin Lutyens and erected in 1920 to replace a temporary structure that had proved very popular with the public during peace celebrations in 1919.

Harley Street [77]   Traditional business address of many of London's most prominent medical practitioners.

Royal Academy [77–78]   The Royal Academy of Arts is England's oldest art school, founded in 1768.

Sophia Jex-Blake [78]   The first officially licensed female physician in Great Britain, Jex-Blake (1840–1912) was a key lobbyist for women's entry into medical school. Besides running her own practice, she established two medical schools for women and a hospital.

Doctors' Commons [78]   A society of ecclesiastical lawyers.

Tom [79]   Thomas William Jex-Blake (1832–1915) was the older brother of Sophia Jex-Blake. He was a secondary school educator and led the exclusive Rugby School for thirteen years, until 1887.

Pierpont Morgan [82]   John Pierpont Morgan (1837–1913), a wealthy American banker and art collector whom Woolf's close friend Roger Fry periodically advised on purchases.

Rockefeller [82]   John D. Rockefeller (1839–1937), an American capitalist who founded Standard Oil.

Christ's words about the rich [84]   Matthew 19:23–24.

Dean Alington [86]   Headmaster of Eton, and later dean of Durham Cathedral (1872–1955).

Dean Inge [86]   The Very Reverend William Ralph Inge was dean of St. Paul's Cathedral from 1911 to 1934 and published many gloomy philosophical works.

Deceased Wife's Sister Bill [87]   This 1835 act of Parliament banning marriage of a widower to his deceased wife's sister was repealed in 1907 after much debate.

Bishop Gore [87]   Charles Gore (1853–1932) was successively bishop of Worcester, Birmingham, and Oxford.

Mors Janua Vitae [90]   Latin, "death is the gate of life."

F.R.S., F.C.S. [91]   Fellow of the Royal Society, Fellow of the College of Surgeons.

Anne Clough [92]   Anne Jemima Clough (1820–1892) was a pioneer in the education of women and presided over the house that became Newnham College, Cambridge, in 1874.

Oriel [92]   A college of Oxford University.

Josephine Butler [92]   Butler (1828–1906) was a friend of Anne Clough's and a leader in the movement for educational reform for women. She also campaigned against the regulation of prostitutes by the Contagious Diseases Acts, which allowed the police to arrest prostitutes and force them to undergo tests for venereal disease.

Gertrude Bell [93]   Bell (1868–1926) was director of antiquities in Baghdad and writer of many books on Persia (Iran).

Bourget's The Disciple [93]   Paul Bourget (1852–1935) published his novel *The Disciple* in 1889.

Florence Nightingale [94]   Nightingale (1820–1910) was famous for her reform of army hospitals during the Crimean War and subject of Lytton Strachey's sharp portrait in *Eminent Victorians* (1918).

Emily Brontë [96]   English poet and novelist (1818–1848) who wrote *Wuthering Heights.*

Christina Rossetti [96]   Author (1830–1894) of *Goblin Market and Other Poems,* and the subject of Woolf's essay "'I Am Christina Rossetti.'"

Creon [98]   The king of Thebes and uncle to Antigone and Ismene in Sophocles's *Antigone.* He sentences Antigone to death for her disobedience.

Antigone [98]   The title character of the last play in Sophocles' trilogy. In the play, Antigone defies Creon's edict prohibiting the burial of Antigone's brother Polynices, who has been deemed a traitor. Creon's law, however, not only rebels against the gods' mandate that no individual should remain unburied after his death but also deprives Antigone of her right as a female relative of the deceased to mourn her brother with proper ceremony.

arrange the hare and the coffee-pot [101]   The speaker is referring to the only way women of her class have had to raise money for their causes—holding a bazaar. The suffragettes were famous for their bazaars. This enforces the notion of women's relative poverty no matter what their class and their habit of giving money to their husbands' colleges, a situation that remains true to this day in the United States. This section of the book may well have been a draft for her "Professions for Women" speech, since that is its subject, and the text is full of asides and jokes suggesting it was meant to be read aloud. This part of the book also works rhetorically very hard to draw in the "you" as a woman reader or listener.

manifesto [102]   A *manifesto* is an open expression of one's tenets, goals, and plans, particularly with respect to politics but also a form used for declarations of artistic intent. Readers in the late 1930s would invariably have connected the word with Karl

Marx, whose *Communist Manifesto* (1848) championed the rights of the working classes and encouraged the proletariat to overthrow the bourgeoisie.

"protect culture and intellectual liberty" [102]   See David Bradshaw, "British Writers," for an account of the organization For Intellectual Liberty, whose meetings Woolf attended.

Duke of Devonshire [102]   Victor Christian William Cavendish, the ninth Duke of Devonshire (1868–1938). In 1891 he became a member of the House of Commons; nine years later he became treasurer of household. In 1909 he became the vice president of the Navy League, and in 1916 he became the governor-general of Canada. At the time of his death in 1938, he was still high steward of Cambridge University and chancellor of Leeds University.

Pindar [103]   Ancient Greek poet (c. 522–438 B.C.), best known for his odes.

1262 [103]   Naomi Black suggests Woolf may here have inverted the date 1226, the "year when the first clear record of the university lists a 'chancellor' at its head" (Black, *Three Guineas* 202).

1870 [103]   See the note to *colleges* [35]. Girton College of the University of Cambridge was founded in 1869.

sixpence [104]   Sixpence was equal to 1/42 of a guinea. See the introduction, page xlvi–xlvii.

Seule la culture désintéressée peut garder le monde de sa ruine [105]   "Only a disinterested culture is able to guard the world from its ruin." In the third volume of her 1930s scrapbooks, Woolf pasted this headline beside a report from the International Peace Campaign.

Grub Street [107]   As listed in Samuel Johnson's 1755 *Dictionary of the English Language,* the address of many would-be poets, historians, and reference writers. Although the road became Milton Street in the early decades of the nineteenth century, "Grub Street" is still used as a connotation for London's community of struggling writers.

Lord Chancellor [107]   See the note to page 26.

George Eliot or George Sand [108]   As noted on page 18, George Eliot (1819–1880) is the pen name of Mary Ann Evans, a nineteenth-century British novelist whose works explore the economic and social domination of men over women. Her best works include *The Mill on the Floss* (1860) and *Middlemarch* (1872). George Sand (1804–1876) is the pen name of Baroness Aurore Dudevant, a nineteenth-century French novelist. Her earlier works, like Eliot's, interrogate contemporary roles proscribed for men and women, while her later novels, such as *La petite Fadette* (1848), depict the lives of rural workers. Woolf's casual reference to these two writers underscores the irony of her allusion: She implies that these are generic names, but in fact they are the pseudonyms of two of the most prominent writers of the nineteenth century.

Milton [108]   John Milton (1608–1674) is one of the major figures in British literature, and the most prominent writer in seventeenth-century England. He is best known for his epic poem *Paradise Lost* (1674), a retelling of the fall of Adam and Eve. The poem contains multiple allusions to classical and medieval Western literature, including the *Iliad* and the *Inferno*. Woolf describes the Christian god as "Milton's bogey" in *A Room of One's Own*.

Goethe [108]   Johann Wolfgang von Goethe (1749–1832) was a German Romantic writer. Like *Paradise Lost,* Goethe's most notable work, *Faust* (1808/1832), is a rendering of an older narrative.

Matthew Arnold [108]   English poet and literary critic (1822–1888). His critical volumes focus on major works of Western literature.

Mrs. Oliphant [109]   Margaret Oliphant Oliphant [*sic*] (1828–1897) described in her 1899 *Autobiography* how her voluminous writings were intended to support her own and her brother's children.

Sheridan [109]   See the note to page 18.

Cervantes [109]   Miguel de Cervantes Saavedra (1547–1616) was a Spanish Renaissance writer. He is chiefly known as the author of *Don Quixote* (1605–15).

Macaulay [111]   See the note to page 18.

Ben Jonson [117]   English playwright, poet, and actor (1572–1637).

Mermaid [117]   The London tavern frequented by Jonson and Shakespeare.

Keats [118]   John Keats (1795–1821), English poet.

Josephine Butler [121]   See the note to page 92.

Westminster [122]   Area associated with the government of England; location of Westminster Abbey, where monarchs are crowned and poets are buried.

Downing Street [122]   Where Britain's prime ministers and chancellors of the exchequer reside during their respective tenures in office.

Anne Clough and *Arthur Clough* [123–24]   See the note to page 92. See also note 1 in "Notes and References: One."

William Wordsworth [124]   English Romantic poet (1770–1850). He and his sister, Dorothy (1771–1855), were devoted to each other.

Bath [132]   An English city known for its spas and retirement community.

Cheltenham [132]   An English town known for its spas and retirement community.

Oxford Street [134]   A major commercial thoroughfare in London.

Bishop Gore [140]   See the note to page 87.

Lord Mayor [141]   Elected head of the Corporation of London, which governs the City of London. The Lord Mayor is the highest-ranking individual in London except for Great Britain's reigning monarch.

Mr. Wells [141]   See the note to page 54.

veil of St. Paul [142]   See the explanation on page 145. See also the note to pages 22–23 and note 38 in "Notes and References: Two."

Lydia [145]   "One of them named Lydia, a dealer in purple fabric from the city of Thyatira, who was a worshipper of God, was listening, and the Lord opened her heart to respond to what Paul said. She was baptized, and her household with her, and then she said to us, 'If you have judged me to be a believer in the Lord, I beg you to come and stay in my house.' And she insisted on our going" (Acts 16:14–15). Quoted from *The New English Bible,* Oxford and Cambridge University Presses, 1970.

Chloe [145]   "I have been told, my brothers, by Chloe's people that there are quarrels among you" (1 Corinthians 1:11). Quoted from *The New English Bible,* Oxford and Cambridge University Presses, 1970.

Euodia and Syntyche [145]   "I beg Euodia, and I beg Syntyche, to agree together in the Lord's fellowship. Yes, and you, too, my loyal comrade, I ask you to help these women, who shared my struggles in the cause of the Gospel, with Clement and my other fellow-workers, whose names are in the roll of the living" (Philippians 4:2–3). Quoted from *The New English Bible,* Oxford and Cambridge University Presses, 1970.

Tryphaena and Tryphosa and Persis [145]   "Greet Tryphaena and

Tryphosa, who toil in the Lord's service, and dear Persis who has toiled in his service so long" (Romans 16:12). Quoted from *The New English Bible,* Oxford and Cambridge University Presses, 1970.

pre-Nicene . . . post-Nicene [146]   Before and after the creation of the Nicene Creed (A.D. 325), which outlines the principles of Christianity.

Emily Brontë [147]   See the note to page 96.

salary of a deaconess is £150 [147]   See the note to *an allowance,* page 47.

Oedipus complex [150]   In psychoanalysis, a boy's purported desire to replace his father as his mother's love object.

castration complex [150]   In Freudian psychoanalysis, obsessive anxiety concerning castration.

man manque [150]   Individual who is disappointed or thwarted with respect to the achievement of his goals or potential (correctly *manqué*).

infantile fixation [151]   No specific definition. However, the psychoanalytic definition of a "fixation" is a focus on an improper object of desire stemming from the libido's failure to move beyond the anal or oral phases. What Woolf calls "infantile fixation" is perhaps well enough defined in the ensuing pages.

Crosby [153]   Crosby is the name of the Pargiter family's servant in Woolf's novel *The Years.*

Antigone [154]   See the note to page 98.

Ismene [154]   Antigone's sister. She chooses not to disobey Creon's edict.

Creon [154]   See the note to page 98.

Mr. Barrett of Wimpole Street [155]   Father of Elizabeth Barrett (1806–1861), English poet who eloped with another English poet, Robert Browning (1812–1889), and whose story is told through the eyes of her dog in Woolf's 1933 novel *Flush*.

Charlotte Brontë [155]   English novelist (1816–1855) and older sister of Emily Brontë. See also the note to page 18.

Sophia Jex-Blake [156]   See the note to page 78.

Tom [156]   See the note to page 79.

Maurice [159]   Professor Frederick Denison Maurice (1805–1872) taught English and history at King's College, London. He founded Queens College, London (see the note on Queens College, below).

Elysium [159]   In Greek mythology, the equivalent of the Christian heaven.

Queen's College [159]   Founded in 1848, Queen's College, London, was the first women's college in Great Britain. The writer Katherine Mansfield entered in 1903.

Harley Street [159]   See the note to page 77.

Mrs. Gaskell [159]   Elizabeth Gaskell (1810–1865), nineteenth-century novelist and biographer whose *Life of Charlotte Brontë* was published in 1857.

Bond Street [163]   Many of London's luxury retailers have franchises on Bond Street.

Gertrude Bell [164]   See the note to page 93. See also note 37 in "Notes and References: Two." She was the creator of what became the state of Iraq, and was opposed to women's suffrage in Britain.

Bertrand Russell [165]   Brilliant English mathematician and philosopher (1872–1970) who published in the fields of philosophy, political science, and mathematics. A strong and outspoken pacifist and socialist.

Holloway [167]   A London prison that since 1902 has incarcerated female prisoners only. Emmeline Pankhurst (1858–1928) was repeatedly imprisoned there for her role in advocating women's voting rights. The suffragettes were not allowed the rights of political prisoners and adopted that well-known strategy of the weak, the hunger strike. They were "forcibly fed" by government order to prevent their deaths and subsequent martyrdom.

circle gules [194]   In heraldry, *gules* refers to the color red.

Renan [198]   Ernest Renan (1823–1892) was a French historian whose *Origines du christianisme* ("Origins of Christianity") Woolf consulted while writing *Three Guineas*.

Est-il cependant . . . [198]   "However, is it absolutely impossible that Paul contracted a more intimate relationship with this sister? One could not affirm it."

Jebb [201]   The quotation is from Sir Richard Jebb's translation of *Antigone* (Cambridge University Press, 1888). Black points out that Woolf has placed diacritical marks inaccurately.

Toutes les existences . . . [222]   "All beings are interdependent, and any human being who was to present his own in isolation without attaching it to that of his fellows would only present an enigma to be unraveled. . . . Individuality has no significance or importance whatsoever on its own. It only takes on a meaning by becoming a fragment of life in general, by combining with the individuality of each one of my fellow beings, and it is thus that it becomes part of history."

Appendix: Excerpts from the *Three Guineas* Scrapbooks

From early 1931 until the end of 1937, Woolf pasted into three bound notebooks various materials—press clippings, letters of appeal, photographs, articles—that became important sources for her arguments in *Three Guineas*. In the examples given here, we can see both how Woolf drew directly on reports in the daily paper and also how she herself was that "methodical person" she hoped in *Three Guineas* had "made a collection of the various manifestoes and questionnaires issued broadcast during the years 1936–7" (see note 1 to part 3, page 203). Also included here are the tables of contents from each scrapbook, typed by Woolf herself.

INDEX
&&&&&&&&&&&&&&&&&

1... Times on virtues of Tattoo
1... Womes dislike of same dress
1...Oxford clinging to revenues.
1... College amenities
2... Thackeray On being Found out.
3... Maternity death rate. amenities for nurses
3...The lie detector
3... Blue uniform for soldiers
4... Postemen want smarter clothes.
4... Do wo en want babies to be soldiers? Birth cont.
5...Service at St auls.
6... umber of careers ; arctic inspector.
6... Lady aldwin and pain of childbirth. Andgxx
        analgesics almost unknown in 1929
7...Mr B's last speech
8...Lady Simons snub.
8... Pratt wont be taxgxx x tested driving by women.
9... Almeria Havoc.
10...   ditto
11...W's love of econmix dependence
11...Magdalen fellows attitude to w. in college
11...George Sand on Community
11... Deaths in Childbirth 1937
12... Income of the Socialist party
12...Three womens church colleges closed for lack of funds
13... Middlesex hospital; refuses legacy to found w. scholars
13... Oysters, taste of women growing for.
14... Pippa on conspiracy of silence. Pensions bill.
15... death rate of men and women. metabolism.
16... Task of Churches.
17...vicar resigns because the congre; wont turn to the east
17...why wom. wont have childiren. War.
18... perfumers on woms. nail varnishing.
19... Outsiders ex s. Miss larke on no cups.
20... The martyrdom of Madrid
21... Cleaning five miles of floor. Avergae working w
22 Poor porspects for women vets
23...Pensions bill. Pippas circular
24...Seule la culture desinterress
24... Internat. Peace campaign leaflet
25...Newnhams ball. Sept. 1937. Funds for coll.
26... Ws cricket. No games against men.
26... Labour party on arms. Dalton. Oct. 1937
27...W. MPs have missed their chance. March 1936
28... Soviet w. beat men as air pilots
29...the six point group
30...G. women in prison as hostages for husbands
31... Medical profs. Letters in NS
31.. Mrs Booth on women; Rita on women and chivalry
32... Religion . the great bloodshedd r. White Devil
35. Arch. Jandon & the Play   147
33...Preservin relics. Lenins body.
34...Work of the Nat. Council for Eqaul Citi
36...Comment on Antony. Educating Arthur
37..Beever on me.
38. Hatred of w. 1935 lectures by men.
39 Mrs Drummond on Sufragettes
40   ditto

...penal clause...
...Ordinance have not been enforced.
Henceforward every white man in
Kenya between the ages of eighteen
and fifty who fails to turn out for
service will presumably pay for his
protest by fine or imprisonment—
unless, indeed, the Crown sees fit to
revoke an Ordinance that should
never have been signed.

"MACHINES PREFER GIRLS"

MORE ACCURATE THAN MEN

The New Accountancy

Sir Herbert Austin, speaking at a
luncheon at the Waldorf Hotel, London,
yesterday in connection with an exhibition of British accounting and tabulating
machines, said that it was an interesting
human point in connection with those
highly intelligent machines that they
revealed girls to be much better
operators than men.

"In the new accountancy women have
a capacity for concentration which makes
them far more accurate than men," he
said. "It may be that here we have a
hint of a growing division of labour, in
which men will more and more be
employed making machines, while women
are engaged to work them. Men may be
satisfied with their own superiority, but
the machines are not. They prefer girls.
I do not know whether they prefer
blondes, but, at any rate, they are worked
better by girls.

"I do not favour female labour in the
factory," added Sir Herbert. "Prior to
the war there were very few women
engaged in our factories, but now they
dispute the positions with men, and
certainly we do find that they are more
satisfactory than youths. They are more
attentive to their work when it is of a
monotonous character, as very often it
must be in a factory. The one disadvantage of female labour is that under
the Factory Acts they are not allowed
to work on night shifts."

DAMAGES FOR TOBACCO BLINDNESS

Judge Who Smokes Twist

Mr. Justice Charles, at the Liverpool
...s on Wednesday asserted that he
...smoked twist tobacco. The st...
...made during the hear...

---

want...se...
pundits of the tow...
This year a large
will be on view, and...
for the plan is the pl...
a judge of our chief cr...
and producers by prod...
suffered as much as a...
carry-ons. On Tuesd...
Guedalla will prosecu...
troublesome critics,...
Geral... Gould, Priest...
Hum... ...and...
Miss...
boo...
dru...
aft...

...w...
Q...
Herbe...
and Sir Nigel P...
Wild will judge...
Mr. G. K. Ches...
head masters...
Taylors', Le...
College S...
liberty of th...
to whom
entertainm...
judge.

Irish S...

Mr....
prose...
story...
Bentl...
evide...
judge...
will p...
ing N...
will...
Coop...
Lor...
dom...
The...
Mr....
again...
humou...
Hasse...
Watts...
cost f...
from 1½...
be boo...
Fund O...
at Messr...
Roy's age...
Those...

T...

30

EQUALITY OF THE SEXES ONLY A MYTH

Wives The Law's Favourites

By His Honour JUDGE McCLEARY

THE physical differences between a man and a woman and the essential variance in their objects and ambitions in life render it impossible to compare the one with the other without qualifications.

A man, whether married or single, in the front which he presents to the outside world is the same man. A woman, when single, may elect to fight the battle of life, and she may justifiably claim equal rights with those possessed by a member of the other sex.

If a married woman she is in a somewhat anomalous position. She may elect pursue her career, if she has one, just through she had not married; or she may prefer to re-ard marriage as her career.

The man is always he fighting animal, ghting to maintain himself, or himself and his wife, or himself and his wife and children.

The woman, if single, may be fighting to maintain herself. If married, she may be fighting to maintain herself, with or without the help of her husband, or she may be relying upon her husband to fight for her. If she is a mother she may have abandoned the fight of life and devoted herself to the care of her husband and children. In balancing the equality of the sexes it is impossible to weigh them in the same scales.

How, therefore, can the rights of a woman in her various capacities be compared with those of a man? As a woman she now suffers from little, if any, legal disadvantage.

The Sex Disqualification (Removal) Act, 1919, purported to remove her disadvantages. By virtue of its provisions she is no longer disqualified by sex or marriage from the exercise of any public function, or from following any vocation or calling.

HUSBAND'S LIABILITY

As a married woman she is not deprived of any of her legal rights so far as the outside world is concerned. She may still pursue her career in life, if she should think fit so to do, with the same freedom she enjoyed before her marriage.

If she is an employed person her employer may object to employ her on the ground that she is a married woman, just as he may object to employ a one-eyed man. He may consider that her earning capacity is not equal to that of a man, but these are not considerations which have reference to her rights.

When a woman marries she adds materially to her rights. Her husband, on the other hand, materially increases his obligations. Whatever may be said of the rights and obligations of a single woman compared with those of a single man, the position of a married woman is immeasurably superior to that of a married man.

In law she has forfeited little, if any, of her freedom. Her husband in law has little, if any, control over her. And yet his obligations to her and his responsibilities for her are enormous.

He is bound to maintain her according to his estate or condition in life. Even if she leaves him he may in certain circumstances be compelled to contribute to her support. She has no duty to support him even if the necessity should arise and she is well able to do so.

It is true that if he becomes chargeable to a poor law authority and she has means the magistrates may make a maintenance order against her separate property, but unless he throws himself on the parish, as it were, she is under no obligation.

A wife has an implied authority to pledge her husband's credit for necessaries suitable to his station in life. It is a right which is freely exercised, and, as may be well imagined, few husbands will dispute their obligations in this respect, though their wives may have grossly exceeded their authority.

A husband may be sued jointly with his wife in an action for damages for any wrong committed by her. If she inflicts injury upon a third party he may be made liable for any damages, though he knew nothing of the wrong which she committed and strongly disapproved of her conduct in that respect. And he has no right of indemnity against her for separate property, if she has any, in respect of those damages and the costs that may be incurred.

OBLIGATIONS

It is a wife's duty to live with her husband. If she refuses his only remedy is to petition for restitution of conjugal rights. He is not entitled to restrain her by force or to keep her in confinement. He may obtain a decree in his favour, but poor will be his consolation if this has to happen.

It is a fundamental principle in jurisprudence that equal rights connote equal obligations. On a consideration of the rights which women now possess, as compared with those of a man, someone may, perhaps, be heard to say that they are not called upon in life to shoulder equal obligations.

Perhaps it is right that their obligations should not be as great as those of a man. Possibly "equality of the sexes" is but a myth and can never, the conditions of life being what they are, become a reality.

We have to face the hard facts.

> In his first article in "The Daily Telegraph" Mr. H. G. Wells discussed the achievements of woman since her recent "emancipation."
>
> In the light of this, Judge McCleary here surveys her legal rights—rights which, he insists, since her in an immeasurably more favourable position than her husband or her unmarried sister.
>
> Mr. Wells's fourth article—it is concerned with the obsession for sport—will be published to-morrow.

A Leid to South Africa.
Remitted Peerage

19th February 1936.

Dear Mrs Woolf,

The Prime Minister, who is also Chancellor of the
University of Cambridge, has most kindly consented to
arrange for a Meeting concerned with the needs of
Newnham College to be held under his Chairmanship at
10, Downing Street on March 31st.

Newnham College, founded 1871, is one of the first
women's Colleges to be established and has from the
beginning played an important part in preparing women to
make their best contribution to the life of the community.

The College is to-day faced with the need of raising
funds to reconstruct out-of-date buildings and to provide
additional accommodation, and it is estimated that
£100,000 is required for building and provision for
upkeep. This heavy capital expenditure naturally cannot
be met out of income and for the first time since it
began the College is appealing to the public for support.

It is desired to form a Committee of Patrons to
launch the Appeal at the Meeting on March 31st and it
would be very greatly appreciated if you would consent to
become a Patron.

Former students of the College have already set on
foot a vigorous and promising effort and to them your
support would give much encouragement.

Yours sincerely,

J.P. Strachey

P.S. Would you very kindly reply to me at 11, Little
College Street, Westminster, S.W.1.

"THE THORN OF HATRED"

OUTSPOKEN ESSEN WOMAN ARRESTED

FROM OUR OWN CORRESPONDENT

BERLIN, AUG. 11

Frau Pommer, the wife of a Prussian mines official at Essen, has been arrested and is to be tried on a charge of insulting and slandering the State and the Nazi movement.

Frau Pommer told the girl behind the counter of a confectioner's shop that if her favourite brand of chocolate was not in stock she would have to go to another shop which she mentioned. The girl replied, with some pertness, it may be imagined, that the other shop was "pure Jewish." Frau Pommer is then alleged to have said:—

I and my husband are and remain German Nationalists; but as long as one does not cohabit with a Jew one can safely buy from him. The thorn of hatred has been driven deep enough into the people by the religious conflicts and it is high time that the men of to-day disappeared.

"A NATION OF MEN"

THE FÜHRER'S BOAST

SPEECH TO NAZI OLD GUARD

FROM OUR OWN CORRESPONDENT

BERLIN, AUG. 11

Herr Hitler made an unexpected appearance and speech to-day at the celebration of the fifteenth anniversary of the Rosenheim branch of the National-Socialist Party, the second oldest in Germany. Addressing the assembled "old guard," Herr Hitler recalled his first speech in the town 15 years ago—15 years "filled with a wonderful struggle, such as had never before been waged for the heart and the soul of the German nation." In apparent reference to opponents at home, Herr Hitler said:—

In battle we have won the German Reich, and in battle we shall maintain and guard it. Those who are against us need not deceive themselves. We have never shrunk from the combat. If they want it they can have it. We shall crush them in such a way that they will abandon for the next 14 years all idea of continuing the struggle.

Recalling "the heavy trials of the movement in the last 15 years," Herr Hitler said:—

If fate is to put it to the test again, we should be really hardened by the hammer-blows of Providence. The years since 1918 have taught us: "Woe to the people which is unprepared to take its liberty and independence under its own protection." Nobody will deny that in the last two and a half years Germany has attained a different position in the world. I am convinced that nobody in the world can attack our Reich again. We want peace and reconstruction, but just as we want peace so the other nations ought to want peace. He who wishes to disturb our peace will no longer fight against a nation of pacifists but against a nation of men. This fact alone will contribute more to peace than all the speeches.

HEROIC

Count Ciano in flying kit.

IPC INTERNATIONAL PEACE CAMPAIGN
27, CHESTER TERRACE, EATON SQUARE, LONDON, S.W.1
TELEGRAMS: ADINGSTONE LONDON. TELEPHONE: SLOANE 2300

Joint Presidents
THE VISCOUNT CECIL
PIERRE COT

International Secretary
MISS ROSA MANUS

Vice-Chairman
British Committee
DAME ADELAIDE LIVINGSTONE

S.A./43/

29

August 12th, 1936.

Dear Madam,

    You have perhaps already heard of the International Peace Campaign which is an International movement to co-ordinate the work of the Peace Societies and other Organisations in support of the League of Nations, and is under the joint Presidency of Viscount Cecil and Monsieur Pierre Cot, French Minister for Air.

    This movement has arisen as the result of the success of the Peace Ballot in this country, and has gained great support in Continental countries and in America.   We feel that Britain should not lag behind in the work, and already considerable interest has been aroused in this country, and good progress is being made.

    I write, however, to ask for your assistance in the hope that you will be able to quicken our progress.   We desire to publish manifestos in support of the International Peace Campaign signed by writers, scientists, religious leaders, and others, and with this letter I am enclosing a copy of such a manifesto, which it is suggested writers might sign in this connection.   I should be most grateful if you would sign it and return it to me for publication purposes, or if you prefer to send an individual message, that too would be of the greatest help.   I am enclosing the third issue of our weekly News Bulletin.

            Yours faithfully,

            Adelaide Livingstone

            (Dame Adelaide Livingstone)
            Vice-Chairman, British National Committee.

NEB/MB.

GIRLS' FOOTBALL
IS JUST *TOO* POPULAR

FROM OUR OWN CORRESPONDENT
WELLINGBOROUGH, Northants, Friday.

OFFICIAL football circles here regard with anxiety the growing popularity of girls' football.

A secret meeting of the Northants Football Association's consultative committee was held here last night to discuss the playing of a girls' match on the Peterborough ground.

Members of the committee are reticent about what happened at the meeting, which was attended by officials of the Peterborough United club. The findings have been reported to the Football Association.

One member, however, said to-day, "The Northants Football Association is to forbid women's football.

"This popularity of girls' football comes when many men's clubs in the county are in a parlous state through lack of support. Another serious aspect is the possibility of grave injury to women players."

During the past few months numerous girls' teams have been formed in Northamptonshire to play matches for charity.

They attract large crowds. At two matches in the Wellingborough area this week men predominated in crowds numbering several thousands.

Earls Barton, Irthlingborough, Bozeat, Woollaston, and Higham Ferrers also possess teams.

ALLOTMENTS GUARDED

ALL-NIGHT WATCH
FOR RAIDERS

Police and allotment-holders at Tottenham are keeping all-night watch on allotments, several of which have been raided recently.

From an allotment at Devonshire Hill whole crop of beetroots was removed one night. Wheel marks in the that a cart had been

If We Had Been Pacifists In 1914—

"HITLER WOULD BE IN WHITEHALL"

Good Samaritan Might Have Laid About Him

THE Church Assembly, meeting in London to-day, passed a resolution deploring general world rearmament, welcoming the declared policy of the Government to adhere to the Covenant of the League, and stating:

"This assembly recognises the right of the Government to maintain such force as the Imperial Parliament deem necessary for the pursuance of this policy, and believes that so long as this policy is maintaining Christian citizens may bear arms in the service of their country."

It was also decided by a large majority to adopt the following addendum put forward by the Bishop of Southwark (Dr. R. G. Parsons):

"The Assembly affirms the responsibility of Christian people to support, criticise, or oppose all defence programmes in the light of Christian principles and in relation to their advancement of the Kingdom of God."

During the debate the Bishop of London (Dr. Winnington-Ingram) said:

"The real dangers to the peace of the world to-day are the pacifists.

"There is no great danger of war if we are strong enough policemen with a trun-

The Bishop of London

The Archbishop of York

cheon to keep order, but the policeman must have his truncheon—otherwise he is no good.

"If we had taken the view of the pacifists in 1914, either the German Emperor or Hitler would now be in Whitehall.

"The German plan was first to swallow France and then go on to Great Britain. This little island in the silver sea would be a German province.

"Coming to later times, I should have thought that Abyssinia would have cured every pacifist in the world.

"If we have no force at our disposal the dictators of the world will triumph over the democracies of the world."

Bombs on Children

Dr. Winnington-Ingram referred to the speech made yesterday by the Bishop of Birmingham (Dr. Barnes).

[Dr. Barnes described himself as an "extreme pacifist," and said: "I cannot see myself that war can be regarded as consonant with the spirit of Christ."]

"I hate opposing the Bishop of Birmingham," Dr. Winnington-Ingram said, "because I have a great affection and admiration for him.

"I would rather die than see bombs dropping on the children and burning

(Continued on PAGE FIVE)

FEBRUARY 17, 1937

19lb CLOTHES AT CORONATION

WHAT SOME PEERS MUST WEAR

NEW COIFFURE FOR PEERESSES

FROM A SPECIAL CORRESPONDENT

Peeresses attending the Coronation who—as revealed in THE DAILY TELEGRAPH yesterday—will each have to wear robes weighing more than 10lb, will be fortunate compared with men at the ceremony. Their robes and uniforms will weigh many pounds heavier.

A West End firm making robes and uniforms for peers, Ministers and officers gave me the following weights of the robes:

Full dress coatee of a first-class Minister	8lb 8oz
Peer's robe	6lb
Full court dress	2lb 8oz
Court knickers	1lb
Court shoes	1lb 8oz
Dress sword	1lb 8oz
White silk satin waistcoat	8oz
Cocked hat	10oz

First-class Ministers who are also peers will wear clothes weighing about 19lb—nearly twice as heavy as the robes worn by the average peeress.

HEAVY SWORDS

Many other peers will wear a 6lb robe, which is 2lb heavier than the corresponding train and cape of the peeress. A peer's appurtenances will weigh more, and he will also carry a sword and a heavier coronet.

I was told that men wish to keep to tradition in their robes, while women prefer to have them adapted to present-day fashions. Peeresses, while abiding by the rules laid down by the Earl Marshal, are demanding some conformity to the latest mode.

The difficulty of perching coronets on the modern coiffure has been overcome by a new hair-dressing style. This Coronation coiffure will consist of a sleek top waving, with side and neck curls to support the coronet.

WATCH TO BE

Mayoress Would Not Darn Socks for War

SPEECH UPSETS ARSENAL EMPLOYEES

From Our Own Correspondent
WOOLWICH, Monday.

THERE is a mild storm in Woolwich because of remarks made by the new Mayoress of Woolwich, Mrs. Kathleen Rance.

Speaking at a bazaar last week at the Plumstead Common Baptist Church, the mayoress said: "So far as my husband and I are concerned, we shall do all we can for peace during our year of office. We are both members of the Peace Pledge Union, and neither of us would take part in a war. I myself would not even do as much as darn a sock to help in a war."

These remarks are resented by the majority of the Woolwich public, who hold that the mayoress was, to say the least, rather tactless. Some 12,000 Woolwich electors are employed in Woolwich Arsenal on armament making.

The objectors also point out that the Mayor and Mayoress are supposed to serve all sections of the community and not any particular sect or party.

HER PRIVATE VIEWS

A prominent Labour Party official in Woolwich said:

"The views Mrs. Rance expressed were her own personal ones, and not necessarily those held by the Labour Party as a whole. We have many Peace Pledge Movement members in our ranks, but we are sensible enough to see that armaments at the present juncture are a necessity and should war come the majority of Labour people in this borough would be as eager to help the country as they were in war days.

"It is interesting to note, however, that although Mrs. Rance has expressed this view about her antagonism to war, she is frequently present in an official capacity at military functions at Woolwich, whilst she has a son making good progress in the R.A.F."

Suggestions for Further Reading:
Virginia Woolf

Editions

The Complete Shorter Fiction. Edited by Susan Dick. 2nd ed. San Diego: Harcourt, 1989.

The Diary of Virginia Woolf. Edited by Anne Olivier Bell. 5 vols. New York: Harcourt, 1977–84.

The Essays of Virginia Woolf. Edited by Andrew McNeillie. 6 vols. [in progress]. San Diego: Harcourt Brace Jovanovich, 1986–.

The Letters of Virginia Woolf. Edited by Nigel Nicolson and Joanne Trautmann. 6 vols. New York: Harcourt Brace Jovanovich, 1975–80.

Moments of Being. Edited by Jeanne Schulkind. San Diego: Harcourt, 1985.

A Passionate Apprentice: The Early Journals, 1897–1909. Edited by Mitchell A. Leaska. San Diego: Harcourt, 1990.

Biographies and Reference Works

Briggs, Julia. *Virginia Woolf: An Inner Life*. San Diego: Harcourt, 2005.

Hussey, Mark. *Virginia Woolf A to Z. A Comprehensive Reference for Students, Teachers, and Common Readers to Her Life, Works, and Critical Reception*. New York: Facts on File, 1995.

Kirkpatrick, B. J., and Stuart N. Clarke. *A Bibliography of Virginia Woolf*. 4th ed. Oxford: Clarendon, 1997.

Lee, Hermione. *Virginia Woolf*. New York: Knopf, 1996.

Marder, Herbert. *The Measure of Life: Virginia Woolf's Last Years.* Ithaca, NY: Cornell University Press, 2000.

Poole, Roger. *The Unknown Virginia Woolf.* 4th ed. Cambridge: Cambridge University Press, 1995.

Reid, Panthea. *Art and Affection: A Life of Virginia Woolf.* New York: Oxford University Press, 1996.

General Criticism

Abel, Elizabeth. *Virginia Woolf and the Fictions of Psychoanalysis.* Chicago: University of Chicago Press, 1989.

Bazin, Nancy Topping. *Virginia Woolf and the Androgynous Vision.* New Brunswick, NJ: Rutgers University Press, 1973.

Beer, Gillian. *Virginia Woolf: The Common Ground.* Ann Arbor: University of Michigan Press, 1996.

Cuddy-Keane, Melba. *Virginia Woolf, the Intellectual, and the Public Sphere.* Cambridge: Cambridge University Press, 2003.

DiBattista, Maria. *Virginia Woolf's Major Novels: The Fables of Anon.* New Haven, CT: Yale University Press, 1980.

Fleishman, Avrom. *Virginia Woolf: A Critical Reading.* Baltimore: Johns Hopkins University Press, 1975.

Froula, Christine. *Virginia Woolf and the Bloomsbury Avant-Garde: War, Civilization, Modernity.* New York: Columbia University Press, 2005.

Guiguet, Jean. *Virginia Woolf and Her Works.* New York: Harcourt Brace Jovanovich, 1965.

Harper, Howard. *Between Language and Silence: The Novels of Virginia Woolf.* Baton Rouge: Louisiana State University Press, 1982.

Hussey, Mark. *The Singing of the Real World: The Philosophy of Virginia Woolf's Fiction.* Columbus: Ohio State University Press, 1986.

———, ed. *Virginia Woolf and War: Fiction, Reality and Myth.* Syracuse, NY: Syracuse University Press, 1991.

Majumdar, Robin, and Allen McLaurin, eds. *Virginia Woolf: The Critical Heritage*. Boston: Routledge, 1975.

Marcus, Jane. *Art and Anger: Reading Like a Woman*. Columbus: Ohio State University Press, 1988.

———, ed. *New Feminist Essays on Virginia Woolf*. Lincoln: University of Nebraska Press, 1981.

———, ed. *Virginia Woolf: A Feminist Slant*. Lincoln: University of Nebraska Press, 1983.

———, ed. *Virginia Woolf and Bloomsbury: A Centenary Celebration*. Bloomington: Indiana University Press, 1987.

———. *Virginia Woolf and the Languages of Patriarchy*. Bloomington: Indiana University Press, 1987.

McLaurin, Allen. *Virginia Woolf: The Echoes Enslaved*. Cambridge: Cambridge University Press, 1973.

McNees, Eleanor, ed. *Virginia Woolf: Critical Assessments*. 4 vols. New York: Routledge, 1994.

Minow-Pinkney, Makiko. *Virginia Woolf and the Problem of the Subject: Feminine Writing in the Major Novels*. New Brunswick, NJ: Rutgers University Press, 1987.

Phillips, Kathy J. *Virginia Woolf Against Empire*. Knoxville: University of Tennessee Press, 1994.

Roe, Sue, and Susan Sellers, eds. *The Cambridge Companion to Virginia Woolf*. Cambridge: Cambridge University Press, 2000.

Ruotolo, Lucio. *The Interrupted Moment: A View of Virginia Woolf's Novels*. Stanford, CA: Stanford University Press, 1986.

Silver, Brenda R. *Virginia Woolf Icon*. Chicago: University of Chicago Press, 1999.

Zwerdling, Alex. *Virginia Woolf and the Real World*. Berkeley: University of California Press, 1986.

Suggestions for Further Reading:
Three Guineas
An Annotated Bibliography

(in addition to the works cited in the introduction)

Alberti, Johanna. "British Feminists and Anti-Fascism in the 1930s." In *This Working-Day World: Women's Lives and Culture(s) in Britain 1914–1945*. Edited by Sybil Oldfield. Bristol, PA: Taylor and Francis, 1994.

Barrett, Michèle. *Virginia Woolf: Women and Writing*. London: The Women's Press, 1979, 1992. Initiated the debate in Britain and then elsewhere on Woolf's politics and feminism, and argued the relevance of her ideas to the new wave of feminism.

Beer, Gillian. "The Island and the Aeroplane: The Case of Virginia Woolf." In *Nation and Narration*. Edited by Homi K. Bhabha, 265–90. New York: Routledge, 1990.

Black, Naomi. "'Women Must Weep': The Serialization of *Three Guineas*." In *Editing Virginia Woolf: Interpreting the Modernist Text*. Edited by James M. Haule and J. H. Stape, 74–90. New York: Palgrave, 2002.

Bowlby, Rachel. *Virginia Woolf: A Woman's Essays*. London: Penguin, 1992.

Bradshaw, David. "British Writers and Anti-Fascism in the 1930s, II: Under the Hawk's Wings." *Woolf Studies Annual* 4 (1998): 41–66.

Briggs, Julia. "Between the Texts: Virginia Woolf's Acts of Revision." *Text* 12 (1999): 143–65.

Carlston, Erin G. *Thinking Fascism: Sapphic Modernism and Fascist Modernity.* Stanford, CA: Stanford University Press, 1998.

Carroll, Berenice. "'To Crush Him in Our Own Country': The Political Thought of Virginia Woolf." *Feminist Studies* 4.1 (1978): 99–129. A classic in the formation of the ideas of feminists in North America in the 1970s.

Chapman, Wayne K., and Janet M. Manson, eds. *Women in the Milieu of Leonard and Virginia Woolf: Peace, Politics, and Education.* New York: Pace University Press, 1998. Indispensable for political background. See especially Marion Shaw on Winifred Holtby, Sybil Oldfield on Margaret Llewelyn Davies, Wayne K. Chapman, and Patricia Laurence.

Cook, Blanche Wiesen. "'Women Alone Stir My Imagination': Lesbianism and the Cultural Tradition." *Signs* 4.4 (Summer 1979): 718–39. One of the pioneering essays on Woolf that initiated the concerns of Second Wave feminists in the United States with Woolf's pacifism, feminism, and lesbianism.

Cooper, Sandi E. *Patriotic Pacifism: Waging War on War in Europe, 1815–1914.* New York: Oxford University Press, 1991.

Feldman, Yael. "From Essentialism to Constructivism? The Gender of Peace and War—Gilman, Woolf, Freud." *Partial Answers: Journal of Literature and the History of Ideas* 2.1 (January 2004): 113–45. Jerusalem: Hebrew University Magnes Press.

Froula, Christine. "St. Virginia's Epistle to an English Gentleman: Or, Sex, Violence, and the Public Sphere in Woolf's *Three Guineas*." *Tulsa Studies in Women's Literature* 13:1 (1994): 27–56.

Gattens, Marie-Luise. *Women Writers and Fascism: Reconstructing History.* Gainesville: University Press of Florida, 1995.

Gualtieri, Elena. "*Three Guineas* and the Photograph: The Art of Propaganda." In *Women Writers of the 1930s: Gender, Politics and History.* Edited by Maroula Joannou, 165–78. Edinburgh: Edinburgh University Press, 1999.

Holtby, Winifred. *Women and a Changing Civilization*. Chicago: Academy Press, 1978. Originally published in 1935.

Hussey, Mark, ed. *Virginia Woolf and War: Fiction, Reality and Myth*. Syracuse, NY: Syracuse University Press, 1991. All the essays in this book are relevant, particularly those by Wayne Chapman and Janet Manson, Patricia Cramer, and Patricia Laurence.

Joannou, Maroula. *"Ladies, Please Don't Smash These Windows": Women's Writing, Feminist Consciousness and Social Change*. Providence, RI: Berg, 1995.

————, ed. *Women Writers of the 1930s: Gender, Politics and History*. Edinburgh: Edinburgh University Press, 1999.

Lassner, Phyllis. *British Women Writers of World War II: Battlegrounds of Their Own*. New York: St. Martin's, 1998. See especially "*Three Guineas* Plus: Virginia Woolf and her War Correspondents," as well as the discussions of other women writers who were Woolf's contemporaries and the differences in their opposition to war: Vera Brittain, Ethel Mannin, Storm Jameson, Stevie Smith, Bryher, Rebecca West, and Naomi Mitchison, among others. The writing of these women on war and peace puts *Three Guineas* in its cultural and historical context.

Marcus, Jane. *Art & Anger: Reading Like a Woman*. Columbus: Ohio State University Press, 1988. Contains the first essay in the recuperation of Virginia Woolf as a feminist, pacifist, and socialist (from 1976 *Women's Studies*), "'No More Horses': Virginia Woolf on Art and Propaganda." The notes to this essay reprint contemporary reviews, including Queenie Leavis's notorious attack in *Scrutiny* called "Caterpillars of the Commonwealth, Unite!" and *Time and Tide*'s response to the vicious review by G. M. Young in the *Sunday Times*. The reviewer notes "the appalling struggle of most reviewers to combine respect and loathing" for Woolf, awarding the palm to Graham Greene's review in the *Spectator*: "While paying all the obligatory lip service to Mrs. Woolf's genius, he contrived to slip in a suggestion that her thesis was out of date, her voice shrill, her outlook provincial and her experience oversheltered." Also notes that a condensed version of *Three Guineas* was published in America in the May and June 1938 issues of the *Atlantic Monthly* as "Women Must Weep—Or Unite Against War," where it was clearly identified as an antifascist document written from a pacifist and feminist perspective: "Her essays, especially *A Room of One's Own,* have endeared her to all militant members of the gentle sex." The use of the word *militant* by the editors of the *Atlantic Monthly* is a significant reference to Woolf's pacifism, as well as to the English suffragettes who were called militant to differentiate them from suffragists who did not endorse the tactical violence of the WSPU in breaking shop windows and burning golf greens with acid. There were a large number of feminist groups working for the vote in England, some related to religious affiliation, some to political parties, some radical and some conservative groups as well. The editor counts Woolf among the militants possibly on the principle that all feminists think alike, or, then again, to sensationalize the articles. This book also contains "Thinking Back Through Our Mothers," which relates Virginia Woolf's politics and her radical and awkward relation to the state to those of Walter Benjamin. "Art and Anger: Elizabeth Robins and Virginia Woolf," a commentary on Woolf's source for the critique of men's dress in Robins's *Ancilla's Share: An Indictment of Sex Antagonism* (1924), also discusses the speech "Professions for Women," another part of what I am calling the *Three Guineas* Documentary Project.

————. "The Asylums of Antaeus: Women, War and Madness: Is There a Feminist Fetishism?" In *The Difference Within: Feminism and Critical Theory.* Edited by Elizabeth Meese and Alice Parker, 49–83. Philadelphia: John Benjamins, 1988.

————, ed. *Virginia Woolf: A Feminist Slant.* Lincoln: University of

Nebraska Press, 1983. Contains Naomi Black's "Virginia Woolf and the Women's Movement" and Brenda Silver's "*Three Guineas* Before and After," as well as Carolyn Heilbrun's "Virginia Woolf in Her Fifties," Susan Squier on the drafts of *The Years,* and Jane Marcus on the influence of Woolf's Quaker aunt on her philosophy and politics.

———. *Virginia Woolf and the Languages of Patriarchy.* Bloomington: Indiana University Press, 1987. Most of this volume deals with Woolf's ideas as a feminist intellectual. "Liberty, Sorority, Misogyny" uses the ideas of Maria-Antonietta Macciocchi to analyze Woolf's antifascism. "The Niece of a Nun" explores the origins of Woolf's pacifism. There is also a rhetorical analysis of the form of *Three Guineas* discussing its failed attempt to introduce the writers of letters to the narrator to each other to form a kind of chorus, as well as a chapter on the politics and allusions in the companion text to *Three Guineas, The Years.*

Mosse, George L. *The Fascist Revolution: Toward a General Theory of Fascism.* New York: Fertig, 1999. All of Mosse's other books on fascism and masculinity are also relevant to the study of *Three Guineas.*

Neverow, Vara, and Merry Pawlowski. "A Preliminary Bibliographic Guide to the Footnotes of *Three Guineas.*" *Woolf Studies Annual* 3 (1997): 170–210.

———. *The Reading Notes for* Three Guineas. The Center for Virginia Woolf Studies, California State University, Bakersfield. www.csub.edu/woolf (launched in 2000).

Oldfield, Sybil. *Women Against the Iron Fist: From Sarajevo to Greenham Common.* Oxford: Blackwell, 1989. Woolf's pacifism in context.

Park, Sowon S. "Suffrage and Virginia Woolf: 'The Mass Behind the Single Voice.'" *Review of English Studies* 56.223 (2005): 119–34.

Pawlowski, Merry. "'All the gents. against me': Virginia Woolf, *Three Guineas* and the Sons of Educated Men." In *Virginia Woolf:*

Emerging Perspectives: Selected Papers from the Third Annual Conference on Virginia Woolf. Edited by Mark Hussey and Vara Neverow-Turk, 44–51. New York: Pace University Press, 1994.

———. "Exposing Masculine Spectacle: Virginia Woolf's Newspaper Clippings for *Three Guineas* as Contemporary Cultural History." *Woolf Studies Annual* 9 (2003): 117–41.

———. "On Feminine Subjectivity and Fascist Ideology: The 'Sex War' Between Virginia Woolf and Wyndham Lewis." In *Virginia Woolf and the Arts: Selected Papers from the Sixth Annual Conference on Virginia Woolf.* Edited by Diane F. Gillespie and Leslie K. Hankins, 243–51. New York: Pace University Press, 1997.

———. "Reassessing Modernism: Virginia Woolf, *Three Guineas* and Fascist Ideology." *Woolf Studies Annual* 1 (Spring 1995): 47–67.

———, ed. *Virginia Woolf and Fascism: Resisting the Dictators' Seduction.* Houndsmills and New York: Palgrave, 2001. All the essays in this book are essential to understanding Woolf's antifascism, especially those of the editor, Marie-Luise Gattens, Vara Neverow, and Jessica Berman.

Phillips, Kathy J. *Virginia Woolf Against Empire.* Knoxville: University of Tennessee Press, 1994.

Riley, Denise. *'Am I That Name?': Feminism and the Category of "Women" in History.* Minneapolis: University of Minneapolis Press, 1988. See especially chapter 3.

Robins, Elizabeth. *Ancilla's Share: An Indictment of Sex Antagonism* (published under the name Anon.). London: Hutchinson, 1924. The source for Woolf's passages on men's love of dress, uniforms, and medals, etc. This text is written as a legal "indictment" (without the whereases), and in its form may also be a precedent for the odd form of *Three Guineas.* Robins uses this unusual structure for her manifesto as a tribute to the style of Christabel Pankhurst, a lawyer who was not allowed to practice because she was a woman, whose speeches in the dock are often constructed this way, as is some of her writing in the weekly

Votes for Women. These connections to other manifestos place *Three Guineas* in an important line of feminist dissent (and descent). Robins was an active feminist, novelist, and playwright. She was a friend both of Woolf and of her mother, and was well known for her play *Votes for Women!* Woolf reviewed some of her novels. Robins's protégée Dr. Octavia Wilberforce was called on by Leonard Woolf to examine Woolf just before she died.

Robinson, Lillian S. *Sex, Class, and Culture.* Bloomington: Indiana University Press, 1978. Contains "Who's Afraid of *A Room of One's Own?*" essential reading for its critique from within Left feminism of Virginia Woolf's arguments in *A Room of One's Own* and *Three Guineas.*

Shaw, Marion. "'Alien Experiences': Virginia Woolf, Winifred Holtby and Vera Brittain in the Thirties." In *Rewriting the Thirties: After Modernism.* Edited by Keith Williams and Steven Matthews, 37–52. Essex, UK: Longman, 1997.

Silver, Brenda. "The Authority of Anger: *Three Guineas* as Case Study." *Signs* 16.2 (Winter 1991): 340–70.

———. *Virginia Woolf's Reading Notebooks.* Princeton, NJ: Princeton University Press, 1983.

Snaith, Anna. *Virginia Woolf: Public and Private Negotiations.* New York: St. Martin's, 2000.

Stewart, Victoria. "Q. D. Leavis: Women and Education under Scrutiny." *Literature and History* 13:2 (2004): 67–85.

Swanson, Diana L. "An Antigone Complex? The Political Psychology of *The Years* and *Three Guineas.*" *Woolf Studies Annual* 3 (1997): 28–44.

Theweleit, Klaus. *Male Fantasies.* 2 vols. Minneapolis: University of Minnesota Press, 1987.

Wiltsher, Anne. *Most Dangerous Women: Feminist Peace Campaigners of the Great War.* Boston: Pandora Press, 1985.

Winterhalter, Teresa. "'What Else Can I Do But Write?': Discursive Disruption and the Ethics of Style in Virginia Woolf's *Three*

Guineas." *Hypatia: A Journal of Feminist Philosophy* 18:4 (2003): 236–57.

Woolf, Leonard, ed. *The Intelligent Man's Way to Prevent War.* London: Gollancz, 1933. Includes essays by Norman Angell, Gilbert Murray, C. M. Lloyd, C. R. Buxton, Viscount Cecil, W. Arnold-Forster, and Harold Laski. Laski's essay is at odds with the other essays in the book because it argues that war is based on capitalism and economic imperialism, a view closer to that of Virginia Woolf. Playing on G. B. Shaw's treatise *The Intelligent Woman's Guide to Socialism,* Leonard Woolf does not include any women's essays in his book, although he was familiar with the work of many women on the topic of war and peace. Gender is not an issue for him here as race is not an issue for him in his most Marxist work, *Empire and Commerce in Africa.* The book is concerned with "preventing war" by encouraging the work of the League of Nations and other forums for international law and justice. Virginia Woolf was not invited to contribute to this volume, and one imagines that this is one of the reasons she wrote *Three Guineas.* Surely her address to readers as "educated men's daughters" is to mimic the rational masculine tone of educated men speaking together on this issue that constitutes Leonard's collection. Doubtless he was as unconscious of the gender bias of his book as she was conscious of it and determined to put the views of women on war and fascism into print. In his appeal to "intelligent men" to prevent war, Leonard Woolf sees the breakdown of civilization in "the economic crisis, in the general political instability, in the growing tension between various nations, the rise of 'ruthless' and savage dictatorships, in the glorification of Fascist mass murders, in the suppression of liberty and all freedom of thought, in the barbarous persecution and torture of Liberals, Socialists, Pacifists and Jews in Germany. . . . 'Fascism,' writes Mussolini in 1932, 'repudiates the doctrine of Pacifism—born of a renunciation of the struggle and an act of cowardice in the face of sacrifice. War alone brings up to its highest tension all human energy and puts the stamp of nobility on the peoples who have the courage to meet it. . . .'" (7, 8). Leonard Woolf was concerned with the triumph of the "barbarians," "one reason they have 'struck the word pacifism from their vocabulary,'" an anticipation of Woolf's burning of the word *feminism* in *Three Guineas,* both clearly influenced by the public book burnings of the Nazis.

Woolf, Virginia. *A Room of One's Own* and *Three Guineas.* Edited by Michèle Barrett. Harmondsworth: Penguin, 1993. Contains a list of textual variants between the English and American first editions, restores photographs, includes the essay "Professions for Women," includes photographs of press cuttings from the *Three Guineas* scrapbooks at the University of Sussex Library and commentary on their composition as sources for the text, noting the humor in the juxtaposition of clippings on a page as a signature of Woolf's style.

———. *A Room of One's Own* and *Three Guineas.* Edited by Morag Shiach. Oxford: Oxford University Press, 1992. Includes a list of works cited in the text of *Three Guineas* and restores the photographs.

———. *Three Guineas.* Edited by Naomi Black. Oxford: Blackwell for the Shakespeare Head Press, 2001. Contains extensive notes, emendations to the text, and bibliography.